THE
BILLY GRAHAM
RELIGION

THE
BILLY GRAHAM
RELIGION

by Joe E. Barnhart

A PILGRIM PRESS BOOK
from United Church Press · Philadelphia

Copyright © 1972 United Church Press

Library of Congress Cataloging in Publication Data

Barnhart, Joe E   1931–
    The Billy Graham religion.

    Includes bibliographical references.
    1. Graham, William Franklin, 1918–   2. Evangelicalism—
United States. 3. United States—Religion.
I. Title.
BV3785.G69B28 269'.2 72–8447
ISBN 0–8298–0242–8

For Mary Ann—
nineteen years an interesting,
rational and delightful wife

And for C. E. Barnhart—
a father who has worked very hard
and enjoys Christmas

Contents

Preface

For years Billy Graham has been asking millions of people to listen with an open mind to his preaching. Some people have, and some have not. Billy Graham and his fellow evangelical Christians believe that those persons who do not have an open mind to his message are manifesting sin and arrogance. Now this raises a question about the evangelist and those who strongly agree with him. Can they be open-minded in reading a book that offers a thoughtful critique of the Billy Graham phenomenon and its evangelical frame of reference?

To write a book about a fellow human being is a serious matter. But it need not be a somber undertaking. Fortunately, regardless of what view one may take of Billy Graham's outlook, there can be little doubt that his life has encountered some fascinating turns of events. Furthermore, to understand this most popular of all American evangelists is to understand something about America itself. It is my hope that when the reader finishes the final page of this book, he will have come to understand himself better, for there is a bit of Billy Graham in all of us.

Fresh out of high school in the summer of 1936, seventeen-year-old William Franklin Graham became an evangelist for the Fuller Brush Company. Grady and T. W. Wilson, who have remained Billy Graham's close friends since their boyhood days in rural North Carolina, went with him to sell the housewives of North Carolina the brushes for which they had been waiting. "Billy was the most dedicated salesman the Fuller Brush Company ever had," [1] Grady Wilson recalled years later. And Dr. Graham himself is quoted as saying: "I had become convinced that Fuller brushes were the best in the world and no family should be without them. Selling those brushes became a cause to me . . . a matter of principle." [2] Billy's quick success as a salesman earned him the right to be called upon to instruct other salesmen in the techniques of selling. To his mother he once remarked that "women . . . need brushes and now I'm going to see that they get the chance to buy them." [3] A few years later the Wilson brothers would once again team up with Graham to sell what they were convinced is not only the best religious faith in the world but the *only* genuine faith. World Wide Publications was set up for the purpose of distributing the literature of their faith around the globe and in many languages. Today Billy Graham is still the dedicated, successful supersalesman that he was in the summer of 1936—only now he offers people a chance at evangelical Christianity and he thinks that absolutely no family in the world should be without it. Evangelicalism is a cause and a matter of principle to him.

Selling is second nature to this tall, impressive evangelist. In Florida in 1937 he took a job which required him to escort a carload of tourists around Tampa. Despite the fact that the then eighteen-year-old youth knew practically nothing about the town, inasmuch as he had just arrived in town, he nevertheless took the tourists on their sightseeing trip and explained to them "the virtues" of the sunny city of Florida. The tourists, Graham recalled, "seemed happy" with his presentation.[4]

Billy Graham was converted in high school and ever since then he has had overwhelming urges to offer to others the same opportunity that he had to receive what he believes is the dearest thing in the world— namely a Christian salvation and a way of life which the Lord of the universe recommends for everyone. Like any alert supersalesman, Graham knows the importance of the "testimonial" of a satisfied customer, and he utilizes this as his primary method in evangelizing. Among Evangelicals, giving one's own testimonial is sometimes called "witnessing to others," and that is what Graham thinks is the heart of evangelistic preaching.

But what about the dissatisfied customers? Or customers who find some other way of life more meaningful to them than Evangelicalism? It must be admitted that Billy Graham appears unable to understand such people. His own religious experiences and convictions are satisfying to him, and he cannot imagine why they would not be satisfying and fulfilling to everyone in the world. Unless, of course, there is something wrong with them. And this turns out to be Graham's answer. Those who do not accept the faith that has meant so much to him are simply— well, they are regarded as proud of heart, lacking in humility, and probably dishonest in some special sense. In fact, every human being is regarded as infected with a disease which Evangelicals designate as original sin. And basically that is what is thought to be wrong with people who do not subscribe to what Graham calls "the good news of salvation."

This doctrine of original sin is used by Billy Graham to account for all sorts of things that do not go the way that he believes God wants them to go. In this book I shall place this doctrine of original sin under the microscope, so to speak, and examine it very carefully. Most of Billy Graham's biographers do not go very far into his convictions and beliefs because they either lack the training to do so or because they apparently think that their readers are interested primarily in the flare and style of the evangelist and not the substance of his theology.

But the Billy Graham phenomenon cannot be profoundly understood if the evangelist's theology is made a sideline interest only. To some people his theology is downright shocking. Others look upon it as simply the result of believing that the Bible represents without error the thinking of the Lord regarding such topics as life after death, absolute moral standards for everyone everywhere at all times, the fate of Russia, the ultimate destiny of modern Jews in the precarious Middle East, and the emergence of an actual Superpresident who will be an evil dictator dominating the entire earth.

In taking the Bible to be infallible truth from God, Billy Graham is led to some unusual notions. For example, he holds that before coming to earth Jesus had no body, whereas now he does and today that body sits at the right hand of God the Father. In Graham's own words, "there is a Man at the right hand of God the Father. He is living in a body that still has nail prints in His hands." [5] On Johnny Carson's *Tonight* show Billy Graham explained that a Christian entering heaven would be able to distinguish God the Father from God the Son by the nail prints in the hands of the Son. Whether this entails that the Father also has hands, feet, knees, beard, and other bodily parts is not clear. The Bible says that Moses saw God's *back*, but some interpreters have taken this figuratively, inasmuch as John 1:18 says that at no time has anyone seen God, and John 4:24 says that God is Spirit.

Taking some numbers and figures from the book of Revelation, Billy Graham once calculated that heaven would be about the size of the state of Florida, although probably governed differently. Rarely has Graham acknowledged any change in his theology but in this case he has changed his mind and now thinks that perhaps the figures in the book of Revelation were meant to be taken figuratively rather than literally.

However, he does *not* hold that hell, devils, angels, and witches are merely figurative expressions in the Bible. He thinks that they are definitely to be taken literally. Hell, for example, is as literal and real as Ford automobiles and certainly more enduring. In this book Graham's thinking about hell will be thoroughly examined. Does he really think that his Jewish friend Joey Bishop will suffer torment in hell forever if he does not "accept Christ as his Savior"? Naturally Khrushchev will be there. But what about Eisenhower? Or FDR?

In this book I will also examine the possibility that Billy Graham is a very popular spokesman of *two* faiths—Evangelicalism and something that might be vaguely described as "Christian Americanism" or "Decent Americanism." This sometimes places the evangelist in a bind, however, and he does not always seem happy fulfilling these roles whenever they come into conflict with one another. Nevertheless, at other times he obviously enjoys being near the front of the parade of Christian Americanism because it gives him an "in." In short, Billy Graham has a strategy. He is not selling his soul to this national religion. He wants to maintain the shell of Christian Americanism so that he can put life and spirit into it. That is, by supporting this civil religion he hopes not only to use it for combating both humanism and agnosticism, but also to use it as a springboard for leading more people into the evangelical faith.

Graham greatly fears the challenge of humanism and he thinks that if the influence of humanism can be held in check, he will have a better chance of converting people to what he genuinely thinks is the one and only way for all mankind. This is one reason why he strongly supports Bible reading and prayer in the public schools: it will combat humanism and also increase the probability that young people will be more inclined toward accepting the evangelical faith which Graham often characterizes as "personal faith in Jesus Christ."

The success of Billy Graham's strategy may be seen in the way Gen. Dwight Eisenhower moved increasingly from a vague religion of "Decent Americanism" to a more definite evangelical faith. In December

1952 the general said: "Our government makes no sense unless it is founded in a deeply felt religious faith—and I don't care what it is." A month later he joined the National Presbyterian Church. Still later his views became more clearly evangelical as he spoke of Christ as the Son of God and of the Deity of the Bible as the true Creator. When the evangelist visited him shortly before his death, the general asked how he could know that his sins were forgiven and that he would go to heaven. Graham reminded him of the evangelical answer and Eisenhower responded that he was ready to die.[6]

To be sure, as a boy Dwight Eisenhower, like Richard Nixon, had been brought up by an evangelical Christian pacifist mother, had attended Sunday school, and had read the Bible. But in the army, Eisenhower's evangelical roots were not always evident. Nevertheless, Billy Graham did have considerable "spiritual" influence on Eisenhower in bringing him closer to the evangelical faith of his childhood.[7] And today Graham would like every child in America to be exposed to Evangelicalism—even if in the public schools—because he believes that such exposure increases the probability of Evangelicals winning converts to their faith. Religion in the schools is currently a "hot" issue. It is discussed in the first chapter as it relates to Billy Graham's "spiritual" role in the United States.

The serious evangelist from North Carolina must not be thought of as a humorless man. Indeed, some rather humorous and sometimes embarrassing things have happened to him. For example, there is the case of his once discovering in his hotel room an uninvited beautiful woman who was shown the exit door pronto! Graham is not one of those saints who claims never to have been moved by a beautiful woman. He freely admits to having had lust in his heart. But he insists that he has always locked it up in his heart, and there is no reason to disbelieve him. Like most people, he sometimes says embarrassing things in public that later he wishes he could have said differently or not at all. He once described Jesus the carpenter as tall and handsome, which may reflect more the influence of Hollywood than of the Bible. Fortunately, when preaching in Korea and Japan he did not speculate about the height of Jesus.

It would be interesting to speculate about Graham's answer if some eight-year-old Sunday school boy or girl should ask him whether Jesus is taller than anybody on the UCLA basketball team. Billy Graham says that there will be delicious food and eating in heaven, but he does not say whether anyone can put on weight or grow taller in the New Jerusalem. Perhaps everyone who goes there will be recreated equal in size, shape, and weight, although the evangelist forcefully insists that they will definitely *not* be equal in every respect. For example, in heaven as on earth, some persons will carry more spiritual weight and status than others. It is a very popular doctrine among Evangelicals, especially in the South, that the person who wins more "souls to Christ" will receive superior status and reward in heaven. If this is true, Billy Graham will be even more popular and influential in heaven than he is now on earth.

Many persons have influenced my thinking over years of study and notetaking with a view toward eventually writing this book, and I am increasingly aware of my debt to them. My wife, Mary Ann, has in her easy and matter-of-fact way made numerous practical suggestions for improving the various drafts of this book. My colleague Ralph Wright was kind enough to proofread the manuscript. The library training of Oragene Addis proved to be invaluable to me. Brenda Brown, Patricia Sikorski, Mary Meeler, and Kathie Alcoze utilized their special skills in transforming a thicket of handwritten notes and inserts into an orderly, readable whole. The pleasure I experienced in writing this book came largely from the efficiency and interest of these individuals.

Billy Graham, I should perhaps say, may not agree with or like a good deal of what this book says. But I hope that he will agree that I have not taken him lightly and have earnestly sought to engage him and evangelical Christianity in responsible dialogue.

Joe E. Barnhart
Denton, Texas
June 30, 1972

THE
BILLY GRAHAM
RELIGION

Chapter 1
CHRIST, LAW, AND ORDER

Evangelist Billy Graham believes that "we are too tolerant of those people who are against the basic principles of this country." [1] With many other Americans, he holds that the Supreme Court under Justice Earl Warren's leadership did great harm by "giving the nation dangerous license." [2] It would appear that if evangelist Graham could have his way, the laws of this land would prohibit many practices that are now acknowledged to be legal. The evangelist is convinced that America is at a critical crossroads. She may either remain a powerful force for good in the world (although God may withdraw this alternative at any moment) or sell out to the recent trend toward the destruction that came to ancient Rome.[3]

Sometimes Graham seems to blend evangelical Christianity and the United States as if they were made for one another. It is as if America were the promised land for Evangelicalism. On New Year's Eve, 1950, the evangelist declared in a sermon, "Communism [is] the avowed enemy of everything Americans stand for—our schools, our social order, our God, our Bible, our churches, our homes." [4] The organization responsible for planning Graham's Rose Bowl rally of September 14, 1950, issued a statement bemoaning "the spiritual indifference which continues to be a threat to the American way of life." The statement continued: "We need a return to God, a hurried return, if we are going to avoid doom in America." [5]

Billy Graham does not profess to know why God has selected him to be an evangelist or to be a voice calling America to return to the paths of true faith, morality, and decency. He thinks it is simply his duty to preach and not to speculate as to why he has been divinely appointed to help save America from destruction. Indeed, at one period in his ministry, Dr. Graham entertained strong hopes of spearheading a worldwide revival, and he has not wholly given up on the hope. He once said, "Although there has never been a worldwide revival, I believe we may be on the verge of one now." [6] Believing earnestly that America may be destined for great moral leadership in the free world, Graham once remarked, "I feel a revival of true Christian faith in America would do more to give us this moral leadership than anything that we could do." [7] This was spoken at a time when much concern was expressed about America's prestige abroad. Late in 1950 the evangelist proclaimed that

> the year 1950 will go down in history as one of the most momentous in the history of the world—a year when our nation began its fight for survival; when American prestige abroad has sunk to the lowest ebb in the history of our Republic; when former friends and allies are deserting us or questioning our leadership. [8]

There can be little doubt that throughout his ministry Billy Graham has earnestly sought to convert the United States into a model Christian nation that would exert her military power to repel the Russians and Chinese, while exerting her mighty moral power on the free world. [9]

However, many people in the United States have questioned just what it would mean in terms of new legislation and new laws if Billy Graham's version of evangelical Christianity should become a dominant influence in the United States. How would Graham's version of Christ and moral reform affect the personal lives of citizens who do not accept the evangelical Christian framework? What does he classify as "moral permissiveness"?

Graham has made it quite clear that divorce ought to be much more difficult to obtain than it now is in most states. This is his opinion in a day when many lawyers and others are pleading for simpler means of divorce. In some states adultery is not considered a crime. But Billy Graham, like the Reformer John Calvin, considers adultery to be one of the lowest forms of immorality, and he often goes so far as to use the terms immorality and adultery interchangeably. [10] Graham clearly believes in capital punishment for murder, and he points out that adultery "is one of the few sins for which God demanded the death penalty in the Old Testament." [11] Furthermore, adultery was, Graham notes, punishable by death not only under Jewish law, but also under Roman law and Greek law.[12] He does not mind that his attitude has been described as puritanical. In fact, not only does he himself prefer to refrain from any form of extramarital sexual relations, he goes so far as to say that practices such as adultery create a national security problem. It "threatens the very security of the nation." [13]

Graham longs for the time when "a divorced man would have no chance in politics." [14] Doubtless it would have been a great dilemma for Billy Graham had his long-time and close friend Richard Nixon taken a divorced person like Ronald Reagan to be his running mate in 1968. Graham deplores the fact that "with our shifting ideals of today, whether or not a person is divorced seems to make little difference." [15] The evangelist would place moral and social stigmas on the divorced. He could never agree with such students of marriage as Morton Hunt and Bernard Steinzor that for some people divorce is "a highly moral act." [16] If one of Graham's married daughters should become a divorcée, he would naturally suffer considerable anguish of mind and heart. Graham's pastor, W. A. Criswell, does not talk against divorce in the way that he used to since his daughter divorced her preacher husband.

While divorce has doubtless been oversold as a cure for personal problems, Graham still holds that there is only one justified grounds for divorce—adultery. He would use social and legal means to put a stop to many divorces in the United States. This could backfire by generating more adultery, however, which would present the evangelist with a perplexing dilemma.

When the issue of racism comes up, Evangelist Billy Graham often states his position very emphatically: Morality cannot be legislated. He insists that the right attitude or behavior toward people of different nationalities or different skin pigmentations must come from the heart. Morality must come from within.[17] This does not mean, however, that the evangelist opposes law and order imposed by the state. He believes that some people have to be compelled to behave properly even though they do not want to do so. For example, the thief must be forced to comply with the law against stealing. Certain forms of killing must be prohibited by law. In Dallas, Texas, in September 1971, Dr. Graham said plainly in a television interview that there ought to be laws against pornography. He favors strict censorship of what he regards as pornography.

Like Martin Luther King, Graham has a dream—a vision of the United States as a Christian nation. He knows that she is not now Christian, but throughout his ministry of over thirty years he has entertained this intermittent vision nevertheless. It is useful to speculate as to what kind of laws would be on the books if Dr. Graham's evangelical Christianity were in a position of greater political influence. The influential Protestant Reformer John Calvin had a vision of a Christian city; and in sixteenth-century Geneva, Switzerland he succeeded in influencing the government to enact at least part of his vision.

One of the laws that Calvin desired to place on the books was the death penalty for adultery. The same Bible that prohibits stealing and certain forms of killing also prohibits adultery. The Old Testament records that those found guilty of adultery in Israel were simply executed. Calvin wanted to continue this practice in Geneva. In Texas the law permits a husband to kill on the spot anyone caught in the act of adultery with his wife. It is likely that this reflects the ancient and primitive notion that a wife is a piece of property which the husband has the right to protect from trespassers. Until a few decades ago in the United States the wedding band was worn by the woman only, as if it were her husband's brand on her. As late as the 1940's the suggestion of a wedding band for men was greeted with the same disapproval that the suggestion of an engagement ring for men would receive today. The idea of two adults freely consenting to adultery has not been taken seriously publicly. Today this is, of course, a very important moral question. But Billy Graham seems to suggest that extramarital sex relations by consenting adults ought to be regarded as a crime against the state.

John Calvin, though not able to attach the death penalty to adultery, was successful in making it a criminal offense. The Protestant lawmakers of Geneva, while rejecting Calvin's sterner measures, passed a law to punish married persons found in the act of adultery by feeding them a diet of bread and water while they were imprisoned for nine days. A small fine was also imposed. The unmarried found engaging in sexual intercourse were given a lighter punishment.[18]

In the United States adultery is not increasing drastically, but it is making a steady rise—sufficiently to raise questions as to its legal status. Jesus is said to have made at least an exception to the law against adultery in his own time when he, upon forgiving the woman taken in adultery, thwarted those who would have carried out the letter of the law by stoning her to death. Calvin was unmoved by this story, however, and claimed that while Jesus Christ could himself make an exception to the Mosaic law on occasion, no other person possessed the authority to do so.

Of course, the woman taken in adultery was apparently sufficiently sorry for her sin to repent. But today we may ask what Dr. Graham would want to do with someone who, found in the act of adultery, refused to repent or even to agree that he or she had done wrong in having an extramarital or premarital sexual relationship. The problem of legislating certain kinds of morality is indeed thorny. Graham has certainly indicated that he would resist attempts by conservative Roman Catholics to make illegal the sale of birth-control devices and pills. On television he once stated very plainly his disagreement with the papal view of birth control.

While the Bible has nothing explicit to say about birth-control devices, it does have something very emphatic to say about adulterers and also sorcerers. Graham believes that sorcerers really do exist. He thinks that we are today witnessing an enormous increase in the number of sorcerers, witches, and wizards.[19] Satan is believed to be sending forth fresh troops to make a last-ditch stand against the forces of righteousness on earth. But the Bible says that sorcerers ought to be killed! (See Exodus 22:18.) Most Evangelicals regard sorcery, witchcraft, and the like to be, not simply very strange forms of human behavior, but literal communication with supernatural beings of the cosmic underworld. Billy Graham has not made a statement as to what the state's position regarding sorcery and witchcraft ought to be. Adultery and sorcery are, according to the Bible, capital offenses. Moreover, the Bible says that anyone who offers a sacrifice to any deity other than the God Yahweh is supposed to be "utterly destroyed (Exod. 22:20)." Heretics among Christians were once destroyed, atheists have been denied full citizenship, Jews have suffered legal blows, especially in Europe during the Middle Ages, and, as the Evangelical Roger Williams learned in Massachusetts, some Evangelicals have wanted to outlaw other Evangelicals.

Billy Graham seems to possess no consistent and explicit principle by which to determine how far to go in turning morality into laws of the state. It is one thing to profess, as Dr. Graham does, to know what the

Bible teaches; however, it is another to know how to apply these teachings in practical social and political situations. Graham says that the Holy Spirit helps to apply the Bible to everyday experience, but this, too, has its practical problems. It is even a more difficult problem when Christians have to live in a pluralistic society where compromise is essential if a measure of social and political harmony is to prevail. *Religious* toleration came not so much from moral conviction as from practical necessity. *Moral* toleration is also a practical necessity, although it need not entail moral approval of what is tolerated. In a pluralistic society Christians of whatever variety learn to compromise, just as non-Christians have to compromise some of their moral convictions in order to live in peace with Christians.

The complicated question of religious worship in the public schools illustrates well the difficulty of legislating one's own morality and religious practice. Billy Graham's own religious group—the Southern Baptist Convention—seems to be split over the issue. A number of Billy Graham's fellow Southern Baptist clergymen have expressed their support of the United States Supreme Court's decision regarding religious worship in the public schools. Carl Bates, president of the Southern Baptist Convention for 1970–72, joined not only the president of the American Baptist Convention, but also leaders within other denominations, to say that the Supreme Court's decision regarding religion in the public schools does not interfere with freedom of worship and freedom of religious expression. Furthermore, Bates and the others opposed the proposed constitutional prayer amendment because they saw it as a "threat to religious freedom." [20]

Dr. Graham, however, has thrown his support in the opposite direction. He has joined with those who charge that the Supreme Court's decision takes "God out of the schools." In the biting words of the evangelist:

> A generation or more ago we took God out of our educational system and we thought we could get away with it. We laughed at God, religion and the Bible. Now the Supreme Court has ordered the Bible out of our schools. We are sowing the wind and we are surely going to reap the whirlwind.[21]

Graham strongly supported the prayer amendment as a way of countering the harm which the Supreme Court was thought to have done.

He thinks that prayer and Bible reading should be encouraged in public schools during the regular hours. Yet even here an uneasy compromise seems inevitable. In the Boston area a large number of Roman Catholics might prefer the rosary or Hail Mary as their prayer, but that would offend many Protestants and others. Would Graham want his grandchildren to be exposed daily to Hail Mary or to devotional readings from Mary Baker Eddy's *Science and Health with Key to the Scriptures*? West of the Rockies the *Book of Mormon* is regarded by many as divinely revealed scripture.

What seemed to be taking shape among those favoring the prayer amendment was "a nondenominational consensus prayer," which, according to its critics, "reduces prayer to its least common denominator." [22] Billy Graham wants to have religious devotions in the public schools sometime during regular hours, but he has failed to say what specific arrangements could be made for those children who are not of the religious persuasion that the daily devotional material reflects. Shall the Jew, for example, be placed under social pressure to listen to prayers ending with "in Jesus' name" or "for Christ's sake"? Should Billy Graham's grandchildren be exposed to the Muslim prayers to Allah, especially when the Muslim thinks there is only one God, Allah, with Mohammed as his prophet? And what of Black Muslim prayers in the schools?

Graham likes to quote statistics as to how many people in America believe in God, but he quotes no statistics to indicate the great diversity of opinion regarding what people think the Deity is like. And Graham would be among the first to say that what a person believes about God is at least as important as simply believing that God exists. In 1970 the delegates to the Arkansas Constitutional Convention voted to accept the following amendment: "All men have a natural right to worship according to the dictates of their consciences." Another amendment would have inserted the word God after the word worship, but it was rejected 56-32, primarily because disputes about the various views of God broke out and could not be resolved. The sponsor of the defeated amendment warned the delegates that they would have to answer the question, "Where were you when they took God out of the Constitution?" [23]

Billy Graham clearly has an image of himself as God's prophet proclaiming the unequivocal and simple message of God. He has often been advertised by his team as "God's man with God's message." Unfortunately, the will of God on complex political and social questions seems to be differently interpreted by various men who regard themselves as messengers of God in some sense. In the United States there are prophets of other faiths who claim to speak for another God than that which Billy Graham claims to represent. In ancient Israel the prophet Elijah could simply order the people of Israel to slaughter the prophets of Baal. But in the United States followers of the God Yahweh have to make political adjustments to what they regard as wicked false prophets, infidels, and the like. The early American Puritans wanted to establish a theocracy, with God as king of the state. Billy Graham talks of a "Christocracy," but he is not very clear as to whether or not this is a political doctrine or in what sense it is political.[24]

The trend of his political thinking seems to be to affirm both Christocracy and democracy. This fits well with his view that if all citizens in America were dedicated Christians, then they would have a Christocracy. And it would have come through the democratic vote and democratic procedures. But of course the probability of America's becoming totally Christian in Billy Graham's sense of Christian is very low, which then raises the question of what he would do if Christians of his particular variety were in a simple majority. What rights would the minority have to live life-styles not in harmony with evangelical Christianity? Would adultery be punished? Premarital sex outlawed? These are hard practical questions, and they raise even more difficult questions. A case against murder, stealing, rape, and certain kinds of fraud could more easily be made because they involve one person or group of persons imposing its will in a flagrant way upon another or others. But in cases of sexuality outside marriage, there is usually mutual consent. Could the Evangelicals accept this form of mutual consent as legal even though they regard it as immoral? Such a question deserves careful attention because it eventually raises the issue of other kinds of freedom—for example, freedom to worship in different ways, freedom to refrain from worshiping, and freedom to propagate new faiths and new moralities.

In cities and towns of Billy Graham's South a few decades ago there were laws that prohibited opening a movie house on Sunday. Graham once remarked that when he was a boy he was not allowed even to "pitch ball on the sabbath." He went on to say that we today have lost much by not keeping the old-fashioned respect for the sabbath.

The business of turning one's own morality into laws of the state is not a simple matter either in theory or in practice. It has exercised the minds of the best legal experts as well as of other persons vitally interested in the question. Graham and many others, both Christian and non-Christian, abhor X-rated movies. Graham seems to want to shut them down, and he speaks favorably of some Christian young people of the Calvary Baptist Church of New York City who organized a picket protest against the showing of "I Am Curious Yellow." [25] One picket sign read: "I Am Furious Red." But no sign was found to read: "I Am Envious Green."

It seems that Graham has not clearly distinguished between individuals' having the political liberty to make their own choices about certain questions of right or wrong, and individuals' having political liberty to choose what Graham thinks is right for them and everyone else. One Southern Baptist editor states the matter boldly: "True liberty is liberty to do the will of God—and nothing else." [26] He adds that "liberty is never license for the lower nature to take over." [27] This is also Billy Graham's view. Unfortunately, one person's lower nature may be another's higher self, at least in his own opinion. And one man's God may be another man's devil. The point here, however, has to do with the degree to which "true liberty" can tolerate what it regards as "false liberty." [28]

Billy Graham seems genuinely concerned about this question but appears not to have any clear principle from which to make judgments about specific cases, even though he often takes stands on specific cases.

The hard and cold fact seems to be that America as a whole simply will not come close to measuring up to Graham's ideal for her. Doubtless this is frustrating to Graham's prophet image, for the burning message of God through the prophet often ends up in the hands of politicians and lawyers. Next to Jesus, the prophet Daniel is the person most admired by Graham, because Daniel was both a prophet and the "prime minister" of what Graham insists was the greatest empire that ever existed on the face of the earth.[29]

A more recent example of a religious empire is that of the Mormons in the United States. Joseph Smith, founder of the Church of Jesus Christ of Latter-day Saints, managed to become a kind of prime minister of his group; when he died, Brigham Young, a masterful organizer of people, led the Mormons to what is now Utah, where they were able to set up their own religio-political system. However, the federal government stepped in during the latter part of the nineteenth century in order to make the Mormon practice of polygyny a crime against the state.

Billy Graham regards polygyny to be not so much poetic justice, or a human experiment, but a special abomination before God. In contrast, Mormons argue that God allowed polygyny on practical as well as theological grounds, for they thought it was better to have many frontier women attached to one man than to have unclaimed women running loose as fair game for every undisciplined male. Curiously, among Mormons, extramarital sexuality was and is regarded as worthy of excommunication from the faith, although if he repents, the offender may re-enter the church and start over again. Adultery is regarded by Mormons as a sin second only to murder.

As Mormons move from Utah into other states, the question comes up more and more as to whether the *Book of Mormon* can legally be read daily to, say, fifth-grade students by a teacher who happens to be of the Mormon faith. Billy Graham says that after reading the *Congressional Record* regarding religion in the public schools, he has concluded "that every teacher in America has the right to stand up and read the Bible in front of the class." [30]

It has been suggested that the various faiths might take turns in the public schools. For example, on Monday the Jew could read from the Old Testament, the Talmud, or the Mishnah and could offer a Jewish prayer. On Tuesday a Muslim could read from the Koran and offer a prayer to Allah. On Wednesday a Buddhist could read and pray; on Thursday, a Protestant or Catholic Christian; and on Friday, a humanist or Unitarian. But Dr. Graham is not at all happy with this sort of plan. Exactly what plan he is happy with other than simply that of his own faith receiving preferential, if not exclusive, treatment is not clear. In one high school in Texas, the reading of passages from the Bible over the public address system was practiced for a while. But when some of the students requested that scriptures of other religions be read also, the teacher in charge resigned her role as adviser in order not to have to bother with this time-consuming issue and its numerous entanglements.

It is doubtful that the United States Supreme Court's decision on religious expression in public schools prohibits private groups who want to gather together voluntarily and unofficially in some unoccupied area in the school, in order to offer prayers or to do whatever their religious faith requires as religious expression. [31] The Supreme Court seems to have had in mind striking down any *official* religious expression. In that way the threat of any established religion was presumably undercut.

Dr. Graham and others, however, have charged that in effect the public schools already have an established religion: secularism or humanism. This charge raises an interesting question: Could the public school system in practice ever be neutral regarding religion? Some Roman Catholic priests have gone so far as to denounce the entire system as "godless." Perhaps this means simply that to be neutral or impartial is to be godless. Billy Graham thinks the public schools should be politically nonpartisan, which is doubtless a step in the direction of impartiality of some sort.[32]

The public schools are clearly in trouble on this point. We do not demand that our mailman profess some religious faith, but we do seem at times to expect the schoolteacher to profess the religious faith of the parents. This proves to be very difficult for the teacher, inasmuch as the parents themselves are not in agreement as to what the "true" faith is. Unitarian parents and evangelical Christian parents cannot rationally expect the teacher to agree with both of them on every religious and moral point. So the teacher must either present every side possible, or attempt to be somewhat neutral, or select what he or she thinks is right.

After the prayer amendment bill was defeated, Billy Graham announced in April 1972, that he could no longer support the "Wylie" prayer amendment, which he had previously supported. According to page 17 of the April 27, 1972, issue of the *Baptist and Reflector*, Graham's change of position came about because of his further study of the Supreme Court's 1963 decision, which he now believes has been variously misinterpreted by the lower courts. Whether this announced change in Graham's position is substantial rather than verbal alone remains to be seen. Apparently the evangelist is just beginning to see how very complex the issue of religion in the public schools really is. While he now wants religious instruction and prayer in the schools to be "voluntary" rather than forced, he seems to be genuinely confused as to who it is that is *voluntarily* engaging in religious expression. He sometimes seems to think that this choice belongs to the teacher.

Also the evangelist appears to be willing to restrict this religious instruction in the public schools to something that Catholics, Protestants, and Jews would, in his mind, more likely agree upon. This compromise turns out to be instruction in the ten commandments, some of which may also be regarded as central to the civil religion of Christian Americanism.

According to page 5 of the June 1, 1972, issue of the *Baptist Messenger*, Evangelist Graham called for a rehearing of the school prayer issue before the U.S. Supreme Court. If the Court should fail either to change its 1963 ruling or to give an opinion more favorable to Graham's position, then a protest march on Washington led by Billy Graham himself might become a real possibility. At least that is what Dr. Graham said at a meeting in Birmingham, Alabama; and he promised that this march would be the largest of all such marches.

In Birmingham, Graham was also heard to say that God has been ruled out of the schools and that demons are moving in. He did not specify whether the demons were certain school principals, PTA presidents, or teachers. Sometimes he seems to be using words like "demons," "Satan," and "devils" to refer to certain publicly observable practices and patterns of behavior of which he strongly disapproves. As will be seen in chapter 11, Satan is a kind of catch-all scapegoat for Billy Graham. Sometimes the evangelist suggests that Satan is a very efficient cosmic administrator who delegates his work to various beings ranging all the way from devils to bacteria. Sometimes Graham gives the impression that he believes Satan is fairly well represented in the U.S. Supreme Court—or at least used to be.

Billy Graham has thrown his considerable weight behind those who say that they want to "restore God to the schools," but what this means in precise terms and how this is to be implemented in practical programs remain somewhat obscure. In fact, some groups have given up any attempt to work out a compromise and have taken the radical step of recommending that public schools be forsaken and that private schools be established everywhere so that parents may send (or bus?) their children to the schools that most faithfully represent the religious, educational, political, and other requirements of the parents.[33] In the fall of 1971 the large First (Southern) Baptist Church of Dallas, Texas, announced that it would begin a twelve-year school to compete with the public schools. Billy Graham has his membership in this church. The pastor, W. A. Criswell (who was president of the Southern Baptist Convention in 1968–70), insists that his school is not designed to outflank desegregation, but instead is designed to be a school where religion will be taught.

A less radical approach, however, is to maintain the public school system but eliminate at least some required courses by turning them into electives. Furthermore, if enough parents think that one of the courses in biology, for example, is not being taught properly because it teaches evolution, then an alternative course in biology could be offered in order to guarantee that the children of these parents will not be taught evolution as anything other than a false theory. Billy Graham rejects the theory of evolution and thinks that it is the work of Satan. Many of those agreeing with the evangelist would prefer that their children be taught biology from an evangelical Christian point of view. Or in the case of history courses, a United Christian, a liberal Baptist, or a liberal Catholic might want history courses to include fewer stories of warriors and more stories of musicians, physicians, and religious leaders.

We are now in a time when America appears to be becoming increasingly pluralistic. Even the idea of a solid middle-class morality is not as clear as we once were led to believe. Or perhaps, to be more exact, the lines of agreement and disagreement seem to be redrawing themselves. In 1969 conservative Catholic Francis Cardinal Spellman welcomed Graham's ministry to New York City after having told Graham earlier that the city needed a spiritual renewal. Only a dozen years earlier the evangelist received no encouragement from Roman Catholic officials in New York and had expected none. In fact, one Catholic prelate had warned his people at that time not to go to Graham's meetings or to listen to him in any way. But now the times have surely changed, and new lines have been drawn. Among Catholics and Protestants are liberals and conservatives, ultraliberals and ultraconservatives, and even left-wingers and right-wingers. Even in the 1950's a right-wing Catholic, Senator Joseph McCarthy, claimed that he had received considerable material and help from a "great preacher," who turned out to be a right-wing fundamentalist Protestant from Tulsa, Oklahoma. His name— Billy James Hargis.[34]

The old feud between Catholics and Protestants is rapidly on the decline in the United States. Disputes between liberals and conservatives within each denomination are more likely to occur. Liberal Catholics and liberal Protestants seem to share a great number of dearly prized values. Within this confusing state of change, Billy Graham would appear to be a dynamic symbol of what many conservative and ultraconservative Catholics and Protestants regard as ideal Christianity and even ideal Americanism. He speaks for many values that are very dear to them, and he opposes what they consider to be rising influences threatening the very foundation of Christian Americanism. He gives voice to many of the religious and ethical beliefs of those who like to think that they are either solid middle-class Christian Americans or the true remnant of old-fashioned patriotism, righteousness, and religious faith in the land. It is as if Billy Graham were the unofficial, but nevertheless highly influential, representative of a great number who seem nervous about what they take to be their favored status in America. Resenting any hint that they are not the sum and substance of the American dream, they seem to harbor the secret fear that they are not the "insiders" they claim to be. They know that they *ought* to be. But are they in fact? That is the question that haunts them. Graham is very important to them because he symbolizes their longing for power and influence on the public and national level. He is their St. George doing battle with the forces of evil. He is to them a kind of Ralph Nader keeping vigilant guard over the spiritual welfare of America.

In October 1971 the city fathers of Charlotte, North Carolina, set aside a special day of parade and celebration for Billy Graham. One of the speakers at this joyous occasion was Billy Graham's long-time friend Richard M. Nixon. Also attending was John Connally, waving enthusiastically from the motorcade and giving the appearance of a politician running for office. President Nixon could not praise Evangelist Graham enough, and the evangelist in turn told of how Mr. Nixon had been a source of moral inspiration to him. A few weeks before election day in 1960 Graham had decided to write a magazine article for *Life* in support of Mr. Nixon for President over John Kennedy. But the evangelist reversed his decision when the late Frank Clement, then governor of Tennessee, and other Democratic friends of Graham urged him to forgo writing the article. Soon thereafter Graham denounced preachers and clergymen in general for becoming involved in politics. In the 1968 race between Nixon and Humphrey, however, Graham announced a few days before the election that he had cast his vote for Nixon by absentee ballot. Newspapers carried this story prior to election day.

Graham himself has often been criticized for revealing his political preferences. But such criticism seems to be based on the dubious premise that the evangelist is supposed to be a kind of impartial League of Women Voters. Granted, Graham exerts great influence on a number of people; it does not thereby follow that he ought to be silent as to his political preferences. But by the same token Graham is inconsistent when he criticizes other clergymen for expressing their political preferences. He charges that they should be more concerned with the gospel than with politics and social issues. But like Dr. Graham, these ministers believe that their concern for the gospel has social and political ramifications. Graham and those of his persuasion have often taken their particular stand, while other clergymen have done likewise. So the real difference between them would seem to turn on what they consider the essence of the gospel to be and what it means to be a Christian in practical terms.

Billy Graham sometimes seems to many persons to be making his version of Americanism a cardinal doctrine of evangelical Christianity. The late Calvin Bulthuis, who was editor of the Wm. B. Eerdmans Publishing Company, collected a number of newspaper and magazine pictures showing Graham side by side with various leading political figures. Some Evangelicals are unhappy with what they regard as the evangelist's excessive ties with political potentates. Every president of the United States since Truman has courted his favor. Eisenhower, Johnson, and Nixon have been numbered among Graham's personal friends, and in many ways Graham has served as unofficial chaplain of the White House.

But Graham's closeness to political leaders need not be viewed with either alarm or cynicism. What is wrong with politicians having friends among the clergy? After all, even political leaders have worries about their own spiritual welfare. Truman was the first president to invite Graham to the White House. Granted that Truman, like other presidents, could see some political value in gaining the friendship of the popular evangelist, we still would be excessively cynical if we failed to consider the human fears, anxieties, and feelings of guilt endured by the very president who dropped the first and only atomic bombs on his fellowmen. After Truman came presidents who committed American advisers and troops to an Asian war. Even John Kennedy had his Richard Cardinal Cushing. If we ask why Presidents Truman, Eisenhower, Johnson, and Nixon had to call in such a popular public and national figure as Billy Graham in order to talk religion, we forget that politicians tend to think in terms of public figures and popularity. It is very easy for them to confuse popularity with moral approval. It was doubtless quite natural for them to think that Graham's great popularity in America must indicate such approval.

Clearly, it cannot be denied that throughout much of his ministry Billy Graham has tended to regard the United States as a messiah-nation, as a nation with a very special spiritual mission in the world. Indeed, during the Joe McCarthy days, it was not unusual to note Graham making the assumption that the future of Christianity in the world was tied in with the future of America. By America Graham usually meant, not Canada, Mexico, or South America, but the United States alone.

"Christian Americanism" (let us call it) tends to become for Graham a kind of added fundamental doctrine to evangelical Christianity. Even his tours around the world and his revival successes in England and Scotland have not significantly deposed his Christian Americanism. (It might perhaps be fruitful to compare this Christian Americanism with Japan's Shintoism before World War II. There are some major points of similarity, points which disturb some Evangelicals.)

It is not difficult to see how Graham became a prophet of Christian Americanism. First, he grew up in an area that stresses superpatriotism. Second, he saw how the United States was very influential in helping to save Europe from nazism. Third, the United States has been the major power in the free world. And it is very easy for an Evangelical from the South to assume that leadership in the free world is identical with leadership of the Christian thrust in the world. Indeed, when Graham was reaching considerable fame during the Eisenhower years, church attendance in the United States was said to be rising, while in Europe it was on the decline. This alone would have suggested to Graham that God was doing a special work in the United States and that the "land of the free" is also the land of special divine blessing and evangelistic opportunity.

Graham sees himself as a modern prophet Isaiah in the court of an American Israel. Israel's kings consulted Isaiah about politico-spiritual matters, and politicians and presidents have consulted Graham. Isaiah thought of Israel as God's special and chosen nation to be a light to the gentiles, and Graham came very naturally to think of the United States as the major source of light to the heathen around the globe. In some ways Billy Graham has been preaching on and off a gospel of Christian American Zionism.

Billy Graham says that the United States was founded upon God. Presumably he means *belief* in God; for if God is as evangelical Christians say he is, then every nation (no matter what its origin) was and is founded upon God. That is, God's power was and is the absolutely necessary condition for the existence of anything—whether it be a nation, a tree, a mosquito, or an institution. If there is a God who is the foundation of all that exists, then whether or not people believe in him would not in the slightest change the fact that everything depends on him for its existence. Our belief in God does not make him come into existence. Our disbelief in him does not eliminate him. Whether or not there is in reality a God of the universe does not depend on the beliefs of men.

Strictly speaking, the Evangelical's God could not be put out of a school, a nation, or anything else. The Supreme Court could not have removed God even if its members had wanted to. What, then, do Graham and others mean when they say that God has been left out of the schools or out of some other institution? Apparently they mean that certain *forms of religious expression* have been left out. If that is what they mean, few people would disagree with them.

This brings into sharper focus the question of what forms of religious expression *ought* to be found in our schools and in other public institutions. As previously suggested, practical answers to this question are not easy to come by. Unless some children are induced to pray and execute other forms of religious behavior in the public schools, they might not be very religious in Billy Graham's sense of the term. But is it the government's prerogative to step in to do the job of religious instruction for the parents or the churches? It has been argued that if the churches are greatly concerned about the children's religious exposure, they will seek to persuade the parents at least to permit their children to attend church, where they can receive religious training.

Of course, many parents do not want their children to receive the kind of religious conditioning that would be promoted in the public schools. They prefer either another and different form of religious conditioning or none at all for their children. Some of the early settlers left Europe in order to escape an official and established religion, although others came to make their own religion the established and official religion of the state.

Billy Graham believes very sincerely that this nation was founded on belief in God, and he is fearful that this belief is on the wane. Actually, the notion of widespread evangelical Christian belief among the early Americans is a bit of fiction. Even in Massachusetts, where the Pilgrims landed on Plymouth Rock, church attendance was not nearly as high as it has been in twentieth-century America. One church historian estimates that at the start of our national life less than 10 percent of the population was in all the churches of whatever denomination. Thanks in part to revivalism in America, the church habits of Americans have been changing since those early times. Numerically the churches today are far stronger than they were in the past.[35]

Settlers came to America for freedom to do all sorts of things—make a better living, start a new church—or to escape the law in Europe. It is a caricature to picture early America as a land where the great majority of the people were Evangelicals. From the very beginning America was, for good or ill, a coat of many colors, a land of pluralism and variety among its people.

Graham makes much of the fact that the word God appears here and there in the nation's Constitution. But he fails to tell his audience that what Benjamin Franklin or Thomas Paine or Thomas Jefferson meant by God is far removed from what Billy Graham means. Neither Franklin nor Paine believed that God had given a written revelation to mankind. They rejected the Bible as divinely inspired revelation. Franklin belonged to no church. In fact, he believed in the existence of many gods, which is absolute heresy to evangelical Christianity. According to Franklin, among those gods is one who is sufficiently outstanding to be designated as "the Supremely Perfect" or "the Infinite Father"; however, he "expects or requires no worship or praise." Franklin went on to explain in a paper written in 1728 that the Infinite Father is not actually in charge of our planet but rather has delegated that responsibility to one of the other gods.[36]

Thomas Paine wrote a manuscript which strongly attacked much of the religion of his time, including evangelical Christianity. Paine was so strong in his attack that even Benjamin Franklin, for reasons of expediency, advised him in a letter to burn his manuscript in order to escape "a great deal of mortification by the enemies it may raise against you." [37]

Paine rejected the Christian doctrine of the Trinity, the doctrine of the deity of Christ, and the divine inspiration of the ten commandments. His view was that God revealed himself in the orderly behavior of nature rather than in a written scripture.[38]

However, Patrick Henry and George Washington were closer to evangelical Christianity than these other founding fathers. Henry, in fact, advocated "a general [tax] assessment in Virginia for the support of the Christian religion," and George Washington went along with this plan for a while. But the plan never was realized.[39]

George Washington was an Anglican. John Adams, the second president of the United States, began as a Congregationalist but moved into Unitarianism because he became convinced that religion ought to be more of a morality than a theology. He had little use for the theological distinctions which Evangelicals regard as utterly crucial and imperative.

The third president of the United States, Thomas Jefferson, often came under the criticism of many of the more orthodox Christian spokesmen because he was not an evangelical Christian. As a deist he rejected the view that God is involved in the affairs of men. According to Jefferson, the Gospels of the New Testament distorted the real Jesus by making him into a deity. It was Jefferson's view that Jesus was only human, a view which Billy Graham strongly condemns.[40] Regarding Calvinism (which many Evangelicals today subscribe to), Jefferson was very blunt in his criticism. He said of Calvin that "his religion was daemonism." Like Paine and Franklin, Jefferson denied that any scripture was of direct revelation from God.[41]

The founding fathers, then, were not all of one mind on matters of religion. Even when they could agree to use the word God, wide and significant disagreements remained among them as to what the word meant. It would appear today that Billy Graham is in the very interesting position of serving as popular spokesman for two religious camps in the United States. The first is a loose and vague theism that combines the profession of allegiance to the ten commandments with a version of Americanism which expects the word God to be used on such special occasions as inaugurations, football games, and lunar trips. The second camp for which Graham is a popular spokesman is the more detailed evangelical Christianity with its doctrines of the Trinity, original sin, everlasting hell, blood atonement, virgin birth, infallible Bible, and the Second Coming.

According to the July 17, 1968, issue of the evangelical fortnightly periodical *Christianity Today*, Billy Graham more than anyone else influenced Richard Nixon to run for president. In the winter of 1967 Nixon was very much in doubt as to his chances (his "hopes were dim"). So he "put in an urgent call to Graham to join him." Although ill at the time, Graham obliged Nixon and flew to Florida, where the two walked on the sandy beach, read the Bible together. and prayed. Sometime during the two hours Graham expressed doubts as to whether Nixon could win, but he urged him to run nevertheless. Nixon openly acknowledges that Graham was a determining factor in his decision to seek the presidency.

The tall evangelist regarded Nixon as a very upright man, and it is understandable that he should have encouraged Nixon to run for the office. The two men think very much alike regarding the United States Supreme Court, but it is only a matter of speculation whether Graham had direct or indirect influence on Nixon's efforts to make the court more conservative. Graham has spoken out frequently on what he considers to be the court's excessive leniency regarding criminals. It is Graham's contention that the National Council of Churches ought not to make statements on specific political issues because the issues are too complex. There is some merit to this criticism, for Billy Graham's own comments regarding the Supreme Court and crime in America have by and large been broadside attacks which reveal little understanding of the fine points and crucial matters of law and the delicate process of balancing the rights of citizens.[42] Still, the price for keeping amateurs and interested citizens such as Graham and Art Linkletter from speaking forth and giving their opinions on crime and other public issues involving specialized knowledge would be so enormous as to be itself an outrageous crime.

There is a very serious question as to whether Graham's original version of the Supreme Court was not more a caricature than a portrayal. Sometimes Billy Graham is carried away with moral-appearing rhetoric. For example, he is quoted as saying, "Fifty to 60 percent of all university students are on dope and surveys show the reason it isn't higher is because of the limited supply of heroin."[43] This is far from the truth, of course, assuming that Graham means what his words indicate. Perhaps he meant to say—or did say—not 50 to 60 percent, but 5 to 6 percent, which is serious enough but still hardly the fault of the Supreme Court.

Billy Graham's influence on Nixon has doubtless been exaggerated by some members of the press, as Graham's brother-in-law, Leighton Ford, once said. But the long and close friendship between Nixon and the evangelist is not insignificant. Perhaps one reason for their close friendship is the closeness of their views on moral, religious, and social questions. They do seem to share the same general outlook. In the November 5, 1970, issue of *Baptist and Reflector* is an article on page 5 entitled "Billy Graham Condemns U. S. Report on Pornography as 'Diabolical.' " On page 13 of the same issue is an article entitled "President [Nixon] Hits Pornography Report as 'Morally Bankrupt' Document." In the book *Great Readings from "Decision,"* Richard Nixon's article "A Nation's Faith in God" appears along with articles by Billy Graham, Dwight L. Moody, and other Evangelicals.[44] (President Dwight Eisenhower's mother admired Evangelist Moody and named her son after him.)

When in 1968 former ambassador George W. Ball publicly described Nixon as "a man without principle," Graham lashed back with a public statement in defense of Nixon:

> I reacted strongly to a below-the-belt statement last week by George Ball against my long-time friend Richard Nixon. Mr. Ball reflected on Mr. Nixon's moral character and personal integrity. I've known Richard Nixon intimately for 20 years. I can testify that he is a man of high moral principle. I have not seen one thing in my personal relationship with him that would give any indication that he is tricky.

Graham went on to add that he "would react the same way if someone attacked the moral character of President Johnson or Vice-President Humphrey." [45]

At first it might seem odd that Graham in fact never did offer such an articulate public defense of either Lyndon Johnson or Hubert Humphrey, for there were a few times when Johnson's moral character especially was said to have been publicly questioned. Actually, Graham's eagerness to "help put the record straight" [46] regarding Nixon is not difficult to understand if the extreme closeness between the evangelist and the President is recognized. Even though Lyndon Johnson gave Graham rocking chairs for his North Carolina home, the friendship between Nixon and Graham is much more evident than the Johnson-Graham friendship. It has been said that Johnson offered Graham all sorts of government positions, which the evangelist steadily declined. Nixon knows Graham too well to offer him any official position.

On the back of a large bronze plaque placed at the site of Graham's birthplace is the following inscription:

Birthplace of Billy Graham, born November 7, 1918. World-renowned evangelist, author, and educator and preacher of the Gospel of Christ to more people than any other man in history. "Billy Graham is one of the giants of our time. Truly a man of God, the force of his spirit has ennobled millions in this and other lands. I salute him with deep and profound respect."—Richard Nixon, President of the United States. This marker dedicated on the 15th day of October, 1971.

It has sometimes been charged that Billy Graham wishes to exert great political power. But this criticism is as empty as the answer that Graham and his team members make when they reply that they are concerned only with giving "spiritual" advice to public officials. Billy Graham's extreme critics fail to see that no one in a position such as his could do otherwise than exert some strong political influence in certain areas, although he has nothing of the great influence that some critics imagine he has. By the same token, Graham needs to see that his so-called spiritual advice inevitably carries a political impact.

So the extreme critics of Billy Graham are wasting their time if they think that the evangelist can somehow avoid exerting political influence and yet keep his associations with famous political personalities. And Graham needs to admit that he does in fact have this political pull and that other ministers have to use other means if they too are to have their pull. Naturally some public figures like to imagine that they are above exerting political influence; but as Reinhold Niebuhr often said, man is a political animal, and he therefore ought to admit to it and learn to play the game by certain well-constructed rules and procedures. There is currently a movement to give religious groups and others the opportunity to lobby more directly in Washington.

In the summer of 1971 about thirty religious leaders selected by Billy Graham were invited to the White House for an hour-long briefing on the U. S. foreign policy regarding Red China. Henry Kissinger talked with the leaders, and then Nixon received them into his office for a greeting. Graham himself had already received a private briefing from the President and Kissinger, which motivated the evangelist to ask that a number of his ministerial and religious friends be given a similar briefing.

Most of those in attendance represented "the conservative and evangelical stream of religious viewpoint," and among them were W. A. Criswell, six or seven other Southern Baptists, T. W. Wilson of the

Billy Graham Evangelistic Association, and Paul Harvey, who belongs to the Church of God. Criswell's political views seemed to deviate temporarily from his usual ultraconservative position on foreign policy when, in answer to questions after the briefing, he replied that he was supporting Nixon's attempt to establish a change in relationships with Red China.[47]

Of course, Billy Graham cannot exert political influence in just any way he chooses. And no one knows this better than he. Many times he has been urged by influential people to represent North Carolina in Washington. But he has declined, for then he would be just another professional politician like Walter Judd, who was once a missionary to China. Graham genuinely respects public officials, but he knows that his influence in an arena such as, say, the U. S. Senate would probably not be highly significant. Besides, he thinks that God has called him to be an evangelist, not a senator. Evangelists do not have to be reelected; senators and congressmen do, as Brooks Hays learned the hard way.

Brooks Hays once served as congressman from Arkansas, and he also was the 1957–59 president of the Southern Baptist Convention. On the race issue he took a moderate-to-liberal stance, and in the next election he discovered that he no longer represented the Arkansas Fifth District, which includes Little Rock. Despite Hays's calm and even folksy manner, the tide of the Little Rock racial crisis swept him from office. Billy Graham the evangelist is truly outside this kind of contingent political activity.

What the evangelist wants is to be *in* politics in a sense but not *of* it. He wants to have a "moral and spiritual" influence on politics, but he wants to be above and outside the political activity. Graham cannot be a Daniel to America. He can only admire "Daniel because he was a great prime minister of the greatest empire in the world. . . . Daniel was a combination of prophet and political leader and he wrote about many of the things that are now happening in the world." [48]

A very brief summary statement is now in order. First, Billy Graham would like to see America both democratic and fully Christocratic. But this cannot be. Second, the evangelist knows that compromise is inevitable, yet general norms by which to make compromises do not seem to be explicit in his thinking. Like most people, he wants freedom for himself and his kind. But he seems genuinely ambivalent regarding toleration of life-styles which are greatly foreign to his own code of ethics. Third, to guarantee that his moral outlook will have considerable impact on legislation, Billy Graham tends to reach beyond his own theological framework to a broader circle of conservative Catholics, Protestants, and even some Jews. This is not exactly bloc politics, but the evangelist does seem to function as a kind of symbol of consensus among many people who think of themselves as the "decent people" of America.

What will be very interesting to watch in the future is the evangelist's attempts to bring an increasing number of young people under this tent of consensus. To the degree that he is successful, we may venture the prediction that his version of Christian Americanism will begin reflecting some of the less chauvinistic sentiments of the younger generation. The attempt to blend the evangelical faith with old-fashioned Christian Americanism will perhaps never be carried out to anyone's full satisfaction, because there are elements in each that seem beyond reconciliation. Billy Graham tries hard to bring about harmony, and he has succeeded to a degree that is not likely to be equaled in the near future.

Chapter 2
THE MOUNTAIN THAT
LIES TO THE SOUTH

Billy Graham's spacious house stands on a beautiful mountainside in Montreat, North Carolina, which is only a few miles down the crooked road from Mount Mitchell, tallest peak of the Blue Ridge Mountains and unequaled in both height and splendor in the eastern half of the United States. Billy and his young bride spent their honeymoon in the shadow of this peak. It was in the neighboring mountain city of Asheville that the up-and-coming evangelist first met affable Cliff Barrows, the ordained Baptist minister who soon became the music director of the Billy Graham evangelistic crusades. Within a radius of two hundred miles of Mount Mitchell is the stronghold of what has been called "hillbilly evangelism." About a hundred miles from its peak is Charlotte, where Billy Graham grew up. As a teenager there in 1935 he was converted at a revival meeting directed by the brimstone-preaching hillbilly evangelist Mordecai Ham.

When Graham eventually left the mountain region, he went to Florida and then to Wheaton College in Illinois. At Wheaton he met a sophisticated Presbyterian, Ruth Bell, daughter of missionaries to China. Having once been rejected by a young lady in Florida who thought he was too "immature" for marriage, Billy thought himself to be a very fortunate young man when Ruth agreed to forsake her plans to be a missionary in order to become Mrs. Graham. At Wheaton, Billy studied under Prof. Gordon Clark, who to this day still insists on distinguishing his own "evangelical Calvinism" from what he disparagingly refers to as "hillbilly evangelism." [1]

But no one can hope to gain a profound understanding of Billy Graham the evangelist without understanding the southern mountain Protestantism that so profoundly affected him in numerous ways. In many respects the preacher Billy Graham is the colorful radio and tent evangelist that Mordecai Ham reshaped into a national and international personality rather than a regional preacher. If Evangelist Ham had been given a good dose of "class," a reasonably close approximation of Billy Graham would have resulted.

Graham did take on class, and he has become an international figure. Today there is another ordained Southern Baptist evangelist, J. Harold Smith, who got his start in the ministry at about the time Graham got his. Smith's home was in Greenville, South Carolina, which is southwest of Charlotte but still within the region of southern mountain Protestantism. About thirty years ago, when Graham was taking on his first radio program called "Songs in the Night," J. Harold Smith was initiating his "Radio Bible Hour" in Knoxville, Tennessee. Knoxville, billed as the "Gateway to the Great Smokies," is still amply supplied with visiting evangelists and radio preachers. It is located ninety miles north of Cleveland, Tennessee, where Billy Graham attended Bob Jones University, a fundamentalist school so far to the right as to make even many Southern Baptists appear to be flaming liberals. Cleveland is only twenty-seven miles from Dayton, Tennessee, where Clarence Darrow and William Jennings Bryan in 1925 did battle over the issue of evolution.

One of the regulations for male-female relationships at Bob Jones University was what the students jokingly called the "Six-Inch Rule," which prohibited any physical contact between male and female. Bob Jones University is proudly advertised as "the world's most unusual university." It is. In 1970 the Tennessee (Southern) Baptist Convention struck down the decision of the board of trustees permitting dancing on the Baptist campus of Carson-Newman College. Hayrides, however, have enjoyed a long and respected tradition at Carson-Newman, but Bob Jones University can boast of no such similar tradition. When President Bob Jones, Sr., declared that his school would be for the "spiritual" development of young men and women, he had a strict definition of what it meant to be spiritual. Not long after Graham left Bob Jones University because he thought its president was too rigid in controlling the lives of the students, the university moved across the Blue Ridge Mountains into a new campus located in Greenville, South Carolina, which is Cliff Barrows' home town today.

To come back to evangelist J. Harold Smith, it is informative to compare the route of his career as an evangelist with that of Billy Graham. In many ways Smith was a much more interesting, colorful, and dramatic preacher than Graham. His speech was machine-gun fast, varied, and highly flexible; his stories could straighten the spine with terror or make the sides ache with laughter. His sermon "God's Three Deadlines" was utterly overpowering to many. Jonathan Edwards' famous sermon "Sinners in the Hands of an Angry God" lacks the gripping dramatic build-up of Smith's sermon on God's deadlines. I have never heard or read a sermon with more terror in it. Alfred Hitchcock cannot do with screen and script what Smith could do with words alone. Smith denounced the movies, but he provided better thrillers.

Yet Smith never gained national fame. He has remained a southerner of the Old South variety. Whereas a Hearst newspaper helped to project Graham into national prominence almost overnight, Smith became involved in a bitter controversy with a Scripps-Howard newspaper in Knoxville. And whereas Graham's monthly paper, *Decision*, usually kept clear of direct and forthright involvement in political matters, Smith's monthly took on the National Council of Churches and other bodies and charged them with being pro-Communist. Graham saw rather early in his career that he could not enjoy national success by binding himself permanently to the right-wing politics that pervades the southern mountain region. When Senator Joseph McCarthy needed a knight to represent him against the United States Army in the early 1950's, he found many volunteers in Knoxville very willing and ready to take the job. In one of his trips to Knoxville, Carl McIntyre set out to show that the *Revised Standard Version of the Bible* was a pro-Communist endeavor. For at least a while Graham had no great love for the Revised Standard Version, but he did not feel that he could serve his career by denouncing it. He still preaches from the King James Version. He also likes *Good News for Modern Man*, which is a translation by a Southern Baptist scholar.

Evangelist J. Harold Smith's voice may still be heard, no longer in East Tennessee, but in Dallas, Texas, where he pleads with his radio listeners to let Jesus save them on the spot. Both Smith and Graham still call on their listeners to make an immediate "decision" without delay, for they believe that if anyone dies without having made the decision to "accept Christ as Savior," he will "spend eternity in everlasting hell."

In 1948, at a mass revival meeting outside Knoxville in the foothills of the East Tennessee mountains, evangelist Smith told the following joke, the precise details of which I no longer recall, but the point and thrust of which remain vivid in my mind.

Smith told of three black men engaged in conversation. The first said that he was going to town to buy himself a white hat and a white suit and white shoes, then get himself a white girl and take her to the white theater. The second black man said that he was going to get himself a white suit, etc., a white girl, and then take her to the white restaurant. The third black man informed the other two that he was going to town to buy himself a *black* suit and a *black* tie and a *black* hat and *black* shoes. And then he was going down to the black funeral home to wait for two black dudes in white suits to be carted in.

While I have not remembered exactly each item of this joke, its essence and the impact of it on the gleeful audience are not lost to me. The audience was composed primarily of middle-class and lower-middle-class white East Tennesseans. Smith spoke forcefully to some of their immediate needs, one of which was the assurance that the increasing talk at that time of "race mixing" would remain mere talk and nothing more.

Graham, of course, has steadily kept his evangelistic crusades on a much higher level. Although a good joke-teller from the pulpit, he would never allow such a crude joke to come from his lips. In fact, the lower middle class to which Smith made much of his pitch was and is suspicious of Graham because of his alleged compromises with the world. Unlike many evangelists of America, for most of his career Graham has enjoyed class, which places him more with Charles G. Finney (the lawyer-turned-evangelist) and Jonathan Edwards (an evangelist and university president) than with D. L. Moody or Billy Sunday. True, early in his career Graham was a bit flashy in his attire and somewhat showy in his pulpit manner, like any tent revivalist in the South. But he has toned down considerably since he left the Youth for Christ organization and began mingling with presidents and other dignitaries.

There is an old tradition in and around the southern mountains that a preacher does not reason with his audience. He simply "gives 'em the word." He sees himself, and the congregation sees him, as something of a prophet with a message from the mouth of God. And who would quarrel with God? Today when a person in, say, Syracuse, New York, sees evangelist Graham, Bible in hand, preaching on TV, he may be tempted to think that the evangelist is rather cocky in his manner and attitude. Indeed, as we have mentioned, Graham is often billed boldly as "God's man with God's message." But this apparent self-assurance is to a great extent what would normally be expected of a Baptist preacher reared in the vicinity of Mount Mitchell. If you have God's message on your tongue, you send it forth without hesitation. And you do not use such words and phrases as "probably," "it would seem," or "in my judgment." Prophets are not to be confused with behavioral scientists, counselors, and philosophers. Graham thinks that philosophers as a group speak only man's wisdom, while he, as one of the divinely appointed evangelists, speaks for God. To remind both himself and his audience of this, Graham will often preface his remarks from the pulpit with the formula, "The Bible says. . . ."

It is still true in much of the South that the minister of a lower-class and lower-middle-class church is referred to as "the preacher" or as "Preacher So-and-So." When he is not preaching he might be questioned like any other man, but when preaching he is regarded as having a special gift or power that somehow lifts him above the ordinary level of human fallibility. It is a bit like speaking ex cathedra. Yet even here the preacher must stay within certain limits. He must not say anything which his own group regards as clearly unscriptural. Naturally, the preacher who sprinkles his sermons heavily with passages from the Bible will usually please his people.

It is also thought by many in the South that because the preacher stands in a very special relationship with God whenever he is in the act of preaching, he ought not read his sermon. That would give the appearance that he is consulting just another document from the hand of man, rather than receiving a message from God. Similarly, public prayers must be unpremeditated and spontaneous. There is a natural tendency for the preacher to hold the open Bible in his hand as he "proclaims the word." It is permissible, even imperative, that his communiqué from God be mediated through the Bible.

One of the signs that a lower-class southerner looks for in order to determine whether or not a preacher is becoming "modernistic" (and is moving out of his class) is the use of written preaching notes. That is considered to be a step in the direction of worldly sophistication. If the preacher does use notes, it is usually a tactical mistake for him to depend greatly on them. He is expected to command the attention of his congregation without this distraction. After all, one function of preaching among the lower and lower middle classes is that of entertaining the audience as well as delivering the word. This is understandable, inasmuch as entertainment costs money. Of course TV is changing this, but the entertainment function of preaching is still very much in demand by the lower classes. Yet they have certain restrictions as to what can be done to entertain. The following is an account of a violation of restrictions.

Just a few miles from the Blue Ridge Mountains, on the Tennessee side, a part-time preacher-garage mechanic was holding forth one Sunday morning. Throwing himself into his sermon, he began relating the story of David and Goliath. Lost in the reenactment of the story, the animated preacher stooped to pick up stones, loaded his imaginary sling, and hurled the stones at the Philistine giant. During all this activity, the preacher also narrated. He told in good mountain style how David slung his weapon and how he then turned the stone loose. "And," said the preacher to the spellbound congregation, "David's stone hit that sonuvabitch right between the eyes!"

The closing hymn soon followed.

In his early days as a preacher, Graham quite naturally entertained his audience. And as much as national TV will permit him to do so today, he still spices his sermons with discreet humor and active gestures that some ministers from another background think out of place. One reason that Graham has been such a success on TV, when other ministers seem to be boredom incarnate, is that he has at least a vague image of himself as an entertainer on the entertainment medium. It was not inconsistent on his part that he accepted an invitation to appear on *Laugh-In* and that he is today a friend of many movie stars and famous entertainers. In 1949 he did not fear to initiate a tent revival in Los Angeles itself, near Hollywood. In fact, one of his early converts from southern California was the once-popular radio personality Stuart Hamblen, who was well known along "The Strip."

It is a rare thing to find a Southern Baptist evangelist who is not an entertainer of some sort, although in the 1970's Southern Baptists have moved up the socioeconomic ladder, which means that entertainment in the pulpit is on the wane. One major exception to this, however, is the "revivals" which Southern Baptist churches experience usually once or twice a year. These revivals are a kind of combination church service and religious fair. Anticipation is in the air, and a sense of "a good time in the Lord" seems to pervade the church. The visiting evangelist is given considerable leeway in entertaining and captivating his audience, while the song leader is in some cases expected to be a half-comical performer who functions to loosen up the audience and to make them feel receptive to the message of the evangelist. Sometimes the evangelist will bring his own music director.

In Billy Graham's evangelistic crusades the smooth and masterful song director, Cliff Barrows, comes across less the comedian and more the cordial and friendly master of ceremonies who can tell a light joke for the purpose of maintaining a feeling of mutual acceptance within the large audience. It is his enormous job to transform the mass of spectator-strangers into a spiritual body of fellowship and participation. When he first met Barrows, Graham was immediately struck with Barrows' charm and winsomeness, as well as his ability to relate quickly and warmly to a large audience.

Those who were not reared in the South and especially in the southern mountain region will better understand Billy Graham the man, when they see and hear him, if they keep in mind that the evangelist is to a great extent a product of his southern religious and cultural environment. The southern minister—whether professional evangelist or not—is expected to emphasize evangelism, which is one reason why Southern Baptists have become a major Protestant denomination in numbers alone. Winning converts and new church members is given top priority. A Southern Baptist minister who has baptized a large number of converts within the past year will—other things being equal—enjoy a considerable advantage over other ministers if he wishes to move to a better church. A minister who has baptized few or no converts is by and large considered to be a failure in his work as a pastor. It is for that reason, among others, that a Southern Baptist pastor may invite a specialist —an evangelist—to come to his church to "hold a revival." The evangelist is an expert in getting converts for the church. If the pastor baptizes the converts, he receives considerable credit for having participated in "winning them to Christ."

This is hardly the sole—or even basic—motive among Southern Baptist pastors for "winning souls to Christ." But it has become a minor motive at least. Of all the Southern Baptist preachers, Billy Graham has won more converts than any other, which is one reason he is admired by so many Southern Baptist ministers and is invited to speak at the Southern Baptist Convention and other evangelical gatherings. All of Billy Graham's books, articles, sermons, and writings are located in a special place in the library of my alma mater, the Southern Baptist Theological Seminary in Louisville, Kentucky, which also has the endowed Billy Graham Chair of Evangelism.

One of Graham's admirers once wrote: "It is possible that Billy Graham might have become the kind of evangelist he is even though he had not been born, raised, and had his early education in the South. But it is not very likely." [2]

Billy Graham is not, however, simply a product of the South alone. After leaving Bob Jones University, he went to school in Florida and then to Wheaton College in Illinois, where he met his wife-to-be, Ruth. It was her rather frank Presbyterian opinion that some of Billy's preaching bordered on the "hammy" side, and she told him so. His residence in Illinois and his brief pastoral ministry near Chicago doubtless influenced his pulpit manner. And conversely it is probably true that Billy Graham has so influenced preaching in the United States that here and there it has become less somber and dronelike. Through Graham, the southern mountain region has probably brought a measure of entertainment—however light—into the preaching business.

Entertainment is certainly a part of today's evangelism. For example, on page A-42 of *TV Guide* for September 4–10, 1971, there was a full-page advertisement for Billy Graham's northern California crusade. Among those appearing with Graham, according to the ad, were to be "Broadway stage and screen star—Norma Zimmer." On the opposite page was a half-page ad for "Oral Roberts in Hawaii." Appearing with this evangelist were to be The Surfers and Patti and Richard Roberts. "Starring Mr. Hawaii, Don Ho," the program was also to feature appearances by a couple of state governors. "Something *good* is going to happen to you," the ad promised.

One of the interesting things about Billy Graham is his feeling for what his audiences can take. He has had to shape himself to fit the tastes of those who would hear him preach. He does not want to offend their taste, but neither does he want to lose their interest. It is a tribute to his understanding of public communications that he has been able to adjust to the public media and use them for his purposes. Had he not married Ruth or studied outside the southern mountain area in the late thirties and early forties, however, he might today be known in the South alone or in some even smaller region. He might have remained a J. Harold Smith, a Mordecai Ham, or a mountain preacher like M. D. Garret.

M. D. Garret was a raspy-voiced evangelist in and around the mountains of Tennessee, North Carolina, and Georgia. Once in the late 1940's he announced that he was going to have something special for those who would come to the Sunday afternoon service under his big tent. The special surprise awaiting both the faithful and the curious was a rented casket in the front of the tent, with Garret's wife lying inside the casket as if dead. The audience was invited to file by to behold the strange sight. Soon evangelist Garret proceeded to preach his sermon, "Let the Dead Bury Their Dead."

Needless to say, had Billy Graham even suggested such a bizarre form of entertainment, not only would Ruth Graham have declined to make such a public spectacle of herself, she would probably have informed her husband that such a suggestion was not in keeping with the manner of Christ. Still, all in all, the Gospels do tell of some rather spectacular things done by Jesus—raising the dead, turning water to wine, and even walking on water. Yet there were some limits to what Jesus would do. According to the account of his temptations, he declined to turn stones into bread or to hurl himself from the temple pinnacle in order to gain a quick following. He also refused to call fire from heaven in order to consume hostile Samaritans; and when challenged to come down from the cross, he declined to do that.

Nevertheless, the Gospels do portray Jesus as doing some sensational things. It could be argued perhaps that Jesus preached primarily to the common people, whereas Billy Graham found himself—almost before he knew what was happening—accepting invitations to preach in Boston and to visit the White House in the nation's capital. He was soon to become a speaker at eastern universities, the guest of royalty, and a friend to foreign potentates. His manner and style had to be adapted to his new audience. The tall boy from Charlotte who wanted passionately to play first base in the major leagues had become first-string pitcher in the major league of American preachers and perhaps the most famous preacher in the contemporary world.

Yet Billy Graham is still a southern mountain preacher at heart. The typical southern mountain evangelist seems never to grow weary of predicting the Second Coming of Christ in his own lifetime. It was said that the flamboyant Mordecai Ham canceled all his insurance policies because he believed so strongly that Christ would appear in the sky before Ham would himself taste death. Whether Mrs. Ham, the beneficiary of the policies, had a faith to equal her husband's was not publicly discussed. Evangelist Ham, like many preachers in his area, had a radio program. But the unique mark of his program was his daily sign-off. He would say, "I'll meet you *on* the air or *in* the air." The next day his listeners would meet him on the air, but they genuinely expected someday soon to meet him in the air en route to the heavenly city.

Most of the more established pastors in the area at that time mentioned the Second Coming now and then, but they did not make any predictions regarding the time of the glorious event—whether it would be in their own generation or in another. As more or less insiders of their community, they dwelt more on the First Coming and seemed not to be very eager to have the Second Coming interrupt their reasonably satisfactory lives. Traveling evangelists were appreciated occasionally, to provide some necessary jolting of the complacency of the church people; but the pastors themselves—that is, those of the middle and upper classes—were not expected to dwell on the topic of the Second Coming. Pastors of middle-class and upper-class churches had their stakes in this present world order, whereas lower-class pastors were expected by their people to denounce the world and to proclaim perpetually that Christ would soon come to take away the faithful to be with him, leaving the world behind to suffer "great tribulation."

Until the interstate highway system came to the South a person could not drive his car very far on some of the two-lane southern mountain highways before seeing signs proclaiming "Jesus Is Coming Soon." Very often these words were engraved in concrete. Some revivalists who were noted for their powerful preaching on the "very soon coming of the Lord" were observed planting shade trees in their backyards.

The preaching of evangelist Billy Graham has revealed considerable ambivalence regarding predictions of the Second Coming. On at least one occasion, in 1950, he sought to resolve his difficulty by announcing that he did not know when the Lord would come again. He knew only *that* Christ would return. The Second Coming might take place today;

it could also take place a thousand years from now, Graham announced.

Still, he could not remain content with such suspension of judgment, and soon thereafter he was again predicting that all "the signs point toward the very soon coming of Christ." In our generation, he feels, Christ will return. When things look very bad locally, nationally, and internationally, then Graham begins looking for the Second Coming. Like many other evangelists, he became very interested in the war between the Arabs and the Jews. It is a cardinal doctrine among southern evangelists in particular that serious trouble in the Middle East is a sure sign that the end is very near and that Christ is on the verge of stepping out of heaven and into the human scene in order to summon his disciples to join him in celestial joy. Dick Cavett once hinted to Graham that this attitude was a kind of cop-out. But Graham does not think that there is any hope for peace in this old world. Only the Second Coming can put things in order and restore peace and harmony—at least for the believers.

According to the twenty-fourth chapter of Matthew, Jesus gave his disciples some signs by which they could tell when the world's end was near. Yet he warned them that neither he nor the angels, only the Father, knows the "day and hour" of that final event (Matthew 24:36). During World War II, the South had numerous evangelists who, while disclaiming to know the precise day or hour, were nevertheless quite confident that they could foretell within two or three years when the Second Coming would take place. They even carried charts outlining the future of the universe around with them. Speculation as to who the antichrist was, or would be, became a favorite but serious pastime.

Mr. Cole (I do not choose to use his real name), who lived not many miles from Mount Mitchell, read the Bible daily and then the newspapers. From these two sources he pieced together an ingenious theory as to the identity of the antichrist, who presumably would take over the world immediately after the true Christ had come to take his followers to their celestial abode. According to Mr. Cole, the antichrist was none other than the fat Italian Mussolini. (Some of Mr. Cole's Republican friends opted for FDR as the antichrist, but as a staunch Democrat, Cole would not hear of such unpatriotic talk.) Cole did not like Roman Catholicism, and he liked Mussolini even less. After the Allied armies had invaded Italy and after Mussolini had been captured and ingloriously hanged, Cole sincerely believed that on the third day following that infamous hanging, Mussolini would literally rise up from the grave and begin implementing plans to become the world-dominating antichrist. When Christ failed to appear immediately after the Italian dictator's death, and when the dictator himself failed to rise from the grave, Cole was exceedingly disappointed. He had publicly announced his prediction, and now he had been proven wrong. How would he face his relatives and friends?

His discouragement did not last, however. Soon he was busy recalculating and speculating again about God's detailed plans for the future. When Mussolini failed to break the death barrier on the third day, I happened to be with Mr. Cole and attempted to console him by pointing out that according to the Bible a day with the Lord is as a thousand years. I even suggested the possibility that the prophecy about Mussolini's resurrection might come true sometime between the time of the day of the hanging and three thousand years later. But Mr. Cole was not impressed with so indefinite a prophecy. My efforts to encourage him proved to be as futile as they were unnecessary. Thanks to his quick and fertile imagination he was already off on a new and exciting mental trip of his own. Mere facts alone were not sufficient to bring this fascinating man back down to everyday earthly matters.

In any case, among southern Evangelicals during those turbulent days, talk of the Second Coming and of related events and personalities was widespread. The apocalyptic books of Daniel and Revelation and the twenty-fourth chapter of Matthew became popular reading among Evangelicals. It is not surprising, then, that Billy Graham should have taken this concern about the Second Coming as a major part of his Christian faith.

In his declining years, old Mordecai Ham, looking back over his life as an evangelist, told Graham about one of his own mistakes. "I preached too much on prophecy," he said, and advised Graham, "Don't get involved in speculating about the future." [3] But as late as 1965 Dr. Graham was found complaining that

> few philosophers, politicians, economists, or sociologists . . . accept Jesus' prophetic account of history as recorded in the twenty-fourth chapter of *Matthew*. To one who accepts the Biblical account, it is exciting to pick up a newspaper in one hand and the Bible in the other hand and to watch the almost daily fulfillment of prophetic events. . . . The course of human events is following just as Christ predicted it would. [4]

While living in Austria just after World War I, philosopher Karl Popper kept noticing how the faithful Marxists would study the newspaper and Marx's prophecies. (Marx rather gratuitously referred to these prophecies as "scientific socialism.") Popper made the following observation: "A Marxist could not open a newspaper without finding on every page confirming evidence for his interpretation of history." [5] In 1968 Graham stated that newspaper reports and "headlines" read as if taken directly from the book of Revelation.[6] Throughout his entire ministry this has been one of the evangelist's recurring statements. Sometimes he adds the book of Daniel to the book of Revelation. Marxists have been disappointed again and again that the collapse of capitalism has not yet taken place as Karl Marx had predicted it would, and many evangelical Christians have been just as disappointed that the Second Coming has not come as expected. Some believers from both these camps have fallen by the wayside and given up prophecy altogether. But there are still others who, despite disappointments, set their hearts to continue unraveling the prophecies of "the things that shall be hereafter."

Concluding a four-day Hemisfair crusade in San Antonio in June 1968, Billy Graham predicted the end of the world and the Second Coming. "Everybody knows it!" he exclaimed. "Everybody feels it! It's in the air!" The eloquent evangelist is reported to have warned in 1970 that "the world is 'moving now very rapidly toward its Armageddon' and that 'the present generation of young people may be the last generation in history' unless there is a world-wide revival." [7]

Sometimes it is very difficult to determine whether the evangelist is warning, threatening, or simply predicting when he speaks of the end of this world order. It is very difficult to repress the impression that he sometimes speaks as much from anger as compassion. But that is perhaps the way it is with a persistent lover whose object of love does not always heed or even believe him. Yet Graham's despair does not last for long. Any sign of resurgent belief within America as a whole is enough to stir him with new inspiration. He noted that "in the late sixties the Gallup poll revealed that an overwhelming majority of Americans believed that Jesus Christ is coming back to earth again—and a majority of the clergymen believed it too." [8] Probably a more accurate statement would be that the majority *said* they believed in the Second Coming.

One of the things that discourages many evangelists is the gap between what people say and the way they behave. Sometimes people are like the elusive object of love who might profess one thing with words but indicate something different by nonverbal behavior. Graham has courted America for years—on God's behalf, he would insist—and there is no sign that he will turn away and call her a lost cause. To be sure, he knows that she is a lost cause in some respects, but he always seems to be thinking that perhaps a miracle may come about. Perhaps she will turn around and come back. Perhaps his love for her will not come to naught after all. In any case, the fact that he continues to win individual converts is in itself doubtless sufficient to reinforce him in his evangelistic work. The hope that at least the United States will on the whole turn to God—the way Nineveh did when Jonah preached—is a long-shot hope, a hope against hope, but nevertheless a hope.

Chapter 3
THE FAITH AND THE WORLD

The August 1971 issue of Billy Graham's monthly publication, *Decision*, contains an article entitled "Be Ready!" The author of the article, John Wesley White, sounds very much as Billy Graham did in the 1950's, when he was picturing international events as a raging hurricane moving ever more swiftly toward some great cataclysmic upheaval. The end of it all was proclaimed to be just around the corner. Needless to say, there was and is enough contingency and uncertainty in things to make the end of the human race in, say, nuclear destruction a very real possibility. But Graham in the 1950's seemed at times to think that it was the inevitable and only possibility remaining. However, he did concede that if the world would accept the gospel as outlined in conservative Christianity, then God might spare at least America and possibly other nations as well. In those days Graham seemed to conceive of himself as a kind of latest-word news reporter who happened to be enjoying privileged access to an authoritative inside word from some very important person in a very high position—namely, the Lord God of the universe.

Many of the young proponents of the contemporary "Jesus movement" have a burning preoccupation with the Second Coming, which is considered to be hardly an echo away. There are new Billy Grahams springing up here and there over the country. James Robinson, for example, still under thirty, consciously seeks to follow in the way of Billy Graham. Another example is a rising young Southern Baptist evangelist,

Richard Hogue, who is endeavoring to link the churches with the Jesus movement. In Houston alone, Hogue, through his Spiritual Revolution Now Crusade, sparked off four thousand conversions in three months. At the center of Hogue's preaching is the theme of the imminent end of it all. Some young persons have dropped out of college in order to work with him in proclaiming the Second Coming and the termination of this temporal world. High school students have received him enthusiastically.

"Here Comes de Judge" is one of Hogue's most effective and moving sermons. He and his wife have declined to buy a house simply because they feel that they would not have time to enjoy it, inasmuch as Jesus will be returning very shortly. Like John Wesley White, Hogue is telling the young people to "Be Ready!" Social and political activities are of no great concern to them, for God will soon come to straighten out all things without any political compromises or deals. The essential thing, then, is to become prepared to face God on Judgment Day. This temporal world has about had it. No need to waste time and energy on it. God has a shiny new world, the New Jerusalem, waiting to give to his obedient children.

In his book *Future Shock*, Alvin Toffler says that we are living in the age of the discardable and disposable. Contemporaries easily dispose of automobiles and discard spouses in divorce courts. Adherents of the Jesus movement (and Billy Graham in some of his more pessimistic moods) exemplify this trend toward disposability in the extreme, for they would simply discard the entire temporal life and replace it with a new world altogether. It is as if this earth were a commodity or a machine that does not work very well. And so instead of attempting to repair it and fix it up somewhat, the more extreme followers of the new eschatological upsurge have simply put in an order (a faith-request based on divinely revealed advertisement)—an order for a brand-new world. The old one is to be left as a piece of junk that God will presumably melt down in the cosmic fire referred to in 2 Peter.

Quite understandably, a sense of powerlessness and frustration in coming to terms with this old world can precipitate among Christians the well-known "to-hell-with-it!" syndrome. Billy Graham is not as extreme as some, however; for he, after all, has enjoyed some success in relating to "the power structure"—as shown by his helping to convince

Richard Nixon to run for president (which doubtless was not one of Graham's most difficult assignments). Evangelist Graham has also been called upon to advise Presidents Lyndon Johnson and Dwight Eisenhower. He has been briefed at the White House on a number of occasions.

However, Graham has entertained hopes of turning the entire world, or at least America, to God. Now and then he breaks out with enthusiastic expressions of hopeful prophecy that America will "turn to Christ." But, despite new "upsurges of faith" now and then, here and there, no grand and general drift in Graham's direction seems to be in the making. Hence, his superdream of national conversion seems perpetually to be slipping away from him. God is said to be stirring mightily in this group and that, but things never seem to come to a good boil. The nation, to say nothing of the world, appears bent on going in other directions. And thus Graham's vision inevitably suffers frustration. It might be thought that his rapport with leaders in high places would eliminate this frustration. And indeed it might if Graham's dream were not so grand and sweeping. But given the nature of his vision of general and widespread conversion, Graham seems doomed to frustration. This doubtless accounts for some of his anger against the world. Like a tutor who lovingly wants his students to measure up to the highest ideals but becomes disappointed and angry if they do not, Graham is found to be ambivalent toward the world. He loves it for what it *could be*. But he is set against it because of what it *is*.

According to Graham's frame of reference, the heavenly Father, as any decent earthly father might do, has called upon a tutor to instruct his wayward children. But, alas, because the children have more pressing interests, the tutor's image of himself as an effective and powerful source of influence invariably suffers. Yet Graham has his divine calling and must perform his duty. Perhaps the students will come around. Graham keeps hoping, sometimes hoping against hope; for in his less enthusiastic moments he faces squarely the very real possibility that a sweeping turn to God (as conceived by Graham) is not very likely even in the United States. At these times he sometimes substitutes a lesser dream. Instead of converting the world, he, and those like him, will simply *preach to* everyone in the world—hence his tours not only across America but around the globe. Yet the grander dream keeps haunting him.

He seems unable to get it out of his mind. He is like a baseball pitcher who cannot help dreaming of winning the world series game that he lost. The dream keeps returning.

Graham defends America with holy zeal, for he sees her as the primary locality from whence his worldwide crusade originates. But he also denounces her for being such a poor example. He wants desperately to see the United States as a model Christian nation. But he knows that she is not. In this, Graham is not unlike other reformers who have had dreams for their nation and have been bitterly disappointed in the poor way that the nation has responded. Sometimes Graham becomes so righteously indignant that he prophesies that the judgment of God will visit America in particular because of her special blessings and opportunities. But no sooner has the evangelist denounced her than he boasts of her as if she were very special to the eye of God. Like a lover who cannot win his girl, Graham heaps upon his nation words of condemnation which he alternates with words of exultation and inspiration. He both threatens and woos. And sometimes he says that it is all going to be over. The end of the whole world is predicted to be very close at hand. It is as if the lover would rather see the object of his love destroyed than left for others to woo and win. He cannot endure the thought of her going off in a thousand directions rather than in the one path that has presumably been made for her. A look into the history of Christianity discloses that Christians have often had a kind of love-hate relationship with their country or with the world in general. A classic example is Augustine's book *The City of God*, which was written in part as an attempt to refute the charge that Christianity was the cause of the fall of the Roman Empire.

Not many Christians of the first century would have predicted the church's survival in the world for two thousand years, for they expected the world itself to end very shortly, in their own lifetime or at least in that of their children. The author of 2 Peter felt called upon to give some kind of explanation as to why the Lord has delayed in keeping his promise to take the elect out of the world and then to dissolve totally all temporal creation. But, as 2 Peter 3:8 explains, "with the Lord one day is as a thousand years," which is to say that while the delay may seem long to anxious mortal Christians, it is not very long at all according to God's time.

Gradually the Christians had to learn to live in the world, to make adjustments, and to come to terms with the temporal environment in which they found themselves. The story of this adjustment is a fascinating one, filled with tales of heroic efforts, shameful cruelties, some colossal blunders, and some wise decisions. With both nostalgia for the first century and the practical necessity of living in their own time, Christians had to make do the best they could. Over the centuries they have not always agreed on the way to live as citizens of two realms. Some declared that the temporal world was unreal and that the spiritual realm was the only true reality. Others took the reverse position, and still others proclaimed some sort of union of the two realms.

Every movement of Christianity that has attempted to return to the faith of the fathers has been able to journey only part of the way back. Evangelist Billy Graham preaches "the old, old story," but his evangelistic team is an efficient system of contemporary technology and organization. This does not mean, however, that conservative Christians like Graham think that these new worldly techniques of communication affect the gospel message itself. Sometimes the medium is not the message. They believe that the true Christian message can be presented today in all its original purity and that the intervening centuries between the apostle Paul and evangelist Graham have not modified the Christian truth in the slightest. The times may change, but not the gospel itself.

There are some, however, who believe that true Christianity, far from being a Rock of Gibraltar, is rather like a mercenary whose services are for hire to the highest bidder. Some of these students of Christianity believe that Christianity, and religion in general, do not provide moral leadership but rather hop on whatever bandwagon seems to be offering the best deal. They picture Christianity as a weather-vane shifting with the winds. When the times change, so does Christianity. According to this viewpoint, Christianity is nothing substantial in itself but is like vapor rising off the more substantial economic, scientific, social, and cultural realities. On the surface preachers may appear to be great moral leaders, but at heart they merely report the weather and changing climate of the times. According to these critics of Christianity, Billy Graham favored integration only after he felt the integration winds beginning to stir, just as he was a mere vapor of the times when he and Richard Nixon were beating the professional anticommunism drums during the Joe McCarthy days.

At best, Christianity is pictured by these critics as a handy device for selling a project, a product, or a program. If Martin Luther King quotes Jesus for his purposes, so will George Wallace. Eric Fromm sees Jesus as a nonauthoritarian humanist, while W. A. Criswell (Billy Graham's pastor in Dallas) pictures Jesus as a person of absolute authority and infallibility on any subject from psychology to cosmology. R. Carroll wrote a pamphlet called *Jesus: A Capitalist*, while a certain French film portrays the Nazarene carpenter as a violent revolutionist for the proletarian cause. "Christian economics" is nothing in itself but is simply whatever economic scheme happens to attach itself to the word Christian. Christian Socialists proclaim socialism to be the Christian ideal, while Carroll sees Jesus and his father Joseph as two capitalists living in the joyous time when "there was no labor union to meddle with prices and wages." Those were the days! And Carroll is emphatic in his belief that the return to "biblical Christianity" entails the elimination of labor unions and other such things that interfere with the divinely appointed Invisible Hand. In his book *God, Gold, and Government* Howard Kershner charges that "socialism is anti-God," but other writers are equally strong in their assertion that socialism is the ship on which the divine will is to be carried around the globe.[1]

Now, it is doubtful that we can believe either the claim that Christianity is merely the passive reflection of the times or the claim that the changing times make no impact on Christianity in any essential way. The truth seems to lie somewhere between these two extremes. A vital religious faith makes an impact on its social, economic, political, and cultural environment; but at the same time the environment affects religious faith in various ways. In fact, any religion which ceases to be influenced by its temporal setting will find itself retired to a position of inactivity and powerlessness.

An influential religious personality such as Dr. Billy Graham is interesting to study because he serves as a kind of trading-post agent of this two-way traffic between religious faith and the world of changing codes, technology, politics, medical evolution, and social mobility. Through him flows much of the interchange between religion, on one hand, and the complex of society and culture, on the other. To be sure, this flow back and forth may be so subtle and steady that the intermediate agent is often seldom aware of what is taking place in him. He is, as it were, an innocent tool of complex dynamics which he may little understand or appreciate.

In some cases, however, the man in the middle may understand enough to want to affect the interchange in some way. He may seek to make a contribution of his own special kind. Evangelist Graham's fundamental conscious objective is to open up better ways by which his conservative Christian faith may exert a mighty impact on the world. He thinks that the world has already had far too much influence on the Christian churches.[2]

One of the most difficult facts of life for practically every religion to acknowledge is the following law of human involvement: *To influence other persons is to be influenced by them.* Orthodox Christianity inadvertently acknowledges this in its doctrine of the incarnation; for once God began to create and influence mankind, then God himself became everlastingly involved with that part of his creation. Once the world became an object of divine attention, then God in effect was "touched" by the world.

Aristotle would not allow that his God was even aware that there exists a world of mortal men and cabbages and kings, for Aristotle knew that if God should ever become involved with the world, then it would in one way or another get to him. So Aristotle referred to his God, not as "the God who acts," but as "the Unmoved Mover." Absolutely nothing moves him, not even crime in the streets or poverty in the slums or pain in the hearts of men. He is everlastingly and totally unmoved. It is as if Aristotle's God does nothing but sit on his throne and hum perpetually to himself the song "How Great Thou Art."

But the Christian God relates to the world and is moved by it. At least that is what Christians believe. Their God is, as the author of Hebrews says, "touched with the feeling of our infirmities" (4:15, KJV). Christianity teaches that prayers reach him and influence him. The world of mankind makes such an impact on God that he cannot get this creature out of his mind—not for all eternity. If the Christian does truly believe this to be true about God, then he will have little difficulty in believing that one of God's human spokesmen will inevitably be influenced by the world.

A major purpose of this book is to look at some of the ways in which a man like Dr. Billy Graham affects the world and is, in turn, affected by it. One of Dr. Graham's former friends and teachers, Bob Jones, of Bob Jones University, has turned his back on him and will no longer pray for his success as an evangelist because Jones thinks that "the world" has gotten to Graham. Desiring to keep the gospel absolutely pure and un-influenced by the world, Bob Jones has erected a fence around his university in Greenville, South Carolina. But in so doing, he has not only reduced the flow of the world's influence into his university, he has reduced the flow of influence from his university into the world.

Dr. Graham was criticized by some of his followers for appearing on the TV program *Laugh-In*. The critics feared that Graham would be too greatly influenced by the world. Like Marshall McLuhan, they felt, vaguely at least, that inasmuch as the TV medium manufactures its own message, the TV message might infect the gospel which Dr. Graham wanted to present on *Laugh-In*. But the evangelist, knowing the risks involved, understood what some of his critics did not, namely, that an evangelist has to take the risk of involvement in the world if he is to exert any influence on it. "It's a chancy job," as Marshal Dillon used to say. But Dr. Graham believes that he is justified in gambling for God, especially if God still manages the house when the chips are down.

Naturally, there are some risks that not even Graham will take on God's behalf. In some cases there is too much at stake. For example, the evangelist once declined an invitation to demonstrate publicly that his God was the only true God and that the Islamic faith of the Near East is therefore under an illusion about its exclusive claims. The occasion was reported in the *New York Times*, March 5, 1960:

MOSLEM DARES GRAHAM TO COMPETE IN HEALING

NAIROBI, Kenya, March 4 (AP)—The Rev. Dr. Billy Graham was challenged today to a healing contest to see whether Christianity is more powerful than Islam.

On his return to Nairobi from Ruandi-Urundi on his African trip, the evangelist was handed a letter from the chief of the Ahmadiyya Moslem mission in East Africa, Maulana Sheikh Mubarak Ahmad.

Contending that Islam alone is the living religion on earth through which man can attain salvation and that Christianity is utterly devoid of any heavenly blessing or true guidance for man, the letter suggested that "thirty incurables" be certified by the director of medical services of Kenya and "be equally divided between you and me by lots."

"We may then be joined by six persons of our respective faiths in prayer to God for the recovery of our respective patients to determine as to who is blessed with the Lord's grace and mercy and upon whom His door remains closed," the letter added.[3]

According to the report, evangelist Graham declined to comment, and his associates expressed doubt that he would respond to the challenge. A Christian familiar with the Old Testament might wonder why the world-traveled evangelist did not avail himself of this golden opportunity. The prophet Elijah would have gladly accepted it. It will be recalled that Elijah held a contest between himself and the prophets of Baal. And if the Old Testament story is to be accepted, then we must concede that Elijah's God responded to prayer and produced a publicly observable miracle demonstrating that the God Yahweh and not Baal was the only true God.

Why did Dr. Graham change? The answer is that *he is a man of modern times.* Conservative Christian theologians do not deny that God is the same as he was in Elijah's day. He is "the same yesterday, today, and forever." But apparently God does not work in exactly the same way. His modus operandi has modified somewhat. External miracles are toned down by even conservative theologians of the twentieth century. Basically that is what the feud between singer Pat Boone and some of the leaders in the Church of Christ is about. Boone thinks that God still works miracles in the twentieth century, while some of the Church of Christ ministers are of the opinion that the day of miracles is over. Miracles in Bible times are one thing. Miracles in modern times—especially in the twentieth century—are another phenomenon altogether. Even Oral Roberts, while still believing in "modern miracles," does not come on as aggressively as he once did with his healing campaigns. He has softened his claims and has "spiritualized" the miracles considerably.

Dr. Graham still believes in miracles. But not the kind that raises people from the dead and makes the sun to stand still. (Some conservative scholars now deny that the Old Testament teaches that such a cosmological miracle ever took place.) For Graham, modern miracles are more subjective and psychological in nature. If a former drunk becomes a sober Christian, then that is a miracle—by definition. To be sure, Graham and other Christians pray for their friends to be healed from illness and disease. But they usually concede that God's healing miracles are nowadays mostly mediated through medical science and the specialized arts of healing. Good hard-core, old-fashioned, publicly observable miracles are hard to come by in these modern times. There are not many Elijahs left.

In short, the scientific environment has become a part of Dr. Graham's frame of reference. When he is ill, he still prays and wonders if he has some secret sin for which God is punishing him. But he also goes to Mayo Clinic or wherever he can obtain expert medical care. There are no reports of his going to his friend Oral Roberts for a miraculous cure. Even when his eyes were in very bad shape, Dr. Graham did not expect a healing miracle. Yet he did not think of himself as lacking in faith for not availing himself of a special work of grace, for he is a twentieth-century man who basically does not believe in such a clear-cut miracle. In fact, it is thought by some conservative Christian theologians that even the direct healing miracles of the Bible were given more for signs than for healing per se. Today there is no more need for such signs, it is reasoned.

There is much more to healing than what medical science today knows. There are indeed psychological factors and all sorts of other subtle dimensions; medical science is attempting to explore these various areas in order to expand the domain of science. There exists some likelihood that the human side of prayer can be examined scientifically and perhaps utilized for human good or ill. But Billy Graham and others of the conservative Christian persuasion are ambivalent about attempts to deal with religious phenomena scientifically. It used to be said—and is still repeated today occasionally—that science works in one domain, while God works in another. But this compromise has never been very satisfactory for either science or religion, for science keeps encroaching on the domain reserved for divine activity alone.

This poses a tortuous problem for Dr. Graham and other Christians of his persuasion. We have noted that he and other Christians have come to accept medical science as divine work after all. True, Christian Science is a holdout in this area, but not for long. There are strong indications that medical science is gradually making inroads into the fold of Mary Baker Eddy.[4]

Conservative Christians cannot help but ask what other inroads science will make into the territory of faith. It is a terrible question to have to ask, but it keeps appearing in the thoughts of men like Billy Graham.

It haunts them and will not give them peace of mind. Their response is understandably ambivalent. Unlike earlier Christians who in the name of religious faith resisted anesthesia for a woman about to deliver a child and resisted treating insanity as anything other than demon possession, Graham has not joined the fight against medical science. He hails its advances as the providence of God. But he is not too sure about Charles Darwin. Conservative Christians are somewhat divided on the theory of evolution. They think that science has gone too far this time. Or, in most cases, they charge that the theory of evolution is only a theory, after all—and that it is not "true science." Christian faith, Dr. Graham insists, is not in disharmony with *true* science. Sometimes, however, this becomes circular reasoning which says that if something does not fit with orthodox Christianity, then *by definition* it cannot be admitted as true science.

However, a handful of conservative Christians, while not accepting the theory of evolution, nevertheless set forth something like "threshold evolution," which is a kind of favorable gesture to the more standard theory of evolution. Most conservative Christian theologians profess to believe that the theory of evolution will never be proved and therefore their Christian faith will not have to be modified by the theory.

Currently, conservative Christianity is being pushed against the wall by various schools of mental therapy. Many branches of Christianity have turned pastoral care into pastoral psychology and have openly acknowledged being influenced by Freud, Jung, Rogers, Glasser, and even B. F. Skinner. Dr. Graham must come to terms with this new intellectual environment and attempt to say something relevant to it. Will he resist psychiatry? Or will he let it affect his understanding of the gospel?

His solution is to dig a moat between religion and psychiatry. There is a place for psychiatry—but it must be on the other side of the moat. Fearing encroachment, Graham hopes to contain creeping psychiatry by relegating it to the area of "mental" problems only. This leaves the religious minister to deal with "spiritual" problems. What Graham means by spiritual is not always clear in his writings and sermons. He usually means something like proper attitude toward God, proper doctrinal beliefs, and proper personal ethics. He writes: "It would call for a psychiatrist with real spiritual insight to be able to tell the difference between the purely mental problem and the spiritual problem." [5] In saying this, Dr. Graham triggers a very serious question: Does he imply that a Christian minister needs *psychiatric* insight to be able to distinguish mental from spiritual problems? Graham does not entertain this question. But if he should respond in the affirmative, he would be making a concession of enormous consequences. Pope Pius XII apparently faced the question, and he concluded with an attack on Freudian psychoanalysis; he prohibited Catholics from undergoing it and Catholic doctors from practicing it. Nevertheless, not all of psychoanalysis fell under the papal ax.

We can only speculate as to what Graham's answer would be to the question raised above. Thus far he has said only that "there is a place for psychiatric counselling when the problem is not one of spiritual significance." [6] "Psychiatry, a relatively new therapy," says Graham, "can relieve the mind; physicians can help the body; but only God can save the soul." [7] Paradoxically, both psychiatric counseling and religious counseling have a way of extending their boundaries. The latter (if it is conservative Christianity) tends to diagnose human problems in terms of sin and to propose Christ as the cure.

Having said that psychiatry and psychology specialize in mental problems, while the Christian minister specializes in spiritual problems, Graham cannot remain content with his own division of specializations. He writes:

> Psychologists, schooled in the intricate workings of the mind, are confessing that psychology is helpless to solve all of the mental and nervous disturbances of people today. Sociologists, trained in the interactions of society, are admitting that sociology cannot cope with the tremendous problems in human relationships. They all say "there is an answer somewhere else, but we aren't sure where." I can tell them where the answer lies: in the teachings of Jesus Christ—nowhere else! [8]

It would appear, then, that initially Graham wanted to distinguish the mental from the spiritual in order to protect orthodox Christianity from the impact of the behavioral sciences. What he apparently failed to realize was that this device could also prevent orthodox Christianity from exerting influence in the realm of psychology and psychiatry. Graham wanted to have his cake and eat it too. But the law of influence does not work that way.

In his writings and counseling, Billy Graham usually attempts to spell out what sin is. And Christ as the cure becomes translated into something of a practical program of church attendance, devotional habits, certain intellectual commitments, specially prescribed attitudes toward God, Bible study, witnessing to other persons, and various other forms of behavior modification. Sin comes to be understood in practical terms as failure to measure up to this program. Statements like "Turn to God!" "Come to Christ!" "Surrender to God's will!" "Accept the gift of the Spirit!"—these have to be translated into more specific directions if they are to do more than leave the convert in a state of confusion and guilt. For those who agree with Graham's view of Christianity, the very act of coming down to the front of a mass evangelistic campaign to "accept Christ" may itself be a practical part of the meaning of accepting Christ.

The interchange between religion and psychology is interesting to observe on its own right. Psychotherapists of various schools tend to be more indulgent toward religion than Freud himself was, although this indulgence is not exactly what Billy Graham would want if he fully understood its implications. Dr. Graham has made reference to Carl Jung's comment, "Among all my patients in the second half of life . . . there has not been one whose problem in the last resort was not that of finding a religious outlook." [9] But what Jung meant by religion is considerably different from what Graham means, a point which the evangelist has neglected to make clear in his attempt to add psychological prestige to his preaching. Psychological and psychiatric therapists tend to say that people need some kind of reasonably functional religion in order to give their lives a measure of unity and purpose. But orthodox or conservative Christians insist that there is only one religion. They hold to *the* way, not *a* way, of meaningfulness in life. "The Bible teaches," says Evangelist Graham, "that the cross is God's testimony to the fact that there is no other way of salvation." [10]

Imagine a physician who has on hand a vast supply of a particular medicine. He wants to use it, but no one among his patients has or will have the terrible disease for which the medicine is a cure. So, instead of disposing of the medicine or at least saving it for a later date, the physician simply goes to his patients and infects them with the disease. Sometime thereafter he announces in glowing terms that he possesses for their benefit the perfect cure for their disease, if only they will accept it and commit themselves to be loyal to him in his profession as a healer.

Doubtless we would think such a man unscrupulous and not interested in the health of his fellowmen so much as in ingratiating himself to them and obligating them to him. This is the way Freud looked upon ministers of religion.

He thought of religion as an advertised cure of a disease, a disease which ministers alone have caused. Were it not for religious indoctrination, Freud believed, there would be no need for the cure. What he himself as a physician would offer, therefore, is an exposure of the evil of the religious enterprise itself. In this way he would contribute to human happiness and meaningfulness by advocating a form of preventive medicine. Just as a physician would advise his patients about how to avoid contracting a disease, so Freud desired to help his readers to avoid catching the disease of religious neurosis in the first place. He would inoculate them, as it were, against this dread affliction and thus leave them better able to cope more realistically with life.

It comes as no surprise, then, that Dr. Graham wants to keep psychiatry at a distance. What is significant is not that he resists psychiatry's encroachment, but that he makes at least some concessions to it. To be sure, while his line between the mental and the spiritual bends and curves at times with bewildering ease and convenience, the vague distinction does nevertheless give conservative Christianity some additional time for working out more thoroughly its relationship to psychiatry and psychology in general. Freud has made his way into the churches, no matter how conservative they are. And doubtless to the disappointment of Freud if he were alive today, the churches have had some impact on psychoanalysis and therapy in general. In order for Freudians to exert influence on religion, they had to run the risk of being influenced by it. Indeed, orthodox Freudianism has itself become a kind of religion with its own practical programs of "cure" for such "sins" as neurosis, psychosis—the Oedipus complex being to pure Freudianism what original sin is to Billy Graham and conservative Christians.

"All across the nation," Dr. Graham declares, "hundreds of educators, counselors, psychiatrists and philosophers are finding out they don't have the answers and they are throwing up their hands and crying for help." [11] Granted that the evangelist is somewhat melodramatic and immoderate in this declaration, it is nevertheless true that few of those who work systematically with the nitty-gritty problems of human relations claim to have "the answers." In fact, it is rather doubtful that they are looking for final answers. That seems to be more Graham's own personal concern. Behavioral scientists have to face up to the fact that human problems are multiple, and therefore the approaches to them must be multiple. So, while it is true that educators and social scientists do not have precut answers, this hardly means that they are crying out for Billy Graham to ride in to save them from their state of ignorance. In fact, many counselors, philosophers, and behavioral scientists look upon Graham and orthodox Christianity as a source of some of the *problems* of human relationships.

But many other persons look to orthodox Christianity to answer their life's problems—or, to be more exact, some of their problems. It is because modern man has so very many specific but entangled problems that the interchange between religion and the world will continue, no matter how many walls and moats are constructed in order to prevent it. Those who prophesy that religion will someday cease to be a part of humanity's concern do not take seriously the fact that religion deals with such perennial human concerns as death, failure, hopelessness, despair, frustration, meaninglessness, the woeful sense of finitude, helplessness, and what the existentialists refer to as angst, or general dread of being. The phenomenal success of Billy Graham's ministry in converting over a million people is greatly due to the fact that he gives voice to some of this human sense of finitude and frustration that throbs in every man's heart.

This also accounts greatly for the success of B. R. Ambedker, who won to Buddhism two-and-a-half million of the untouchables of India. Despite their miserable lot in life, the converted untouchables "experienced a sudden sense of release, a psychological freedom" that they had never known previously. "Filled with a new spirit of self-confidence," they were enabled to face their hardships with greater resoluteness and courage.[12] That is what Buddhism gave them.

Orthodox Marxists are forever worrying over the fact that bourgeois morality, politics, and economics keep taking their toll on the pure doctrine of Marx and Lenin. Even Russian Communists, who look upon themselves as guardians of the faith among the Marxist countries, cannot maintain their own purity. Longing to make a thoroughgoing impact on the world, they have repeatedly discovered to their horror that the world has in turn been making itself felt within the gates of orthodoxy itself. It is because religion, friendship, sexual ventures, poetry, music, intellectual curiosity, and a host of other human expressions are attempts to respond—however greatly or poorly—to human needs that Marxism, orthodox Christianity, Buddhism, Freudianism, and other such movements have struck sympathetic chords in the lives of men. But these numerous needs—whether innate or cultivated—are not so easily satisfied with one pat solution. Hence, each of these religions and ideological movements must secretly admit to itself that it is not wholly adequate to the task it has set for itself. This is a bitter pill to swallow, for it is a confession that its promises have not all been fulfilled. Indeed, the promises were not always clearly spelled out.

Frustration and promises are the fuel propelling mass movements, but they are also the source of revision, reform, and modification, if not outright hamstringing of mass movements. In order to continue making itself felt in the world, Marxism has had to revise itself again and again. Lenin started by modifying Marx. The "revisionists" are the "modernists" of the Communist world. The needs and promises that bring men to mass movements of all sorts will also tempt them to grow weary of the faith if it does not make itself responsive to the wider world. Orthodoxy will always suffer apostasy and "a falling away"; and even when there is a revival of orthodoxy, it will come with new and strange elements that make the old orthodoxy a bit uncomfortable, if not secretly resentful and ambivalent. The "Jesus People," for example, are something old and something new, something orthodox and something heterodox, something welcomed and something resented.[13]

It is typical of Dr. Graham's preaching to picture the Bible as a kind of self-contained entity that is self-explanatory, provided the reader is converted and guided by the Holy Spirit. Yet even here the influence of the wider world passes into the heart and marrow of the words of the scripture itself. Not only do the discoveries of new scrolls, manuscripts, and archaeological objects often compel the student of the Bible to revise his interpretations and refocus his theological perspective, but scientific theories in biology, geology, and astronomy sometimes suggest ways of interpreting the Bible that were unknown to Christians of previous centuries. This is a point reluctantly but frankly admitted by the noted conservative Christian scholar N. H. Ridderbos.[14] With a chilling bit of forthrightness, Ridderbos says to his fellow conservatives that historical anthropology has forced on the attention of the scientific world some considerations which "cannot be easily squared with the content of

Genesis." [15] He challenges his fellow believers to give more attention to historical anthropology. And it is no great stretch of imagination to conclude that if today it is biology and historical anthropology making an impact on the exegesis of scripture, tomorrow it will be psychology and sociology.

Dr. Graham is by and large very critical of sociology because, for one thing, in effect it attempts to find specific ways of talking about what Dr. Graham and conservative Christianity have classified under the general heading "original sin." Original sin has been a fixed Christian doctrine for centuries, even though its meaning has varied considerably. Psychological exegesis of scripture has been attempted in various ways, but not very systematically or self-critically. Nevertheless, it is only a matter of time before psychology and sociology make their influence felt systematically in the field of orthodox biblical exegesis and interpretation. At present the consequences of this can only be vaguely anticipated. It is one thing to have an infallible book at the heart of one's religion. But it is another thing to have to acknowledge that the interpretations of the sacred book are in varying degrees subject to the development of the natural and behavioral sciences.[16]

When Oral Roberts was once in extreme pain and thought that perhaps he had a kidney stone, he called for his physician, who examined and treated him medically and also prayed for him on the spot. Roberts' relief came within a matter of hours. And his explanation was that whether his recovery came through prayer or through medical science, or both, the truth is that his recovery was a "miracle from God." Billy Graham, who preached the dedication sermon at Oral Roberts University, in Tulsa, agrees with Roberts that cures for the sick are often miracles, regardless of the particular human methods used. Both evangelists chide those who refuse to consider the possibility that healing can come through prayer and faith.

It would indeed be very narrow of a person to refuse to consider the role that prayer and faith may have on any patient's recovery. There is nothing scientific about turning one's back on empirical data. However, while very eager to have the prayers of Christians regarded as a means by which healing comes about, Graham and Roberts are very ambivalent regarding the role in healing played by the prayers of Muslims, pagans, Hindus, and many other non-Christians who pray for the sick. An open-minded scientific study of healing would, at a preliminary level at least, be compelled to give a fair hearing to every type of claim to healing by prayer. There is no a priori reason why a science for understanding such phenomena as prayer, worship, and meditation could not be developed in the years to come.

Presently, when the word miracle is not used frequently with any strong theological connotation, Billy Graham and Oral Roberts are prepared to use it in connection with healing, conversion, and certain other times in one's life. If, however, the word miracle is used too frequently, then it comes to mean little more than an unusual or unforeseen happening. "It was a miracle that I passed the exam!" exclaims the surprised student. If the term miracle is stretched still further, it becomes diluted to mean hardly more than a highly desirable normal event. Of course, these two evangelists may find that they cannot consistently avoid regarding every desirable event or occurrence in the world as a miracle of God, which would then remove some of the distinction between the natural and the supernatural.

If the supernatural were really understood in terms of natural phenomena, then scientific research could draw out the relevant variables by which things good or ill come about, including such things as religious conversions and special healings. Indeed, science would search for possible laws and would check and recheck the correlations and patterns between events and their relevant conditions. If prayers can improve the probability of healing in some cases, then a scientific study of "healing by prayer" would seek to determine what particular kinds of prayers most often result in cures. It would be important to have this knowledge, which could then be compared with knowledge of cures that come about either without prayers at all or with prayers uttered by Christian Science practitioners, pagans, Buddhists, Catholics, Muslims, Spiritualists, and all sorts of believers of various faiths. Moreover, careful records must be made of the number and kind of prayers offered but followed by no cures. How many prayers are followed by complications or even death? All in all, a scientific study of the function of prayer in healing seems quite possible.

What the results would be is at present a matter of more or less intelligent speculation. It would be interesting to know what their answer would be if Billy Graham and Oral Roberts were asked to give their endorsement and support of an open-minded and thoroughly systematic study of prayer and its relationships to healing.

The scientific study of ESP and paranormal phenomena in general has been very slow to develop, for it has been necessary to overcome considerable fraud, gullibility, and wishful thinking, as well as bureaucratic dogmatism among scientists. Some reports of both paranormal phenomena and faith healings are doubtless sincere, while others are outright attempts at leg-pulling. There are many points along the continuum between these two poles of sincerity and fraud.[17] On Dallas TV Channel 8, October 21, 1971, Evangelist Leroy Jenkins told of a woman with one of her legs shorter than the other. Jenkins claimed that he touched her and performed other religious exercises, whereupon her short leg grew to the appropriate length.

Billy Graham is perhaps the most famous contemporary figure in America who is known for his belief in the supernatural. There have been tendencies to view either all natural phenomena as supernatural, or all supernatural phenomena as natural. Graham seems to split the difference, so to speak, but it is a very uneasy and tenuous compromise that he strikes. The supernatural realm and the natural keep infringing on one another's territory, and men like Billy Graham seem at a loss to determine what specifically is supernatural and what specifically is natural. If *all* phenomena can be regarded as both natural and supernatural, then what is the point of calling attention to certain specific phenomena and designating them in particular as supernatural? If the birth of a baby is a miracle, then is anything uniquely miraculous about the conversion of a criminal to Christianity? Or if we can explain in natural terms the birth of the child, then is it possible that the conversion of the criminal could be explained in natural rather than supernatural terms? These are questions which Graham does not himself verbalize but which are always close at hand whenever he writes or speaks. They are troublesome questions which will be looked at more thoroughly in chapter 10, "The Natural and the Supernatural." Both naturalism and supernaturalism have been charged with inventing a narrow orthodoxy which necessitates surreptitiously introducing new ideas in order to keep the old orthodoxy from atrophying.

It is very difficult to be a prophet and to be at home with the scientific spirit. To be a prophet is to have the truth already packaged and ready for delivery. To be a scientist is to have some of the truth and to be seeking more truth and also to be testing and raising questions about what is already in hand. Sometimes the all-out prophet will give the appearance of being scientific in spirit, but it is mostly just appearance. Karl Marx talked of "scientific socialism," but he held to his dogma without so much as tipping his hat to the scientific attitude of experimentalism and the willingness to entertain objections to his hypothesis or theory or even his methodology. Lenin, too, spoke of science—with his lips; but with his actions he revealed no sympathy with the scientific temper of experimental inquiry, tentative formulations, and revision of one's hypothesis in response to new data and in coming to terms, in a coherent way, with objections and criticisms raised against his view. Although a professing atheist, Lenin thought of himself as an instrument of the life-force that moved dialectically and providentially to attain its aims.

Unlike Lenin, Billy Graham has respect for tradition. Also unlike Lenin, Graham is aware of certain rules of human interaction on earth, and he is careful to respect those rules. Like Lenin, however, Graham believes that he is a special tool of the superior cosmic reality and that he is a major voice of the destiny that will eventually conquer all foes. It is interesting that men like Graham and Lenin seem to have no qualms about dying. Indeed, they flirt with the notion and seem sometimes to welcome it. "Many times," says Graham, "I look forward to death. I have no fear of death whatsoever." [18] Men who believe themselves to be very closely associated with transcendental cosmic destiny sometimes find it easy to think of stepping out of this temporal, finite realm and into the eternal victory of which they claim to be special agents on earth. Indeed, for all we know they may have strong suicidal tendencies; but if they do, they have dressed up the tendencies so well that they appear to have an outstanding superfaith that transcends the normal longing and desire to hold on to life a bit longer.

Lenin thought that destiny had appointed him to use any cruel and brutal means necessary to advance his cause. Graham, on the other hand, has too much of a democratic spirit for that. To be sure, he will not hesitate to use the "hard sell" to win followers of his cause, but he does not regard violence to be an appropriate method to winning men to the Prince of Peace.

The role of violence in maintaining law and order, as viewed by his "Christian Americanism," is another matter, however; and Graham is painfully ambivalent on this point. Indeed, any thoughtful and compassionate human being is going to be painfully ambivalent regarding the use of force to sustain his own way of life. To be sure, Billy Graham believes that in the end God will send all his enemies to the torture pit to suffer agony forever, but that is God's doing, not Graham's.

Billy Graham talks very strictly about the husband's authority and the wife's role of submission. But his practice seems to be much more democratic in spirit than his preaching. He is, in fact, quite outspoken about the authority of the husband over the wife in certain areas, but exactly where these areas are is not altogether clear. Graham is adhering to the old faith of the fathers, which makes the "weaker sex" inferior to the man in some sense. But by not being too precise about the locus of male superiority, the evangelist in effect is yielding to the temper of the times. The "world" is getting to him. Once again, his own personal life seems more democratic in spirit than his preaching, more responsive to new information about women than his preaching would seem to reveal. Ruth Bell Graham, contented wife of the world-renowned evangelist, advises unmarried women to accept as divine fact that the Lord tailors the wife to the husband and not the other way around.[19] Ruth Bell, having spent her childhood in China as the daughter of missionaries from the United States, spoke Chinese before English. Today the role of women in China is considerably different from when Ruth Bell was growing up there. In those days the woman's role was unequivocally that of subservience to her husband. But when Ruth Bell agreed to marry the tall, youthful preacher from the South, she believed that her marriage to him would give her fulfillment, not servitude. She had planned to return to China as a missionary, but after being courted by Billy Graham she became convinced that her calling was that of wife to the evangelist and mother to his children.

It is Billy Graham's belief that wives ought to be submissive to their husbands because long, long ago a wife named Eve, by taking action on her own, plunged the entire human race into utter ruin. Besides, man was not created for woman, but woman for man. Evangelist Graham is convinced that God selected Ruth for him—even when she was living in China with her missionary parents. Having selected Ruth for Billy, God then began preparing her for her future role, even to the point of training her to become accustomed to good-byes, for she would later be saying good-bye frequently to her traveling evangelist husband.

Billy Graham explains:

I didn't know that way out in China, God was preparing a lovely young woman just for me. She was the right one in temperament and in her experience. She had to leave home when she was thirteen to go to school in Korea. She said she never dreamed that God was preparing her for a lifetime of good-byes. God specially prepared Ruth to be my wife for this particular ministry that He called me to.[20]

Such is Billy Graham's answer to Women's Liberation.

With the apostle Paul, Billy and Ruth Graham hold that the male is created in God's image, whereas the female is one further step removed. She is created in the image of the male—a copy of the copy (1 Corinthians 11:7–9). Nevertheless, Paul himself was struggling creatively with the new notion that "in Christ" the distinction between male and female does not exist (Galatians 3:28). Unfortunately, Paul was unable to reconcile this radical view of woman's status with the received tradition of the natural inferiority of the so-called weaker sex. And today Billy Graham experiences this same surging ambivalence that Paul experienced two thousand years ago.

There are other passages in the Bible about woman's place, passages which Billy Graham as an Evangelical must subscribe to, because in 1949 he vowed to take the Bible to be the infallible revelation of God's own thinking about various subjects. One such biblical passage says: "Let a woman learn in silence with all submissiveness. I permit no woman to teach or to have authority over men; she is to keep silent (1 Tim. 2:11–12)." The reason which the biblical author gives to justify this injunction is not that local custom will permit nothing else. Rather, the reason goes all the way back to the first couple in the Garden of Eden. After all, "Adam was formed first, then Eve; and Adam was not deceived but the woman was deceived and became a transgressor (1 Tim. 2:13–14)."

In other words, when Adam sinned, he knew what he was doing, but Eve did not—at least not as fully as did Adam. Some commentators say that Adam went along with poor Eve because otherwise she would have had to bear her guilt all alone, without a man to share her burden and guilt. Woman, therefore, cannot be trusted with authority over man because she got him into the worst sort of trouble the first time an important decision came across her path. And in any case, Eve was only an afterthought, whereas Adam was what God had in mind to begin with. Of course, sometimes an afterthought is better because the first thought serves as a kind of useful experiment. But down through the centuries the male commentators on the Bible have not been impressed with this interpretation.

Some recent interpreters suggest that the biblical writer did not mean to imply that a woman should be given no authority in the business world. Her silence and loss of authority is limited strictly to the churches. For various reasons this bit of interpretation, however, has not been happily accepted among evangelical Christians.

But not all is lost. Women, despite their inferior status in some places, may compensate by bearing children. That is what the Bible says, at least; and Billy Graham believes in all the Bible, even the following verse: "Yet woman will be saved through bearing children, if she continues in faith and love and holiness, with modesty (1 Tim. 2:15)." Ruth Graham has given birth to three daughters and two sons and has continued in the faith with modesty. She thinks that this way is the very highest calling for women. It is her version of Women's Liberation—or Women's Salvation. Ruth Graham has found what she calls "vicarious pleasure" in her famous husband's activities and is convinced that the ideal vocation for a woman is to be a wife and a mother. Every other vocation for a woman is less than ideal. She thinks also that the world outside the home is and ought to be a man's world. The home is woman's place. Contrasting men and women, she says of women, "We have our own field and our role to play, so why compete." [21]

However, the Bible, like the Sears catalog, is a very large book, and there are many passages from which to select. Some of them offer more comfort to women who have aspirations somewhat different from Ruth Graham's. *Peter Freuchen's Book of the Eskimos* shows clearly how utterly dependent Eskimo husband and wife were on one another for their survival. But only the female Eskimo would openly recognize her dependence; the male steadfastly refused to acknowledge his dependence.[22] The apostle Paul was more willing to make this concession regarding mutual dependence between man and woman in his part of the ancient world. The apostle writes: "Nevertheless, in the Lord woman is not independent of man nor man of woman; for as woman was made from man, so man is now born of woman. And all things are from God (1 Cor. 11:11–12)." Simple observation taught Paul that men did not make their entrance into the world without women. So in that sense the male's dependency on the woman is clearly admitted. Billy Graham has gone even further, recognizing his dependency on Ruth to bring up the Graham children while their father was traveling.

Curiously, the Bible has very little to say about the wives of the first disciples of Jesus. Presumably Jesus himself had no wife. Paul is thought to have been single. We deduce that Peter was married because the New Testament mentions his having a mother-in-law. Paul does have something to say about the husband-wife relationship, but not a great deal. A married couple is to be one flesh, the head of which is to be the husband, the body of which is the wife. They, husband and wife, owe each other certain rights of marriage, but Paul is not very specific as to what exactly they are.

And of course that is the crux of the matter. Privileges in one century may be rights in another. On the surface Billy Graham's preaching does not appear to have yielded to the amorphous Women's Liberation movement, but it is interesting that his sermons about the place of women in the world are very different from sermons delivered by evangelists and evangelical preachers before World War II. In short, the world and the changing times probably have very subtly but surely made an impact on Graham's perception of woman's status in the world.

Chapter 4
THE QUICK CURE
AND THE HARD SELL

Television dramas often solve the most complicated problems in short order. Commercials promise immediate relief or even instant transformation of personality. Pills and tablets are advertised as avenues to lightning success of one sort or another. Norman Vincent Peale offers a few simple "magic formulas" for success and happiness. Today the general message seems to be that time is no longer required for attaining some of the most important things in life.[1] Engagements are considered to be too time-consuming, inasmuch as quick marriages and divorces can be obtained at an early age. Instant diagnosis of personal problems is given in newspaper columns, and some of the youths of the world assume that involved and complex human problems can be resolved pronto.

It is in this age of advertised quick and simple solutions that the drug cult has emerged, with its presupposition that a meaningful human existence may be turned on with the same speed that a television show is turned on or a new record is placed on the turntable. Billy Graham is a child of this generation of quick remedies and instant simple cures. He tells young men and women to "turn on with Jesus" and to "get high on Jesus."

As early as 1954 he was revealing in his preaching a longing for a simple escape from the bewildering practical problems that responsible men had to face up to daily. No one who has gone through the period of World War II, with all the trials and the frustrations befalling the

United States since that war, can fail to feel considerable sympathy with Graham's longing to find a simple way out of all the perplexities. In a 1954 interview with *U.S. News & World Report* Dr. Graham was asked and answered a number of questions. The following is one of those questions and Dr. Graham's answer to it:

Q. But haven't the churches made these points [about sin, Christ, and the spiritual life] in their sermons over and over again? It isn't novel, surely. What is it that brings this response now? Is it that they have been absent from church, and you are reviving their interest?

A. I think that the points that I listed a moment ago are the contributing factors—that there's this world-wide hunger and need and the realization, as Sir Winston Churchill said, that "our problems have gotten beyond us."

I mean that the human mind cannot cope with the problems that we are wrestling with today. And when our intellectual leaders begin to admit that they don't know the answers, and that fact reaches the masses on the street, then they are going to turn somewhere. They will turn to all sorts of escapisms. Some will turn to alcohol. Others will turn to religion in want of security and peace—something to hold onto.[2]

Sometimes the evangelist inadvertently portrays religion as an escapism or at least as a superquick, supersimple way to resolve all major human problems. He wants "the answer," and offers Christ as the "miracle that can heal the ills of the world." [3]

Responsible adults and responsible young people in the 1970's are rightly concerned about the fact that some youths are turning to hard drugs. One partial explanation for this escapism is that drugs give the illusion of "the simple answer" to complicated problems. Unfortunately, they divert human energy and intelligence from the tough job of confronting the problems and working out compromises, improvements, and more reforms. Drugs often become a part of the problem because they are an excessive form of escapism. Billy Graham's supersalesmanship is one among many manifestations of the contemporary cult of escapism. Under the name of Christ he promises "the answer," no matter what the problems are. He is like the old patent-medicine salesman who can give you a cure for whatever ails you.

Those who are on "speed" have a longing for a speedy escape from the difficult problems of living. Graham has his own version of speedy escape, which he proclaims in glowing terms. If a married couple seem to be having an especially difficult time of it, Graham rushes in and promises instantaneous marital success:

> Reno can give you a quick divorce, but Christ can give you a quick transformation in your home. The tempers that have flared, the irritations that are evident, the unfaithfulness that is suspected, the monotony and boredom of existence without love can be changed and *transformed in the twinkling of an eye* by faith in Jesus Christ.[4]

When the going gets rough, the drug cult looks for a means of dropping out because political, social, and economic problems seem so terribly overwhelming. "Turn on; tune in; drop out!" (says Timothy Leary) or "Look for the Second Coming!" (says Billy Graham).

Graham seems at times to be surprised that young people attend his meetings and even surrender to his message. But this should not be a great surprise at all, for in desperation some of the young are turning to all sorts of things to find some way of escaping from the hard realities of their lives. They become converted to drugs, astrology, scientology, witchcraft, and a number of other magic-oriented sects and cults. It is a tough, complex, and confusing world that the young are growing up in, and Billy Graham is only one among many with a bagful of stupendous promises of escape. In this way he contributes to the perpetuation of childishness among a number of young men and women. He likes to see himself, however, as one who contributes to their maturation. While there is doubtless some truth in this image, he seems more to be recruiting them for a subculture of children who do not know how to wrestle patiently and intelligently with some of our more pressing social ills of the empirical world that finite mortals have to live in.

However, there is another and equally important side to Billy Graham. He is neither the money-hungry villain that some critics have portrayed him to be, nor the all-American boy that others have imagined him to be. Both have been *misled by his show of superconfidence* and his air of unswerving dedication, whereas to a great extent Billy Graham is a very ambivalent person and is much more flexible a salesman than most observers seem to realize. There is much of the supersalesman in him; and as any sales manager knows, a superior salesman learns quickly to shift his ground just enough to keep appealing to the customers.

One reason that Billy Graham is liked so much in America, even by those who do not buy what he is selling, is that Americans admire a supersalesman. He is Mr. Success, the American dream come true. Many Americans may not like Graham's particular brand of the product, but they like him and identify with his style. They would not themselves take to being pressured beyond a certain point to join his particular salvation club, but they admire his spirit and do not see any great harm in his being an aggressive salesman, so long as he is selling the other guy. After all, the other guy may want what Graham is selling.

Dr. Graham himself does not resent at all being regarded as a salesman. He is quite honest about his methods and goals. "I'm selling the greatest product in the world," he explains. "Why shouldn't it be promoted as well as soap." [5] The point here is that Billy Graham uses a very traditional technique of salesmanship to present his program. It is very simple: Get the prospect to sign on the dotted line as soon as you can. A superior salesman who really believes in his product will not be shy in using enormous pressures and promises to get the customer in on a good deal. After all, it is for the customer's own good!

The following excerpt from the sermon "Will God Spare America?" is just one among many examples of high-pressure techniques used by one of America's most successful supersalesmen:

> Now ladies and gentlemen, we have maybe two more years. *You* might have another day—you don't know . . . you can only be converted when the Spirit of God is moving and speaking and convicting the soul, and He's doing that tonight. He's giving you one more chance to make it right with Jesus Christ. He's giving you one more chance to say "yes" to Jesus Christ. And if you don't, the Scripture teaches that God will spare not—God will spare not, and it means hell, the lake of fiery brimstone. . . . Tonight you say, "Well, Billy, I want peace with God. I want to know, if an atomic bomb falls upon this vulnerable city of Los Angeles, that I'm ready to meet the Lord God." [6]

In short, the deal of a lifetime is being offered for a limited time only. Better sign now. Nothing to lose and everything to gain if you sign up right now. If you wait, the offer may be withdrawn. And you'll lose everything. What a policy! You can't afford not to act on it immediately!

Now, once Graham signs up a convert, he has a follow-up program. It is like joining a record club. There are more benefits to come, and of course a price to pay. Again, like any salesman convinced that he has the supreme deal of a lifetime (in Graham's case, a deal of this lifetime and the next too), he does not think that the price is too high to pay for the sets of products that come with joining the club.

Here is how the plan works. The first commodity is absolutely free to the customer. Salvation is a gift. And it is an outstanding gift—nothing to be ashamed of. But if it is accepted, then the customer is subsequently made to feel very guilty if he lets it go at that. He is made to feel very ungrateful in declining to sign up for the other products. True, salvation is absolutely free. But who wants to be an ingrate? So, once the initial gift is accepted, the customer finds it very difficult to resist other salesmen of the company (personal workers and others) who urge him, for example, to continue subscribing to *Decision*, which is the monthly publication of the Billy Graham Evangelistic Association.

It is this follow-up program that gets new converts involved. And it is through this program that Dr. Graham feels strongly that he himself contributes to the maturation of young people. He gives them a program of Bible reading, some training in witnessing, prayer, and devotional life. And they are supposed to discipline themselves to carry through with the training. Understanding this, we may perhaps now place in perspective the numerous fantastic and seemingly irresponsible promises that Graham makes in his preaching and writings. They are come-on appeals. Granted, they are sometimes outlandish exaggerations. But apparently Graham can justify them to himself by reminding himself he does have a practical program of reforming and reprograming the convert. True, Christ does transform lives—if not quite instantaneously, then at least after the spiritual fitness program begins taking effect and new patterns of behavior modification set in.

Now, it must not be thought that Dr. Graham consciously and deliberately plans to issue these glowing come-on promises in order to obtain recruits for his program. But nevertheless this is the way he functions— as a supersalesman convinced that he must go to very great lengths to get people saved for heaven and recruited for sanctified living on earth. He is very proud of his follow-up program and believes that it balances out much of his evangelical appeal.

If advertisers of soap can make all sorts of promises in order to sell their product, then why should not a Christian evangelist do all he can to sell his product? Billy Graham is convinced that he is selling the greatest product on earth, and he does not question hard-sell methods of advertising. In that sense the evangelist is definitely both in the world and of the world. For Graham, there exists an abundant supply of salvation, and what he sets out to do is to create a need for the product. Or, to be more faithful to the evangelist's frame of reference, he conceives of himself as laboring to bring prospective customers around to seeing that they really do need the product that is in superabundant supply. If a prospect is feeling finite, anxious, or alienated, Graham steps forth to tell him that what he is really suffering from is sin and that Christ is the only miracle drug on the market to cure this deepest ailment.

Chapter 5
THE HUMBLE AND MORAL MAN

A couple of Jehovah's Witnesses called on a Baptist family in the summer of 1964. After discussing their faith for a while, the couple realized that they could not deal with some of the questions raised by the Baptists. Instead of calling a halt to their attempt to win two new converts, the Jehovah's Witnesses promised to send someone else to deal with the difficult questions. A day or so later someone else did appear at the front door and was invited in. The questions were raised, and the discussion was on its way. After a while it became apparent that the discussion was not progressing smoothly. The Baptists had even more pointed questions, and some of them were rather disconcerting to the Jehovah's Witness expert.

Finally, disgusted with the Baptists, the man picked up his case containing the Bible and other literature and announced that his audience of two lacked sufficient humility to receive the truth. The Baptist couple smiled, and one of them said as he walked the guest to the door, "I think what you mean when you say that we lack humility is that we simply disagree with you."

If Jehovah's Witnesses (or anyone else, for that matter) should say that Billy Graham has repeatedly refused to be converted to their faith because he is not humble, Graham would not be very much impressed with the charge. Even when the Witnesses charge that pride prevents him from accepting the truth and that he clings to his fame and influence with politicians and other members of the worldly kingdom of men, Graham remains unwilling to yield. He rejects their charge that pride and lack of humility keep him from becoming a Jehovah's Witness.

Yet again and again Billy Graham uses this same charge against humanists and others who do not agree with the evangelist's own particular theological stance. In fact, like the Jehovah's Witnesses, he finds it quite difficult to entertain even the possibility that humanists and others might simply be as humble as he, while at the same time remaining in disagreement with Graham's fundamental conservative Christian outlook. Like a person who cannot help but squint his eyes whenever the sun hits them, Graham seems unable to check his automatic charge of "pride" when he thinks about humanists, naturalists, and even other theists who hold a perspective greatly different from his own.

In 1966 an agnostic was present at a large auditorium in an Iowa town where a theologian and a few others were engaged in a panel discussion on the topic of the existence of God. When time came for comments from the floor, the agnostic stood up and stated that the entire discussion that had just taken place was entirely useless, because nobody knows anything definite about whether there is a God or what he would be like if he exists. The conclusion that the agnostic then drew and stated to the panel was that, inasmuch as he did not go around attempting to make statements about the nature of a God whom no one knew anything definite about, he as an agnostic was more humble than the members of the panel. The agnostic recommended this humility for the panel members and then sat down.

Now, labeling either oneself or others as humble or not humble is a rather precarious venture. In a great number of cases men designate as humble those who agree with them in their thinking or general outlook. Billy Graham is not immune from this practice. Hence, when he claims that a certain group does not accept what he preaches because the group lacks humility or is swollen with pride, Graham is not really giving an explanation at all. Rather, he is giving a *definition*. He is telling his readers or listeners how he is choosing to use words like humility and pride.

The complicated thing about this practice, however, is that anyone can demand the same privilege to define a certain word to his own special advantage. If the conservative Christians can do it, so can agnostics, liberal Christians, Jews, Muslims, Marxists, Hindus, or any and every group on the face of the earth. In this sense, everyone lacks humility when judged from frames of reference other than his own, inasmuch as no one can accept every frame of reference.

Now, some people think that Billy Graham is a very arrogant man to allow his ad men to refer to him in public and on posters as "God's man with God's message." To be sure, this may indeed be a very arrogant thing—when judged from another frame of reference. But inside Graham's framework it is not necessarily pride at all. It is simply letting oneself be used as a humble servant of God, who, Graham believes, sometimes chooses the humble to do great things for him. The last shall be first, and so on. Mormons do not think that Joseph Smith was a proud and arrogant man simply because he gave them the *Book of Mormon*, which they take to be the word of God along with the Bible. On the contrary, they believe that he was one of the few men sufficiently humble to receive this revelation.

Billy Graham thinks that Mary Baker Eddy was a very arrogant woman to found a new faith to compete with orthodox Protestantism, but Christian Scientists look upon her as one of the humble vessels of God. In fact, leaders from almost all religious groups—from Roman Catholicism and Hinduism to orthodox Protestantism and Seventh-day Adventism—have been regarded as very humble persons by those who accept their special outlook on things. The same leaders have also been regarded as extremely proud and arrogant by outsiders. Many Englishmen thought Gandhi was intolerably arrogant. His followers thought he was humble before God and true to his convictions.

> You are pig-headed and obstinate.
> He is mulish and stubborn.
> But I am a committed defender of truth and righteousness.

It seems evident that moral choices and value judgments are made within some frame of reference, and we shall be inspecting here and there some of the crossbeams and foundation stones of Billy Graham's framework of conservative Christianity, in order to test what they are made of and how well they hold together.

One of the biggest problems in understanding any framework is that of distinguishing it from the furniture and accessories that are placed inside it. Presumably the furniture is less essential to the structure and is in some cases a matter of preference and individual choice. For example, are rules against smoking, dancing, and drinking a part of the essential framework of conservative Christianity, or are they simply pieces of movable furniture? Graham seems to take them as furniture only—important furniture—but nevertheless not a part of the basic structure itself. In fact, some conservative Christians go so far as to insist that any attempt to argue for total abstinence must be set aside as fruitless because it conflicts with the fact that Jesus himself drank wine. Conservative Christians take Christ's life and words to be infallible guides for believers.[1] It is important to see here that this moral opinion regarding drinking is not based on scientific and medical evidence but on scripture.

However, Sherwood Wirt, editor of *Decision*, which is published by the Billy Graham Evangelistic Association, claims that "there is actually Biblical warrant for both temperance [i.e., total abstinence] and moderation."[2] This is perhaps another way of saying that the issue of abstinence versus moderation cannot be resolved on biblical grounds. Graham reluctantly acknowledges this, although in his preaching he sometimes gives the impression that drinking of any sort is contrary to the conservative Christian faith. To be sure, total abstinence may indeed be a very wise road to take. If so, it would seem to be less a biblical matter and more a question of scientific and medical knowledge coupled with some understanding of social and personal consequences.

If the issue of abstinence versus moderation is not an essential part of the conservative Christian structure, the injunction against adultery surely is. For Graham and conservatives there cannot be any choice between total abstinence and moderation on this question. And presumably there are absolutely no extenuating circumstances. If a man's wife is imprisoned or separated from him in one way or another (except in death or biblical divorce), the Christian man will simply have to do without the sexual relationship, no matter how long the deprivation lasts. As for a compromise in the form of masturbation, contemporary Christianity is rather reluctant to deal with the issue in any explicit and systematic manner.

For conservative Christians divorce is out of the question, of course, except when one spouse engages in an extramarital sexual relationship. (Fundamentalist preacher Harvey Springer once stated in a sermon that a person could justly separate from a spouse who had been guilty of premarital sexual intercourse and had failed to report the fact to the partner before the marriage took place.) Unfaithfulness is very strictly defined by most conservative Christian scholars as sexual intercourse with someone other than one's mate. Anything short of that does not count as grounds for divorce. If, for example, Robert Jones has physical intimacy with another woman but does not have intercourse with her, then presumably his wife, Betty, cannot use adultery as a cause for divorce.

However, what Robert did will be counted against him as adultery even though Betty cannot use it. That is, if Robert looked upon the other woman and lusted after her, then he committed adultery in his heart. But adultery in the heart, while a sin, is not grounds for divorce. Actual penetration is, for conservative Christianity, the sole cause or grounds. However, some conservatives are more flexible than this in actual practice, depending somewhat on the circumstances and situations.

Evangelist Graham is very fond of saying that conservative Christians do not have as great a percentage of divorce as does the general public. This, of course, is true of a number of groups. What it means is not always clear, however. In some cases it suggests that spouses with values and beliefs in common tend to remain together. In other cases perhaps it means that because of religious rules against divorce, many conservatives, Roman Catholics, Mormons, and the like are simply forced to live in a mediocre marriage rather than do something about it. But these are only tentative suggestions. For all his hostility toward sociology, Billy Graham does not hesitate to propound sociological conclusions, intuitions, and impressions. Like a supersalesman, he will quote figures if they can help him sell his product. When the figures are unfavorable, however, he becomes less willing to make reference to the behavioral sciences.

In his preaching Billy Graham has spoken of the marriage ceremony which God performed for Adam and Eve in the garden, but it is doubtful that he would insist on this as a literal fact. It is more of a poetic expression. Most conservative Christians assume that a marriage ceremony is a necessary avenue to marriage, although the Bible does not seem to come out explicitly as to the necessity for a third human party to perform a marriage ceremony.

This raises an interesting and increasingly relevant question about the idea of a young couple living together and refraining from having children. What will conservative Christianity's attitude toward them be? Until fairly recently it has been assumed that the ideal Christian marriage includes having children. But this assumption may be changing.

Unlike the pope, Billy Graham has come out very much in favor of birth-control devices—for married persons, that is, inasmuch as the unmarried should not be having sexual intercourse at all.

The question is, should the young couple living together be regarded as married if they have not obtained a legal marriage? Does *Christian* marriage depend upon *legal* marriage? The Bible is hardly explicit on this question. Conservative Christianity will have to begin dealing with the question—especially if the "Jesus People" and their cousins begin making an impact on conservative Christianity, for theologically the Jesus People seem to be very conservative—even fundamentalist—in outlook.

Conservatives could perhaps resolve their problem by saying that living together *is* Christian marriage if the two who unite in the relationship do so with a lifelong commitment of loyalty to one another under God. Doubtless in some countries the requirements for legal marriage are less in conflict with the Christian ideal of marriage than in other countries. In his eager concern to win converts and to recruit for his program (or some similar program), Billy Graham would probably do well to avoid tying the Christian ideal of marriage (or at least the conservative version of it) to unnecessary legal encumbrances.

Billy Graham is among those who insist that ethics and morality cannot float except on board a theological ship. Take away the structure, and ethics will sink to the bottom of the sea.[3] It is undoubtedly true that men cannot make very many moral decisions without some frame of reference. But what is the proper frame of reference? We shall be moving into that question bit by bit, but here it is important to note that men of various frames of reference can sometimes share certain common moral principles.

Naturally, there is a tendency for each man to think that his framework best accounts for these commonly held moral principles and that the other frameworks are only parasitical. Some humanists contend that attempts to tie ethics to the theological ship do great injustice to ethics. Ethics is too important a concern, they say, to permit it to sink with theology and religion. Peter Caws is convinced that for most men the theological structure is no longer viable. It is a waterlogged old ship that is sinking despite the singing and confidence still put forth on deck by those souls reluctant to get off while the getting is good. Men like Caws do not want morality to go the way that they think Christian theology has gone. They want honest morality to be on its own, independent of outdated theological and religious planks.[4]

A former Christian, Alasdair MacIntyre, believes that theology and talk about God could never get off the ground without a moral vocabulary. Hence, the theological structure has to obtain much of its lumber from an independent supply of ethics and morality.[5] Without this stockpile, the theological framework would be hardly possible. Some of those taking this position oppose Christianity on both intellectual and moral grounds. They contend that Christianity takes morality and perverts it, making people feel guilty when they should not, and letting them off the hook when they should not be let off.

The controversy between Christianity and, say, humanism has too often been polarized by hard-sell apologists on both sides. It is a fruitless pastime to define Christianity in such a way as to make it essentially evil and ignorant, and it is equally fruitless to define humanism as the essence of immorality and meaninglessness. After all, there are many shades of both Christianity and humanism; and on some moral issues, there are some Christians and some humanists closer to one another than to those of their own group.

For example, on the birth-control question, Billy Graham and liberal Christians are much more in harmony with most humanists than with some Catholics and certain other conservative Christians. On the question of abortion, however, there are some conservative Christians and humanists who are together in opposition to other Christians and humanists. The same is true on the question of welfare and questions of social ethics. Pacifists are found in practically every camp, and unethical businessmen may be found under almost any tent of religion and nonreligion.

Graham sometimes preaches that morality is impossible without a prior conversion to Christianity. What this means is not as clear as it sometimes appears on the surface, for it would seem to suggest that Jews, humanists, liberal Christians, Buddhists, and indeed most people in the world lack what Graham thinks is a necessary requirement for morality. Are they immoral? Are they less moral than Graham and other conservative Christians? [6]

There seems to be some confusion in Billy Graham's preaching as to what he means by Christian, which is perhaps surprising, inasmuch as it is one of the key terms of his preaching and ministry. In some contexts, being a Christian entails belief in the "fundamentals" set forth by the fundamentalists early in the present century. Graham says: "I believe in the inspiration of the Holy Bible, the Virgin Birth, the resurrection of the Christ from the grave, the atonement by His blood of the sins of mankind, and the return of Christ to establish a kingdom on earth." [7] If believing in these fundamentals is essential to being a Christian, and if being Christian is a prerequisite to being moral, then there are very few moral people in the world. This is all the more true when it is realized that believing in all these fundamentals does not itself guarantee morality. All that is guaranteed is that if a person does *not* accept these doctrines, he cannot possibly be moral. That is Graham's conclusion.

Actually, Billy Graham would not deny that there is very little morality in the world. He does believe, nevertheless, that there are some good people in the world. Once when he described Jesus of Nazareth, he pictured him as robust, tall, and handsome—very much like Billy Graham. There is some indication that the evangelist regards himself to be among the good persons in the world. He fits most of the qualifications that he sets forth, including believing in the fundamentals. He regards himself as a Christian. However, Graham does not give himself credit for his being what he is. He gives God the credit. That is what a humble Christian would do.

There is in the evangelist's preaching a second meaning of the term Christian. Sometimes when talking of a person's becoming a Christian, Dr. Graham seems to mean that one need not believe explicitly in the fundamentals so much as to believe himself to be a sinner and Christ to be his savior. In fact, many new converts do not know what the fundamentals are. In essence, there is a minimum number of *explicit* teachings associated with a larger spread of *implicit* teachings that the new convert must be willing to believe in due time. For example, a new convert may not have even heard of the teaching or doctrine of the virgin birth, and he may not understand the atonement in any explicit sense. Yet he can still be a Christian if he is willing to believe as his faith matures. His heart and mind are open and receptive. If the prospect professes belief but later does not develop by believing certain fundamental doctrines, then that may be taken as a sign that the prospect did not really believe in the first place.

This raises a fascinating question. Suppose there is a person who is quite honestly willing to accept the conservative Christian doctrines, and whatever else is necessary for being a Christian, provided he can *honestly* do so. The only thing preventing him at present is that he cannot honestly do so. This does not mean that he thinks that all those who do accept the doctrines are dishonest. It is simply that he and they see things differently, and he would be untrue to the principles of truth and reason if he should accept what these others accept. Now, is this person to be counted a Christian because of his willingness to believe the truth and because of his dedication to the truth? As was suggested earlier, Billy Graham has an extremely difficult time facing this question because he simply cannot embrace the position that someone could both be honest and disagree with what Graham believes to be the essential truth of religion. Would Graham want this person to be dishonest and thereby become a Christian? That would be a curious predicament.

Sometimes Billy Graham uses the word Christian in a third way. It may be called the gerrymandering definition because it is a way of gerrymandering non-Christians out of the possibility of being regarded as moral. When used in this way, Christian means not only the proper doctrines, beliefs, and repentance, but also the virtues and moral rules and principles. But that is not all. These virtues, moral rules, and principles are made the exclusive property of Christianity.

This needs to be made more explicit. When Graham declares that only the Christian can be a truly virtuous and moral person, he sometimes is saying two things. (1) Built into the definition of being a Christian are the virtues and moral rules and principles. And (2) these virtues and rules belong *exclusively* to the definition of being a Christian. They can apply to no other term.

What the evangelist is doing is defining his key terms in such a way that anyone who does not accept the conservative doctrines and attitudes is *by definition* excluded from the circle of morality. Hence, in purporting to be making a statement of empirical fact about the inability of non-Christians to be moral, Graham is actually making no statement of fact at all, for there is no conceivable way of testing his statement to see if it is empirically reliable. The reason that the statement cannot be tested is that it is a prescriptive statement, even though it gives the illusion of being descriptive. That is, Graham is prescribing how the word non-Christian is to be used. He defines morality in such a way as to contrast it with all non-Christian frames of reference. He does not show that this is true empirically, however. In short, under what appears to be an empirical and factual statement, Graham stipulates how to use words like Christian, non-Christian, and moral. Needless to say, like Humpty Dumpty, anyone can arbitrarily stipulate whatever he wants a word to mean. Anyone can play the gerrymandering game. The only trouble is that it breaks down communication whenever a person prescribes his own meanings and ignores the general and common meanings of words.

Let us see how Dr. Graham's gerrymandering definition works in a practical situation. Suppose that an employer desires to hire a secretary. He has two applicants, both of whom have letters of recommendation testifying to their honesty. This is an important virtue in this case in particular, because the secretary hired will be handling much of her employer's money and may eventually succeed him as an executive of the firm.

But he also needs the secretary to be very proficient at typing and to have had some experience in filing, shorthand, and making important executive decisions.

Of the two applicants, the first not only is honest but also meets the other requirements. She is also a Jew. The second is honest but lacks skill as a typist, can take shorthand only fairly well, and has no executive experience. But she is a Christian. Now, it is essential that the secretary be honest, otherwise the employer could lose a lot. Proficiency and experience without honesty are useless to him.

What will he do? If he were to take Billy Graham seriously, he might say to himself, "Well, the first young woman is a Jew, a non-Christian. Therefore, she cannot possibly be moral, which means that she is not honest. Her letters of recommendation are obviously the product of forgery or misstatement." Clearly, Dr. Graham himself would not engage in this sort of hiring practice, which is to say that his practice would belie his preaching in this instance. June Hunt, an active member of the First Baptist Church of Dallas and daughter of perhaps the richest man in the world, was asked about her tendency to surround herself only with Christians. She was also asked what she would do if she found herself sitting on top of her aging father's business empire. June responded that she "would not go through the organization discharging nonbelievers." However, she went on to explain that if she were putting together her own company from scratch, "I would see to it that my associates had a right relationship with God. . . . God would be my Board Chairman and Jesus Christ my President." [8]

What Billy Graham seems to want to say is that morality is lacking something if it is not accompanied by belief in God, the virgin birth, repentance, atonement, and the Second Coming. This may or may not be true. In any case, however, it is very misleading and confusing to imply that morality is not morality unless it is accompanied by these other matters. It becomes even more confusing and misleading whenever Dr. Graham's own practices indicate that he really does bank on the morality of many persons who are not Christians and certainly not conservative Christians. And are there perhaps a few conservative Christians who now and then bear watching?

In closing this short chapter, we may ask why it is that Christianity has been denounced by some as a terrible evil on earth and praised by others as the great source of goodness on earth. A tentative answer is at least twofold. Those persons denouncing Christianity may have one notion of what goodness is, while those praising it may have another notion. Or they may differ in their understanding of what Christianity is.

Some people define Christianity in such a way as to close the door to any possibility of demonstrating it to be anything other than corruption and evil. Others define Christianity in such a way as to make fruitless any serious empirical inquiry into possible merits and demerits of Christianity. The result is that useful and intelligent communication is practically destroyed. This, then, leads to the self-stultifying consequence that both sides, pro and con, deny themselves the opportunity to improve their understanding of Christianity in many detailed and practical ways.

Christianity is a very large tent with many acts going on inside. Some people insist that Christianity must be either taken in toto or rejected in toto. This becomes in some sense a practical impossibility because the more basic problem is to determine what the essential ingredients of Christianity are. It is often said that humanists, personalists, and others cannot pick and choose whatever they want from Evangelicalism. They must go either all the way or none of the way. The reason for saying this is that Evangelicalism is regarded as a *system* of beliefs. Each belief or doctrine or view leads into the others. The doctrine of God's love eventually leads to the doctrine of the resurrection of Christ, which in turn leads to the doctrine of the virgin birth, which eventually leads to the teaching of a belief in hell, and so on.

Doubtless it is true that one belief leads to another in some sense. But it is essential that the "leads" be examined critically to see where they do go, and are not simply taken on faith. Much of the remainder of this book is an attempt to look at a few crucial doctrines of Billy Graham's evangelical theology for the purpose of tracing them out, so to speak, in order to see where they lead. It will do no good for a person to denounce as lacking in humility all who do not trace out a doctrine in the way that he himself has traced it. If they are wrong, then he ought to go back over their journey with them and show them precisely where they went wrong. Instead of his hurling the charge "Hypocrisy!" it would be more useful simply to point out plainly what appears to be inconsistency. Instead of attaching the word humble to those who agree with him, it would be more useful simply to say that they are in agreement.

Now, there is no doubt that, taken in toto, Christianity of whatever historical mode is responsible for both great evil and great good, as well as mediocre good and evil. It is true that a fanatical mob of Christians in 391 burned the priceless library in the temple of Serapis and that Christianity failed in some ways to encourage learning and has encouraged useless wars. But it is also true that Christians have sponsored hospitals and colleges, have insisted on better treatment of oppressed peoples, and have opposed brutalities around the world.

This sort of score-keeping could go on forever. What is more important is to take note of the good that is done, regardless of who does it. And as men effectively communicate on ways of working together in promoting more good, they can at the same time perhaps learn to communicate more effectively their specific and precise disagreements in doctrine.

Billy Graham has done well in cooperating with various diverse groups to promote his crusades. He has also cooperated with various groups to promote humane causes in the world. Of course, the tendency of each group is to get for itself more credit than it perhaps deserves, but this is understandable. Each group may insist that it works through humility, while the others work out of envy. But doubtless there is some humility and envy in each party. Perhaps we should rejoice that despite mixed motives, good consequences can nevertheless sometimes be mutually supported.

Chapter 6
HAPPINESS AND
THE MEANINGFUL LIFE

A cult of scientism has begun to develop, particularly in the United States. Whenever a particular problem or a set of problems arises, devotees of this cult will say, "Science can solve all problems!" "Science is the answer!" This bit of quasi piety is a modern form of magic with its own pat formulas. It has little to do with the hard work of scientists and the self-correcting methodology of science. Billy Graham and a number of his fellow Southern Baptists indulge themselves in a similar bit of magical ritual when they pronounce in authoritative voice the formula "Christ is the answer" or "God can solve all man's problems."

The trouble with these kinds of magical sayings is that they announce a prescribed answer before they are reasonably clear as to what the nature of the problem is. Moreover, the formulas are relatively useless as practical programs. If a "flower child" says, "The way for all men to be at peace with one another is for them to love one another," we do not feel that we have been told very much. We would like such a generality to be broken down into specific steps so that we could begin implementing the advice and testing its specific results. To say "Be scientific!" is to say very little, for being scientific on a given problem is something definite that has to be spelled out.

If a Buddhist urges us to follow Buddha, we may not know what he has in mind until he spells out what he means in definite steps and programs. After this is done, then we can perhaps begin testing the steps to see if they produce the promised results. Of course, we have to be very careful here lest we wrap ordinary things in fancy paper. For example, if someone tells us that Taoism will bring peace to all who practice it, he may be saying little more than "Those who act peacefully will be peaceful," which is not a greatly practical and useful statement. Similarly, to say that serving Christ will eliminate thievery is sometimes to say simply that whoever avoids the temptation to steal will avoid being a thief. If serving Christ *means* (in part) not stealing, then obviously serving Christ entails not being a thief.

The point to be made is that much of Billy Graham's preaching is composed of tautologies empty of empirical content or practical import. If within the definition of being a Buddhist is included the practice of refraining from stealing, then of course Buddhism does away with stealing. But it does so only *by definition,* not by testable procedures in the empirical world. Suppose that we catch a Buddhist robbing a store. Have we found evidence contrary to the Buddhist claim? A Buddhist evangelist might say of the thief, "Well, he was not a true Buddhist, not a genuine Buddhist. A true Buddhist doesn't steal, you know."

Similarly, when "followers of Christ" are caught doing what the evangelist promises that they will not do, then his response is that they are not genuine Christians—at least not at the time when they do evil.

Now, what is happening here is that Graham is making what appears to be an empirical claim that presumably could be tested. But as soon as someone points to contrary evidence, Graham will not allow that contrary evidence is even conceivable. In taking this route he reveals that he is not making an empirical or factual claim after all. It only seems that way at first glance.

Suppose that a leader in the Moose Club exclaims, "All members of the Moose Club are good family men." And then when one of his fellow members is exposed as a very lousy husband and father, the leader announces, "Well, the man must not be a Moose, otherwise he would be a good family man." After a while, the person making the charge may give up attempting to discuss the matter because he sees that this particular leader is not actually making a factual claim but rather is making the quality of "being a good family man" a part of the very definition of Moose Club member.

In his essay entitled "Has Religion Made Useful Contributions to Civilization?" Bertrand Russell contends that all the major religions of the world, including Christianity and communism, have done enormous harm to mankind.[1] Billy Graham sometimes likes to distinguish Christianity from religion in order to conclude that, whereas religion has done much harm, Christianity—*true* Christianity—has been a source of great good in the history of mankind.[2] Wherever it would appear that Christianity has contributed to evil in the world, Graham resorts to denying that this is true Christianity. But he will not allow other religions and humanists to resort to this same device. That special privilege is presumed to be reserved for Christians alone.

There are some persons who can see no good in Christianity because they have defined Christianity in such a way as to include all evil and no good. Billy Graham, however, like a boy in a state of romantic passion, frequently sees the good in his faith and is blind to the harm caused by it.

To be sure, it is altogether fair to argue that the principles of one's faith would, if applied perfectly, bring perfect happiness to mankind. But it is sometimes difficult to maintain a clear distinction between the principles themselves and those who profess to practice them. Billy Graham does not always keep this distinction clearly in mind when he attempts to show how much good Christianity has done for mankind. But when Christianity comes under attack he sometimes does make the distinction and then insists that the apparent failures of Christianity are really the result of the poor application of the perfect Christian principles and teachings.

According to Evangelist Graham, life without Christianity (by which he means the conservative definition of Christianity) is meaningless. Without Christ, life is absurd and void of significance.[3]

Lovers have exclaimed that without their "one and only," life is emptied of all meaning. But experience shows that most of these lovers nonetheless find meaning even when they lose their "one and only," although it is true that a few do fail to recover. Among these few are some who drag out the rest of their existence in bitterness or repression, and in some cases they commit suicide.

Now, it seems empirically true that many men find a meaningful life without being Christians or without Christ in their lives (in Billy Graham's sense of Christ) or without belief in God at all. Billy Graham denies that these people who are so very different from himself do find a meaningful and happy existence. But can his claim be factually substantiated? As a matter of fact, many formerly conservative Christians have found Billy Graham's religious way of life to be a source of meaninglessness and unhappiness. This is why some of them have journeyed on to another way that they believe gives greater happiness and meaning.

In examining this notion of a meaningful life, let us look into something a bit less general. Let us talk about a meaningful marriage. This will perhaps throw some light on what is meant by a meaningful life. A marriage that is meaningful, let us say, includes mutual respect, deep intimacy, and enjoyment of one another. This intimacy comes through many hours, days, weeks, and months spent by the marital partners in one another's company and in profound communication with one another. If this special definition of a meaningful marriage is accepted, then a salesman who is at home very infrequently is not likely to be intimate with his wife in this special sense of the term. Many corporation executives are said to be so busy in their work as to have little time for developing marital intimacy. As a very busy crusader Billy Graham has been at home only a few days a month. Does this mean that his marriage has not been very intimate and therefore not meaningful?

Now, just as there are many kinds of marriages, so there are many life-styles. If we should choose to do so, we could insist that a life-style of a certain kind provides the only possible meaningful life. But that would be a matter of arbitrary choice, not a matter of reasoning to a conclusion or establishing an empirical generalization. We could, if we should so choose, declare that only the kind of life that includes the enjoyment of Mozart is meaningful. In fact, we could add any requirement that we so desired. But so could anyone. Billy Graham can say that only the Christian has a meaningful life. But he is not establishing a case; he is arbitrarily choosing to make being a Christian part of his personal definition of a meaningful life.

It would seem that we could have no way to discuss rationally who enjoys meaningful life unless we find some common and general agreement as to what constitutes it. Perhaps the most widely accepted general tests of the meaningful life of an individual are (1) the enjoyment which the individual has in his own life and (2) the contribution he makes to the opportunities for other persons to have enjoyment too. If serving Buddha, the Communist party, baseball, Christ, mankind, the nation, or the cause of cleaner air meets these two tests, then such service, we may conclude, gives meaning to life.

However, what gives individual enjoyment to some persons may provide boredom or worse to others. For some, a meaningful life may include a good marriage. For others, it includes being devoted to teaching school and not being married. Still other persons find both marriage and teaching together to be a source of enjoyment. It seems that individuals all around the globe find all sorts of ways to meaningfulness in the sense of personal enjoyment and social usefulness to others.

It is rather strange that Evangelist Graham cannot easily bring himself to think that there are numerous routes to human happiness and meaningfulness. Regarding those non-Christians who seem to be happy, he carries the suspicion that they are not "truly happy" or "really happy." After all, Dr. Graham has already proclaimed that only a Christian's life can be happy and meaningful! Once again the evangelist appears to be making an empirical statement, when in the final analysis he is merely stipulating a definition. That is, he is taking an ordinary word and giving it his own personal definition, thus reasoning in a circle.

In this chapter and the previous one, I have attempted to show that Dr. Graham has a pattern of taking ordinary words with ordinary meanings to make empirical claims. So far so good. And so long as his claims seem to be supported by the empirical facts or data, he performs no verbal tricks. But whenever his claims seem to go contrary to fact, he sometimes switches from the ordinary meaning of a word to his own personal and special meaning. This is like playing according to the rules until you start losing the game and then switching to your own set of rules without warning. Of course, a person may give any private meaning to a word that he wishes. But in the interest of clarity and efficient communication he ought to let his readers and listeners know when he is taking an ordinary word and giving it his own special twist. It would reduce confusion, reasoning in a circle, and equivocation.

Some people insist that human life is empty of meaning unless the whole universe is moving toward some ultimate or cosmic goal. These people believe further that their own personal lives are meaningless unless they somehow share in this grand goal. Billy Graham agrees with them. If at one time in their lives they are brought to the point of facing the alternative view that there is no ultimate goal for the entire universe, they may fall apart emotionally. Others, however, may adjust and find meaning (i.e., happiness, enjoyment, and social usefulness) in goals that are less grand and cosmic.

Billy Graham thinks it is very sinful even to entertain such an alternative. Or, as has been said of him, he is afraid to face it squarely. Be that as it may, the fact seems to be that some people cannot avoid great depression, despair, and moral paralysis unless they believe in a grand, sweeping cosmic goal of some sort. Others, however, seem to manage fairly well without it. Most of those who have to have a cosmic goal to hitch their lives to have been taught that there is such a goal which must be at the center of all their concerns. This is a part of orthodox Christian upbringing. Humanists, naturalists, and personalists sometimes suggest that if children were not led to expect to share in such a grand cosmic goal, they would not suffer the great mental disillusionment and emotional depression brought on by serious doubts as to whether there is any cosmic goal. Instead of caring about an ultimate goal for the entire universe, children might fare better if they were taught to work with more realistic and believable goals of a less pretentious nature.

No preacher knows a sufficient number of human beings to declare what will make them all supremely happy and their lives supremely enjoyable. Neither does anyone else. We have to look and see. It is dictatorial to take upon oneself the burden of telling other persons what actually makes them happy. What brings a sense of peace, power, fame, conviction, goodness, humility, usefulness, and security to Billy Graham may bring to another person a feeling of intellectual dishonesty, moral guilt, and general uselessness. One man's relevancy may be another man's cop-out. Doubtless, some things are more or less common sources of happiness to men everywhere. Sometimes these are called basic needs. It does not seem to be true, however, that knowledge of the *Book of Mormon*, the Bible, or any other scripture is a basic need for *every* man's earthly happiness. For some men, it may be necessary—depending on what they grew up to expect and what their special circumstances are. Man seems to be the most adaptable and flexible species on earth. He can find many avenues to happiness of varying degrees of intensity and duration.

The Mormon faith is at or near the top in percentage of growth among all religious bodies. It claims to be meeting human needs. Some Mormons take their success as a sign that they have the only true faith, while other persons outside the faith suggest that more natural factors account for this growth. Bob Jones would say that the devil is the cause of it. Growth, of course, does not prove divine favor; otherwise the cockroach (whose duration and universal appearance is phenomenal) would be one up on every religious body in the world. Sometimes Billy Graham treats his crusade successes as a manifestation of divine favor. Others take them as just one more sign of human gullibility. Still others hold that Graham is speaking to some of the basic needs of men, or at least of some men. What he gives them may be unworthy of them, perhaps, but at least he gives them something—a promise, a cause, a hope, a challenge, a discipline, and encouragement. And these are all a part of what makes life meaningful.

Doubtless, most persons in today's world do need these things if they are to have enjoyment and to feel useful to others. But just as the need for nourishment may be satisfied by various kinds of food, so there seem to be various kinds of promises, causes, and disciplines that can satisfy men. Beans and rice may not satisfy everyone. And just as some tasty foods are harmful, so it is possible that some religious faiths may be greatly harmful to intellectual, moral, and emotional development. In short, what a person eats makes a difference, and likewise what he takes as a religious faith makes a difference. The fact that many people will eat whatever is set before them proves only that they have a need of some sort, not that what they eat is necessarily good for them or is what they would choose if they had, and knew of, other options.

It will do no good to denounce men like evangelist Graham or Joseph Smith, for they have understood what many of their critics have not, namely, that those who entertain the vision of infinity and eternity cannot endure the thought that there is nothing of lasting value transcending the finitude of their temporal existence. Men like Graham and Smith see how time and change unravel the threads of human efforts, and they refuse to believe that such is the final word about their lives. There must be something more enduring. Their hearts demand more than this temporal existence. Their hearts are restless, and they must either embrace eternity or watch their personal lives break into a thousand pieces. Their vision is what holds their being together, providing them momentum and order. Without the vision they might perish as a sound in the night or become lost somewhere in a desert of aimless wanderings void of enjoyment and contentment.

In such individuals the vision destroys the very possibility of earthly happiness without the vision. Those who are touched by its spell are like the man who could never find a happy marriage with an earthly woman because of the hounding dream of a perfect woman, a paragon, who makes all his earthly relationships appear as nothing.

Because of the overwhelming importance of their vision, those who cannot live without it seem totally unable to understand those who *can* live a reasonably happy and meaningful life without it. Those possessed with the vision cannot bring themselves to believe that other people can go about their business and ignore it. Surely these others must be very wicked persons. Stiff-necked! Hardhearted! Insincere!

Those who dream perpetually of infinity cannot help believing that all persons—all people everywhere—really want the vision of eternity if they could only allow their worldly minds to surrender their ruthless grip on their souls. And to some extent the visionaries are correct, if not regarding all earthly men, at least regarding those who have been programed always to hope for the perfect ending to the story.

Hope is a source of great joy and agony. It is when the hope of something infinite and immortal is finally believed to be *mere* hope that intense agony sometimes settles over the land of ecstasy like a killing frost. For many persons there comes a time when transcendental hopes, reaching beyond this finite realm of being, must either be embraced with passionate devotion or turned loose to float away. In this respect the choice is like that of two lovers who come to the fork of the road where they must either commit themselves to one another for life or go their separate ways.

In 1949 Billy Graham came to have some doubts about the infallibility of the Bible. But rather than devote years to the study of biblical Greek or do sufficient research in the field to satisfy his own intellectual unrest, he allowed the throbbing vision to override his doubts and questions. On what was to be a momentous day in his life, the evangelist, opening his Bible and placing it before him as he knelt alone, offered a resolute prayer of promise to God. It was a promise that he would "by faith" take the Bible as the flawless revelation of God and that he would continue to follow the path to which he had already committed himself.

Intellectual questions and problems sometimes reformulate a vision or even dispose of it. But not for Billy Graham. His vision of "winning men to Christ," as he so frequently states it, forced the intellectual problems either to disappear or to go deeply underground. Since that "hour of decision" when he chose not to examine the doubts about the Bible, but rather to treat all such doubts as the stirrings of a sinful mind, Graham has never profoundly questioned his primary vision. To be sure, doubts do arise at the outer edge of his mind; but never at the center. He will not permit doubts to enter, for he conceives of them as ventures in sinfulness. Doubts regarding the truth and worth of his vision are regarded as evil thoughts to be shunned and abhorred. Anyone who would attempt to bring forth evidence contrary to the claims of the vision is rebuked in no uncertain terms. To tell a man deeply immersed in romantic passion that his fiancée is in fact already secretly married is to invite the man's scorn, not his gratitude. Similarly, to present what might appear to be evidence challenging the trustworthiness of the vision is to invite denunciation.

But what is this "vision" that drives a Billy Graham, a Lawrence of Arabia, a Joan of Arc, or a Brigham Young to face the world that seems so distant from their vision? It is really not something unknown to most men, for it lies perpetually at the door of their hearts as an eager messenger to be summoned for a sacred and holy duty. In essence the vision is nothing other than man's longing for the perfect relationship, for the ideal state of being in which the wrecked endeavors that humans and their fellow humans have suffered will somehow be restored to wholeness. It is Camelot. Heaven. The dream of the perfect mountain, the perfect brotherhood, utopia, the New Jerusalem, the supreme love affair. Men and women may have suffered broken romances, even broken marriages, and broken lives; but they still hope just once more for that second chance, that second opportunity, to find the perfect love.

Graham writes of the utopia of eternity and promises that the end of the rainbow can be reached:

> Heaven will be the perfection we have always longed for. All the things that made earth unlovely and tragic will be absent in heaven. There will be no night, no death, no disease, no sorrow, no tears, no ignorance, no disappointment, no war. It will be filled with health, vigor, virility, knowledge, happiness, worship, love, and perfection.[4]

Here, in this vision, the restraints of finite living are all thrown to the wind, and there is no sane person alive who would not wish to believe in this vision if only he could. Especially for Americans with a restless pioneer background, heaven is not static; it includes progress too. Graham quotes Ian McClaren: "Heaven is not a Trappist monastery. Neither is it retirement. No, it is a land of continual progress." [5]

Romantic passion and religious conversion are two expressions of this vision, which promises to disperse the clouds of contingent human existence and to flood the soul with sun and warmth. Both the love song and the hymn testify to the power of this vision to change the fortunate individual's world. The beauty of life may have been present all along, but only in the powerful vision do the scales fall from the eyes so that the beauty may be beheld. In the song "Till There Was You," from *The Music Man*, Marian gives voice to the unleashed romantic passion:

> There were bells on the hill,
> But I never heard them ringing;
> No, I never heard them at all
> Till there was you.
> There were birds in the sky,
> But I never saw them winging;
> No, I never saw them at all
> Till there was you.
> And there was music,
> And there were wonderful roses.
> . . . .
> There was love all around,
> But I never heard it singing;
> No, I never heard it at all
> Till there was you.*

This simple but moving song may be compared to the words of the nineteenth-century American evangelist D. L. Moody when he tells of being converted: "The morning I was converted I went outdoors and fell in love with everything. I never loved the bright sunshine over the earth so much before, and when I heard the birds singing their sweet song I fell in love with the birds. Everything was different." [6]

Both romantic passion and religious conversion reach down into the depths of men and women, young and old, and offer them what promises to be a new life, a defiant song about overcoming the dead flesh of the past, and a fresh declaration that this time things will be altogether different and truly wonderful. The old ways of frustration and of one defeat after another will be forcefully challenged by the power of love or by the power of Christ, Allah, Jean, or Alfie. When you are in love you can conquer every obstacle; or you can do all things through Christ. Dreariness and boredom will give way to the upsurge of life and hope

---

* "Till There Was You" by Meredith Willson. © 1950, 1957 Frank Music Corp. and Rinimer Corporation. Used by permission.

and joy. The vision rolls back the clouds so that flowers may bloom and birds may sing as never before.

It seems to be the nature of this vision to defy empirical ties that resist it. In intense romantic passion the loved one may become deified as a god or goddess, an idol of worship and adoration, "my life," "my all." So-called love songs praise the loved one as everything, as the meaning of life, or even as life itself. Similarly, in the climax of religious enthusiasm, Christ (or whatever the loved one is named) is the all-in-all, the source of all life, the alpha and omega, the joy of man's desires.

Sometimes preachers will compare the new birth of religious experience to falling in love. In the 1950's among Southern Baptist youths in particular the song "In Love with the Lover of my Soul" [7] was quite popular. One could hear it sung and talked about at church gatherings and youth conferences. It spoke of being in love with Jesus, who was described as the soul's lover. It seemed to express sentiments, emotions, and levels of belief that were fairly widespread among youth. The idea of a divine-human love affair, as represented in this way, appears to embody both a yearning for and promise of a permanence, steadfastness, depth of emotion, and timelessness that surpass all human love. Such a love becomes the anchor or mainstay of life for the lover.

In his book *The Affair*, the writer Morton Hunt reports the words of Mary, who was having an extramarital romance with Neal: "In Neal I had found that combination of traits I had always dreamed about but thought didn't exist. . . . Loving him, I was like someone who has just had a religious experience; how could I not believe?" [8] In temporarily contemplating the possibility of breaking off his relationship with Mary, Neal muses:

> How could I repudiate the person I had finally become? Give up the love I had only begun to know? Turn away from the new life I had scarcely tasted? A retreat back into the torpor, the flatness, the desiccation of my former ways, would be accepting an imprisonment for life, with only my few recollections as a tiny window through which to look out upon the dear lost world.[9]

To give up Mary would have been a betrayal of life, a sin of omission—backsliding!

There can be little doubt that special religious experiences and romantic involvements touch the deepest nerves of the human soul and powerfully stir youths and adults alike. It is no wonder that in the throes of romantic passion or at the peak of religious fervor, men and women (again, young and old alike) become involved with idealized images that may not in some cases touch ground at all. The love-sick person is one who cannot begin to face reality about the object of his or her romantic passion. Speaking of a past involvement with Jennifer, a man called Edwin confesses: "I made myself believe everything she told me, despite all the evidence to the contrary." [10] In short, at the heart of the romantic involvement appears an almost irresistible "will to believe." The lover is swept off his feet as if under the force of an "irresistible grace." "I was," Edwin explains, "like a man in a poker game who's been losing and losing, and insists on playing for higher stakes because he has to win it all back." [11]

Another example is the case of the religious believer who, though entertaining serious doubts about his commitment, feels nevertheless that he has already come too far to turn back now. He has placed too much on the table already. To prove that he did not make a mistake, that he has not thrown away much of his life on a poor bet, he must throw himself more energetically and thoroughly into the work of his faith. He will win all or lose all, he tells himself; and he insists that he will win it all!

It is not easy to break this sort of romantic spell. And when it is broken, it is not easy to react moderately to the brute intrusion of reality. Similarly, for many, it is not easy to give up on a religious faith. It has offered many moving promises and has involved the individual profoundly and significantly. But if and when the faith is seen to be not altogether what the believer had once imagined, a tendency to be resentful at having spent one's energies on illusions or false leads develops. Sometimes this process of scaling down is made less painful, however, if the individual can see that perhaps his faith did at one time meet his needs, in some sense at least. Moreover, just as a new lover can sometimes ease the pain of the lost involvement with the former lover, so a new religious faith or a new moral cause can often compensate for the loss of the old faith. Many of those finding conservative Christianity to be inadequate have journeyed on to a new religious faith, or a different version of Christianity, or at least a new framework which purports to meet needs and answer questions which evangelical Christianity was unable to cope with.

The comparison between religious conversion and romantic involvement provides a very fruitful line of study. In movies and TV dramas the love scenes are frequently enhanced by music that brings the scene to a powerful pitch. In Dr. Graham's crusades the music is woven into the events with masterful skill, aimed at enhancing the moment of decision. In a day when alienation is part of the environment, the singing in the evangelistic crusades offers the individual a possibility of significant participation. Just as a viewer of a surging *Love Story* may identify with the lovers, so in Billy Graham's revivals the music may assist the individual in identifying with the entire sacred hour of decision as a holy happening. Like the romantic sexual experience, the holy happening is something dearly prized and special, something for which there is a build-up in anticipation—anticipation of that which is far beyond the ordinary. The unordinary is made to seem both desirable and acceptable.

The entire crusade experience is geared toward positively reinforcing this feeling of belonging and of participating in anticipation of something supremely special that may usher in new being and new meaning. The crusade also gives negative reinforcement against holding out, against not joining in. Those who bring to the crusade a feeling of alienation often leave with a far more intense feeling of alienation if they do not "make a decision for Christ." In fact, in recent years Dr. Graham seems to have toned down somewhat the notion of hell as fire and brimstone in order to portray hell as a living death cut off from the joy of life, as endless remorse, isolation, and alienation. Those who do not "accept Christ" at the crusade are reinforced to experience a foretaste of hell everlasting.

Graham tells what hell is like:

No matter how excruciating or how literal the fire of hell may or may not be, the thirst of a lost soul for the living water will be more painful than the fires of perdition. Hell is, essentially and basically, banishment from the presence of God for deliberately rejecting Jesus Christ as Lord and Savior.[12]

Billy Graham regrets that in the present generation the number of sermons on everlasting hell has declined considerably.

The experience at the crusade meeting is a tribal experience, giving acceptance to those who cooperate and agony to many who do not. It is a rare experience in America, except perhaps for Woodstock and some of the other rock festivals. In China there are similar crusades—gigantic ideological crusades which take on the overwhelming air of religious passion and hope in the power of something like a transhistorical, transcendental realm. Instead of a follow-up program in Bible reading, the Chinese Communist party urges the faithful reading of scripture from the handbook of Mao Tse-tung.

Once in a sermon Billy Graham made reference to the popular song "Honey." He was trying to show how even among the younger generation there is a longing for heaven as the ultimate stage of meaningfulness. According to this song, which tells a story, a recently married couple are happily enjoying their new state and are living a life of playful, gentle delight. But the young wife, Honey, soon dies. The young widower then sings:

And it was in the early spring
When flowers bloom and robins sing
She went away.
And, Honey, I miss you. . . .
And I'd love to be with you,
If only I could.
. . . .
Now all I have is memories of Honey.
And I wake up nights and call her name.
Now my life's an empty stage
Where Honey lived and Honey played
And love grew up.[13]

Sensing the agony of loss that a newly married man would suffer at the death of his wife, Evangelist Graham proclaims that the heart's desire for perfect and immortal love will be wholly satisfied in heaven. And on another occasion he writes that heaven "will be as wonderful and beautiful as only the Creator can make it. Everything for your personal happiness and enjoyment is being prepared. Every longing and every desire will have perfect fulfillment." [14]

However, there is a serious qualification to this beautiful vision. According to Dr. Graham, God "says plainly that certain people will not be allowed to enjoy the glories and joys of heaven. . . . They are the ones who said 'No' to Jesus Christ." [15] Then he adds: "This is still an age of grace. God's offer of forgiveness and a new life still stands. However, the door will one day be closed. Someday it will be too late." [16]

Evangelist Billy Graham believes that there really is a Camelot. And the worst conceivable grief that could come to any individual is to be left out of it, to be alienated from the banquet of perpetual love, to be isolated in the dark of abject loneliness. For Graham, the apex of a meaningful life is to be transported from this earthly existence to heaven, to Camelot, where perfection is the normal state of affairs and where the vision becomes the reality and where the mortality of finite creatures fades into a mere passing shadow which citizens of Camelot will hardly remember, except perhaps as it reminds them that they have gained everlasting victory over all defeats.

In his book *The Kingdom of Love and the Pride of Life* the evangelical spokesman Dr. E. J. Carnell has written that children's fairy tales are simple expressions of the Evangelical Christian's faith.[17] Dr. Carnell has been criticized by some fellow Evangelicals for saying this, but I think he unwittingly has come up with something that throws light on the strong appeal of Billy Graham's preaching. Carnell noted that the elementary fairy tale expresses the human heart's conviction that in the end the good people will triumph over evil and will live happily ever after, while the wicked will suffer their just deserts.

The broad appeal of the fairy tale is something that every child and adult can easily understand and appreciate. In rather dramatic form it gives voice, in the first place, to our primitive desire to even the score with those who frustrate us in our endeavors. The wicked witch symbolizes those who have done us in, cheated us, deceived us, or taken what we regard as unfair advantage of us. The neighbor threw rocks at our cat or jeered at our baby brother. The carpenter whom we contracted to build us a good house did not live up to his promise. The automobile mechanic charged us considerable money but failed to make the necessary repairs. The teacher or friend betrayed our trust. The hospital staff treated us as if we were intruders rather than customers. Most of us have the urge to see the score evened, and the fairy tale very readily provides a mental picture of the bad character getting his deserved punishment in the end. Second, the fairy tale allows the good character to be rewarded by living happily ever after. In the fairy tale everything turns out as it should. All the records are set straight. All is right once again. The good characters of the story are taken to the enchanted land to live, where they will never again be forced to associate with wicked villains and witches.

Uncovering more truth than he perhaps realized, Carnell let the cat out of the bag when he compared the evangelical faith to fairy tales. Graham and his associates keep saying that his sermons appeal to something down deep in the heart of individuals everywhere, not only in the United States, but throughout the world. (His largest audience was in South America.) Everywhere people respond to his appealing message. And to a great extent Graham and his associates are correct in their claim about his wide appeal, although *what* it is that Graham appeals to "down deep" is a matter of debate. Dr. Graham contends that there is a longing for Christ in every man, even in people who have never heard the name "Christ."

Another way of approaching this, however, is to take Carnell's lead and follow through with it in a way that he himself did not. Graham's sermons very simply denounce bad characters and proclaim that goodness will triumph ultimately. The score will be settled! In Graham's preaching, those who do not "accept Christ" are simply identified with the class of those despicable characters who lie and swindle and cheat their neighbors out of their rightful belongings. Graham holds that "rejecting Christ" is worse than committing murder or rape. The uncomplicated "invitation" that Graham offers is for a person to step out of the camp of evil characters and into the camp of those whom the Prince of Peace transforms by grace into redeemed Christians. As if by magic (or miracle) a frog is turned into a human, that is, a sinner into a Christian. "Christ," like a fairy godmother, can make this transformation instantly and on the spot.

The child's world is neatly divided into the wicked and the good. To a great extent Billy Graham's preaching is an appeal to this simple childhood expectation. The evangelist, in effect, is telling people that their deep and early childhood fantasies are really true, that the world in the final analysis is as simple as children imagine it is, that their dearest and noblest dreams will all come true in the end. Those on the side of the fairy godmother will live happily ever after.

The word Christ in Graham's preaching means various things, but in some contexts it is a symbol of the gentle and kind Prince who restrains the wicked powers and accepts all who are willing to accompany him into the royal court where goodness and happiness will be enjoyed perpetually.

Billy Graham openly acknowledges that his preaching does not appeal greatly to the intellect. He says that his message is directed to the "heart" and is "so simple that a child could understand it." And indeed this is true because the "heart" is in reality the childhood wishes which the child's fairy tale expresses so vividly. In his preaching, Graham does not mention the evil witch of fairy tales, but he talks openly of her theological counterpart—the devil—whom adults are permitted to believe in so long as they do not carry on conversations with him in public. Satan and all who do not enter the gates of Camelot will eventually suffer an agony worse than what any earthly being could imagine. Payday some day! Evangelist Graham promises that Christ's kingdom is ultimately going to triumph and that those who believe in him can share in the victory. "Come as a little child," Graham says frequently to those who in their heart long for the time when the disorder of the world will be restored to perfect order.

Such a simple faith often makes it possible for certain kinds of believers to adjust to some of the inequities of their present temporal lives. After all, some day the score will be settled. Other Evangelicals, however, having had the "vision," cannot be content with the present life and so become activists as either "witnesses" or reformers. Still others are affected differently.

Earlier in this chapter reference was made to a man and woman who had been having an extramarital affair. The woman compared the relationship to a religious conversion for her, while the man indicated that giving up the relationship would be a betrayal of something dear and meaningful. Doubtless many Evangelicals will dismiss such individuals as simply violators of God's commandment. But perhaps their extramarital experience can illuminate the religious experience.

What those who engage in extramarital affairs often seem to be saying is that life is passing them by, and they want to live before it is too late. Wisely or foolishly, they sometimes see the extramarital affair as a new opportunity to enjoy again, to be alive, to change and develop a new dimension of human exploration. Some look for a deeper living. Others long for an escape, just as some people seek in religious experience an escape from their drab existence or escape from their responsibilities. People profess to find a new self and a new outlook in their conversion or their extramarital affair.

Billy Graham tells those in his audience that without Christ in their lives they as individuals are not really alive. That they are dead in sin. That their lives are flat and meaningless. Then he promises them that they can come alive inside. They can live again. They can experience a new birth, have a new life, and enjoy a new and beautiful relationship with a new Person.

Studies of extramarital affairs show that they usually last for only a few months or a few years. Doubts settle in. Confusion emerges. Indeed, the social structure serves to destroy the intense extramarital relationship. But Billy Graham promises that the new relationship with Christ need not be a short-term affair. It can last forever. One can come alive at this very moment and live for eternity. And to help guarantee that the new venture will not become flat and disillusioning, the Billy Graham Evangelistic Association utilizes a follow-up program designed to reinforce the convert's new commitment. Whereas the extramarital affair is pressured to remain concealed, the new religious experience is drawn out in the open. New converts are urged to give public witness to their commitment to Christ, and to join openly with others who have made such a commitment. Whereas the affair is to be done discretely and privately, the conversion experience is supposed to be boldly and openly acknowledged. Indeed, the new convert is urged to tell others about his new love, whereas the participants in an extramarital affair are by numerous social forces sworn to secrecy.

It is no wonder that the extramarital affair usually has a short life. What is more surprising, however, is the fact that often the religious experience seems to lead to disillusionment or disenchantment despite the numerous forces designed to sustain it. Billy Graham thinks that Satan is working mightily to turn the evangelical religious commitment into a misadventure. Some persons, however, believe that other natural factors of life simply become more interesting and rewarding. A good religious faith, like a good marriage, is one that can grow and develop. But when a religious faith has certain built-in limitations that prevent growth along certain significant lines, then the believer may discover his interests turning him in a new direction. Indeed, he may himself be an incurable romantic looking for a better religious love, a richer faith, a more genuine and meaningful commitment than his old commitment could provide. To walk away from his old faith may be a sad experience, but the lure of Camelot sometimes seems irresistible.

If the promise of a better faith draws someone into Evangelicalism, the same promise may also challenge him to journey on further to a different faith. Indeed, even the cynic seems to feel the pull of the vision of Camelot. His cynicism is the groans of one who, having come to his last rainbow and finding no treasure, cannot yet erase from his mind the vision of what never was but surely ought to have been. This suffering cynic, sick with love and desperate to believe but still unable to, has not yet learned to supplement his ethereal vision with mediating visions that reflect a broader range of reality than does the fantasy freedom of fairy tales.

Chapter 7
DID HELL SURPRISE GOD?

WHAT IS THE EVANGELICAL'S HELL LIKE?

Evangelical Christians of every variety are still in strong agreement that hell is both unending torment and very much a living reality. It is definitely not a state of sleep or suspended consciousness. For Billy Graham, on one side of the great chasm stands glimmering heavenly Camelot, while on the other side the horrible abode of the damned sprawls out in absolute mental anguish, misery, and remorse. Among some of the more sophisticated Evangelicals a tendency has developed to underplay the physical dimension of hell. F. C. Kuehner, himself a staunch believer in the torments of hell, rejects the following attempt by Charles Spurgeon to describe hell: "In fire exactly like that which we have on earth thy body will lie, asbestos-like, forever unconsumed, all thy veins roads for the feel of Pain to travel on, every nerve a string on which the Devil shall forever play his diabolical tunes of hell's unutterable lament." [1]

Usually Billy Graham may be numbered among those who, like Calvin, regard the "worm" and "fire" of hell to be figurative or metaphorical symbols.[2] Only the cruder minds among Evangelicals, fundamentalists, and conservative Catholics are supposed to believe that the fire of hell is literal and that sinners will actually be forever scraping worms from their bodies.

But this entire debate as to how physical hell may or may not be turns out to be academic at best, for almost all Evangelicals, fundamentalists, and conservative Catholics believe hell to be the worst conceivable of horrors and to be everlasting. Billy Graham states the matter bluntly: "No matter how excruciating or how literal the fire of hell may or may not be, the thirst of a lost soul for the living water will be *more painful* than the fires of perdition." [3]

Graham's fellow Southern Baptist minister H. H. Hobbs writes that "hell is more terrible than its symbols describe it. If hell is not fire, it is something infinitely worse." [4] In contrast to the ontological argument for God, the evangelical version of hell may be stated as follows: Hell is that than which nothing worse can be conceived. In the opinion of Evangelist Graham himself, hell is worse than the descriptions of it. "It is all these and more." It will "exceed any and every description of hell anywhere in the Bible." [5]

Hell is unspeakably terrifying, according to evangelical theology. Fundamentalists emphasize its literal fire, whereas the more sophisticated Evangelicals emphasize "the terrors of eternal banishment from God." [6] But they all agree on one thing—nothing could conceivably be worse than the endless, hopeless, torturous hell that awaits the damned.

Evangelicals resist all attempts to tone down the mental and psychological horror of hell. The former president of the Charles Fuller Theological Seminary, E. J. Carnell, one of evangelical Christianity's most gifted writers, defines "hell [as] that place beyond which nothing more awful can be conceived." Like his friend Billy Graham, Dr. Carnell used to make it clear that nothing could equal hell in misery and agony. Again like Graham, Carnell holds that the agony of hell will *exceed* the physical pain of burning in a literal fire. "Sorrow in the soul," Carnell explains, "is worse than discomfiture in the body." "A severity of suffering beyond all . . . mentioned" is to live forever in guilt and to be lost from God's love and fellowship. Such utter grief and agony is "a form of pain so incisive in its slashing of spirit that it forms the only persuasive analogy of what the second death is like." [7]

The vice-principal of Clifton Theological College, J. A. Motyer, holds that those in hell are to be "tormented day and night for ever." [8] Hell received its name from an area outside Jerusalem known as the Valley of Hinnom, a section of which was used as "a common refuse dump, a place of perpetual fire and loathsomeness. . . . The final indignity offered to the executed criminal was that his body be flung into" this dump.[9] The New Testament term Gehenna is the Greek equivalent of Hinnom. It is the symbol of "the final spiritual state of the ungodly in Matt. 10:28 and Mark 9:43." [10] Another evangelical theologian explains that "the reality [of hell] will exceed, not fall short of, the figures employed [in the Bible]." [11] In a sermon entitled "The Generation Gap," Graham declared to a Dallas audience in September 1971: "The hell of hell is to be totally rejected—separated from each other and from God."

The Evangelicals insist that hell is not "remedial or corrective." It is better not to have been born than to go to hell. God's holiness is infinite, and the punishment of hell must be literally everlasting, for it is punishment for those who have never repented of their defiance of divine holiness.[12] There is no ease, no rest from the torments and anguish which citizens of hell must endure.[13]

> Could any material torments be worse than the moral torture of an *acutely sharpened conscience,* in which memory becomes remorse as it dwells upon misspent time and misused talents, upon omitted duties and committed sins, upon opportunities lost both of doing and of getting good, upon privileges neglected and warnings rejected? It is bad enough here, where memory is defective, and conscience may be so easily drugged; but what must it be hereafter, when no expedients will avail to banish recollection and drown remorse. Cecil puts the matter in a nutshell when he writes: "Hell is the truth seen too late." [14]

In short, hell is conceived of as God's full wrath felt to the fullest—without any distraction or diversion.

Some Christians have held that those whom God cannot win over to his way will simply be annihilated at death rather than kept alive in some hell to be tormented endlessly. Like a candle blown out, they will be no more. But Graham and other Evangelicals will have nothing to do with this alternative, for they regard it as an insult to God's holiness. In other words, man's sin is considered to be a direct assault on divine holiness, which cannot be satisfied by simply eliminating the sinners. Rather, they must be kept fully conscious—forever—in order that they may suffer torment and agony to the fullest. That is what God's holiness demands!

Some Christians hold that a certain amount of suffering is necessary if a higher order of good is to come about. In other words, this greater good needs this lower order of evil and misery. In Billy Graham's theology, this new order of good does indeed come about, but only at an unbelievable price; for the lower order of evil makes possible not only a higher level of good, but also a new and intensified degree of evil and misery.

In what is perhaps the saddest passage that Graham ever wrote, he seems to find no avenue by which to escape the conclusion that his God loses more of his human creatures than he saves. It is as if man, burdened with a "free will" beyond his finite capacity, cannot live up to the divine hopes. The utopian venture proves to be a tragic mistake. God is said to have once repented having made man, and Graham's most pessimistic mood seems to lead to the cold and sad conclusion that God once again must be having second thoughts about man. The venture in human free will has proved to be at best ambivalent and inconclusive. Graham writes: "There has never been a generation in history, nor will there ever be a generation, in which the majority of the people will believe in Christ. Statistics indicate that the church is rapidly losing in the population explosion. There are fewer Christians per capita every day." [15]

It is no wonder, then, that the evangelist longs for the Second Coming, for every day's delay means that God loses more than he wins. Graham's religious faith has this morbid, pessimistic underside which belies the ultimate optimism that the evangelist seeks to project. The triste tolls are more persistent than the trumpets. C. S. Lewis is quoted in *Decision* as saying that "the sole purpose of creation is to create joy." [16] Graham's God seems not to have greatly succeeded if this is his purpose.

Perhaps it would be revealing to gain a better understanding of what is involved in the Evangelical's version of holiness, which is a major theme of Graham's preaching. In fact, his preaching can be understood only superficially if his doctrine of divine holiness is not grasped. (In the next chapter this doctrine will be explored more thoroughly.) But we must now ask how, in Billy Graham's view, hell came about in the first place.

WHAT KIND OF PARENTS?

Let us suppose for the moment that through some remarkable gift or power modern parents could, before conceiving their children, know how the children will fare in life. Suppose that Tom and Beverly know beyond a shadow of doubt that they can have ten children if they want them and that five of their children will fare quite well in life, while the other five will suffer unbelievable agony, bitterness, grief, and remorse for the major portion of their lives. Moreover, Tom and Beverly have the amazing power to foresee exactly which particular children would enjoy life and exactly which particular ones would find life on the whole to be utterly miserable, full of woe, and hopeless. Not only that, Tom and Beverly are given the freedom (and the heavy responsibility) of choosing which particular children they will bring into the world and which ones they will never allow to be born.

Will Tom and Beverly conceive all ten children and bring them into the world? Let us suppose that this husband and wife are on the verge of choosing to bring all ten into the world. In justifying their future choice, Tom and Beverly argue that the five children who would suffer long and excruciating horror in life would have the same free will that the other five would have. Therefore, Tom and Beverly deny any responsibility on their own part to give birth to *only* those children who would use their free will to gain happiness rather than misery in life.

Another married couple, however, see it quite differently. Mark and Lois cannot bring themselves to conceive and give birth to the five children who would surely spend the overwhelming portion of their lives in utter sorrow, grief, and misery. Like the first couple, Mark and Lois can foresee what would happen to their children. But unlike the first couple, the second choose to give birth only to the children who they know would freely choose happiness. Mark and Lois realize that if they so desired, they could bring into existence all ten of the yet unborn children. But they cannot make themselves do it. The thought that five of the children would spend the significant part of their lives in absolute agony and despair weighs too heavily upon them as potential parents. Mark and Lois ask themselves what good could be gained by bringing such terrible misery into the world. They reason further that, after all, the free will of the potentially agonizing five children would not be destroyed if they never came into existence to begin with. They ask if free will is valuable in every case, even if it has to be paid for with such absolute horror and misery. Besides, the five *happy* children who will eventually be born will enjoy free will. Hence, not all free will is to be denied in the world. So Mark and Lois give birth to the five children who will freely choose happiness and deny birth to the five who would choose misery.

There is, however, a third couple. They do not even believe in free will. Bill and Julie have the power to *determine* everything that their children will do and be in life. This third couple decide simply to create five extremely happy children and five horribly miserable children. Why? No reason. This is simply what pleases Bill and Julie.

A fourth couple—Jack and Betty—also do not believe in free will; they, too, enjoy the enormous power to produce either happy or miserable children. But unlike the previous couple, Jack and Betty choose to create only happy children and to leave uncreated what would have been very unhappy and sorrowful children.

Now, in order to understand Billy Graham's view of God better, we may ponder these couples and then ask ourselves the question, "Which of the above married couples would we regard as the most moral?" We could begin to answer this question by eliminating Bill and Julie, who created five happy and five miserable children for no other reason than it pleased them to do so. Creating five children and determining that they shall be excruciatingly miserable in life is a cruel thing to do. It is clearly unworthy of moral approval. Yet some Calvinistic Christians believe that God did just this. He created some for heaven and some for hell.

The first couple—Tom and Beverly—did not *have* to create five miserably unhappy people. Nothing forced them to do it. But they did it nevertheless. Granted, the couple knew that the five children—if given birth—would "freely choose" misery; there is still a serious question as to whether it was moral of Tom and Beverly to produce the five children who Tom and Beverly absolutely knew would end up in the most horrible state imaginable. Jesus is reported to have said that it would have been better for Judas had he not been born (Matthew 26:24). A number of persons have wished they had never been born. Of course, they sometimes change their minds when things improve for them. But what would a person say if he knew absolutely and without doubt that he would live twenty-five fairly happy years followed by a million utterly miserable years? Would he not wish he had never been born?

Billy Graham and other Evangelicals believe that it would have been better for some individuals had they never been born. But this seems to be an admission that *it would have been better had God not created them.* So why did he create them? Let us imagine that unborn children could somehow be given birth and intelligence for only one day, during which time they could choose whether or not they wanted to be born and to live for, say, two million years. Would they choose to be born if they knew beyond a shadow of a doubt that they would be suffering absolute hell for all that time with the exception of about seventy short years on earth? It seems rather doubtful that they would. Moving closer into Billy Graham's doctrine of hell, we might ask what could be said of a God who would bring them into the world despite the fact that he knew infallibly that they would spend forever in the misery of hell (see Matthew 26:24).

Billy Graham and other Evangelicals seem never to be clear as to whether those who presumably go to hell do in fact *want* to go there. If out of free will a person knowingly chooses hell, then presumably he chooses it because that is what he wants. This, however, raises three questions. First, what were the conditions in a person's environment which led to his wanting to go to hell? Second, were those conditions wholly of his own making or was God eventually responsible for them in some way? Third, does every person who knowingly chooses hell know fully what he is getting into? In answer to this third question, it may be said that most of those whom Billy Graham believes have gone or will go to hell are not very well informed as to the details of their eternal destiny. In the final analysis, Graham would seem to be in the position of having to say that God can send people to hell without their having very much advance knowledge about what will happen to them. When they arrive in hell they will be most unpleasantly surprised.

Billy Graham suggests that in some sense even God was surprised to learn that human beings would be going to hell, for the evangelist says that hell was not made for man but for Lucifer and other fallen angels.[17] It is as if a woman, after building an area of a certain size in which to keep her cattle, discovered to her surprise that the area was far too small for the new shipment of cattle. But Graham's orthodox evangelical theology states explicitly that God knows everything, which means that before he made hell for Lucifer, God must have known also that great masses of human beings would eventually end up in hell. Indeed, if Graham's evangelical theology is correct, then God knew about man's plight before the creation of Lucifer. So, God knew about hell all along!

GOD AND HELL
AND PREDESTINATION

Billy Graham does preach that God knows everything about the future—down to the last infinitesimal detail—so that nothing escapes his vast net of omniscience. Before the foundations of the earth were established, God knew "from eternity" precisely who would go to hell and precisely who would not. According to Evangelist Graham, "when God gave the law, he knew that man was incapable of keeping it." [18] Yet Graham is careful to deny that God *predetermined* that anyone should sin and go to hell. Here the evangelist breaks with some of his more thoroughgoing Calvinistic friends, among whom is his fellow Evangelical and former teacher Gordon Clark, whose Calvinism is unyielding on this point.

Clark thinks it is plainly inconsistent of Graham or anyone to hold that God *foreknows* everything but does not *predetermine* everything. Clark thinks that God would not really foreknow every detail if any person could out of free will change something that God had already foreknown. Clark and all Calvinists believe that if something could possibly be other than what it in fact will be, then God's foreknowledge would not be infallible and absolute knowledge after all. It would at best be a matter of probability. Hence, instead of knowing perfectly the future, God would know it imperfectly and statistically only.[19]

But Billy Graham and other Evangelicals who reject this version of Calvinistic predestination answer that God can know everything about the future without at the same time predetermining the future. Parents, for example, can predict what their teenage children will do, but that does not mean that the parents *predetermine* what the children do. Unfortunately, this example does not hold up very well, for the parents' foreknowledge of their children is not infallible knowledge. It is only probabilistic, iffy, and conditional knowledge. In fact, parents often become bewildered because they discover that they did not know their children as infallibly as they had imagined they did.

Perhaps we can find a better example that seems to indicate how absolute foreknowledge can exist without entailing predestination. For example, imagine that a traffic engineer is standing on the top of a corner building. He looks down on an intersection. In the distance he sees an automobile approaching the intersection. From a different direction he sees another automobile approaching the same intersection at right angles. According to the reading of the engineer's instruments, the two automobiles are traveling at rates of speed such that they will collide upon entering the intersection. The engineer *foreknows* that the collision will take place. But that does not in the least suggest that he *predetermines* the collision. Is this not a case of foreknowledge without predestination?

Again, the answer must be that the foreknowledge is merely conditional. A lot of things could happen before the automobiles enter the intersection. One car could run out of gas or have a flat tire. The driver in the second automobile could make a U-turn or simply change his speed. The transmission could fall out, or the pavement could suddenly drop four feet. Hence it turns out that the foreknowledge possessed by the traffic engineer atop the building presupposes that none of the altering conditions will come about. But this is a precarious presupposition, and God's foreknowledge is not supposed to have a stand on such a precarious foundation. Billy Graham and Calvinists alike claim that what God knows is infallible and beyond all guessing. What God knows he knows 100 percent. And he knows everything.

So it would appear that if many human beings will suffer hell forever, as Billy Graham emphatically insists, then not only did God foreknow precisely who would go to hell, but he actually *predestined* them to go there. Graham, however, draws back from such a terrifying conclusion, for he cannot believe that the God whom he serves would actually plan and will to send millions of souls to hell for everlasting agony. But it would seem that Graham accepts just enough of the Calvinistic doctrine of divine sovereignty to make it impossible to avoid this very conclusion that is so abhorrent to him. That is, Graham cannot *consistently* avoid it. Not knowing how to escape it, however, he resorts simply to both affirming and denying God's omniscience and omnipotence.

What Graham wants is to get his God off the hook, which is why the doctrine of free will is so utterly crucial to him. It appears to be the only way to save God from at least sharing the blame for hell. The evangelist explains:

> God conducts himself in keeping with His righteousness. He will never violate our freedom to choose between eternal life and spiritual death, good and evil, right and wrong. His ultimate goal is not only to glorify Himself but also to make happy relationship with His crowning creation —man. Never will he make any demands which encroach upon man's freedom to choose.[20]

If this were true, God would exert no influence during "the hour of decision." Unfortunately, it would seem that at least half of God's "crowning creation" ends up totally and eternally alienated from him and finally in hell forever. The gift of free will turns out to be something of an enigma, if not a scapegoat. Graham treats it as a kind of theological pack mule which is made to carry most of the heavy burden of his theology.

Consistent Calvinists, however, do not worry that people think God immoral in predestining many people to go to hell. These Calvinists deny that the notion of free will is intelligible, and they make it perfectly clear that there exist no moral standards to which God must conform in order to be regarded as moral. God's own will decides what is right and what is wrong. If God arranges well in advance to send some persons to eternal hell, then it is good and just of him to do so. Why? Because God does it! It is that simple. God is the absolute power. His will is sovereign. Who can call him to account? [21]

Evangelist Graham, like many other Arminian Christians, is most uncomfortable with the logic of consistent Calvinism. But what can the evangelist do? He cannot say that God's foreknowledge, while very great, is nevertheless limited. That is, he cannot say this and at the same time be counted among the orthodox evangelical Protestants. So he must continue attempting to ride two horses going in opposite directions.

But even if he could somehow get his God off the hook by placing all the blame for hell on man's free will, the evangelist would probably still have to face some rather embarrassing questions. Our purpose in looking at the hypothetical cases of the parents was to raise at least one of these bothersome questions. Let us now consider it very clearly: Before creating the world, did God know who would go to hell? It is important to understand that Graham believes that God's *absolute foreknowledge* and the doctrine of *predestination* can somehow be unhooked from one another. As previously indicated, this distinction is doubtful; at least the Calvinists think so. But let us assume for the moment that Dr. Graham can separate infallible foreknowledge from predestination. Then the question arises, if God could have foreknown without predetermining what his creatures would do, then why did he deliberately proceed nevertheless to create those who would spend eternity in hell? Why could he not have used his foreknowledge to prevent this tragedy of all tragedies?

Of course, Graham holds with most evangelical Christians that God is omnipotent or all-powerful. So if God did have all this power before creation, then presumably nothing or no one could have *compelled* him to create those whom he knew would go to hell should he create them. So the question remains, why did he create them? Did he perhaps lack some power after all? Was he simply unable to refrain from creating them? It would seem that a truly all-powerful and good God could have created only those who would freely choose heaven and have left un-created those who would freely choose hell if God created them.

Billy Graham does not appear to want to answer simply that it pleased God to create those whom he knew would choose hell. In fact, like many other Arminian Christians who cannot stomach the boldness of consistent Calvinism, Dr. Graham has to duck the question. To be more exact, he diverts attention from it in two ways. First, he insists that man, not God, is wholly responsible for hell. Second, he says that far from desiring hell for man, God has done everything he possibly could do to keep men out of hell. After all, he gave his only begotten Son as a sacrifice. What else could God do? [22]

In seeking to shift total responsibility for hell to man rather than God, Graham says: "God will never send anybody to hell. If man goes to hell, he goes by his own free choice. Hell was created for the devil and his angels, not for man. God never meant that man should go there. And God has done everything within his power to keep you out." [23]

WHO MADE HELL?

Billy Graham does admit that both sin and hell existed before man, which is to say that man's environment from the very start was not truly perfect. Now, it is a cardinal doctrine among Evangelicals that God *cannot* sin. Dr. Graham agrees with this. [24] However, that does not entail for him that God is therefore unfree. He sees no problem in asserting both (1) that God could not possibly sin and (2) that God nev-ertheless is perfectly free in his will.

But for some unclarified reason, Billy Graham thinks that man cannot be free in his will unless he is subjected to temptations and the choice of going to hell. This is all very confusing to many Christians, and Graham confesses that he himself does not know how sin originated. He simply wants to insist that God cannot be held responsible. And yet he says that sin existed before men. He struggles rather heroically with this problem:

> The puzzling question is Where did evil and sin originate, and why did God allow it? The Bible teaches that sin did not originate with man, but with the angel whom we have come to know as Satan. Yet exactly how sin originated is not fully known. It is one of the mysteries the Bible does not fully reveal. . . . For some reason it has not pleased God to reveal the full answer to the mystery of where iniquity began.[25]

Graham then concludes that somehow "iniquity . . . was found in [Lucifer's] heart, but there is no explanation as to how it got there." [26]

Doubtless the evangelist has at least entertained the passing thought that sin entered Lucifer's heart because God put it there. But that is a conclusion which Graham cannot abide. It is so very abhorrent to him that as a last resort he has to invoke a device greatly favored by orthodox theologians: "mystery."

But once again the persistent branch of orthodox evangelical Protestants known as Calvinism does not draw back from the conclusion that so sickens Graham's heart. Again, his friend and former teacher Gordon Clark states the Calvinistic conclusion plainly: "It may sound strange at first to say that God would decree an immoral act, but the Bible shows that he did." [27]

Billy Graham regards the Bible to be the final answer to any topic that it purports to speak explicitly about. The strict Calvinists agree and go further to say that the Bible does in fact tell us where evil came from. In the minds of Calvinists there is no mystery about it, for God has revealed the truth on the matter. But if it is the truth, it is a most difficult one to swallow, and Dr. Graham's reluctance to accept it is somewhat understandable. Calvinists love to quote the following chilling passage, which they take to be a direct quote from God: "I make peace, and *create evil* (Isa. 45:7, KJV; italics added)." Another favorite passage is, "The Lord hath made all things for himself: yea, *even the wicked for the day of evil* (Prov. 16:4, KJV; italics added)."

Graham's Calvinistic fellow Christians will have nothing to do with what they regard as the Arminian game of theological hide-and-seek. Calvinists come out in the open to announce forthrightly that evil and the wicked were made by God himself. There is no secret or mystery about it. Not for the Calvinists.

No matter how many twists and turns are made in attempts to escape from this dreadful conclusion, the fact remains that at least some major portions of the Bible take divine sovereignty so seriously as to render God the cause of sin and hell. B. B. Warfield, the beloved theological master among orthodox evangelical Protestants, fully accepts this version of divine sovereignty:

> It is God that hardens the heart of the sinner that persists in his sin (Ex. iv. 21, vii. 3, x.1, 27, xiv. 4, 8, Deut. ii. 30, Jos. xi. 20, Isa. lxiii. 17); it is from Him that evil spirits proceed that trouble sinners (I Sam. xvi. 14, Judg. ix. 23, 1 Kings xxii, Job i.); it is of Him that the evil impulses that rise in sinners' hearts take this or that specific form (II Sam. xiv. 1).[28]

Many Christians are prepared to say that God is the cause of all the good that Christians do. They even insist that God, not they, executes righteousness. In this connection Paul's words are often quoted: "It is no longer I who live, but Christ who lives in me (Gal. 2:20)." Paul also tells a group of Christians to work out their "own salvation with fear and trembling; for *God is at work in you* (Phil. 2:12–13; italics added)." However, only the Calvinists are bold enough to say that it is God who works in a person to do evil! Many orthodox Protestants prefer to pass the buck to Satan. But the Calvinists do not stop with Satan, for they see that a wholly all-powerful and all-knowing God would simply work through Satan if necessary to accomplish the all-encompassing divine purposes. Calvinists contend that if God had not been at work in Satan, Judas, and Herod, then God could not have been absolutely certain that Christ would have been crucified. And if that pivotal event had been uncertain, then all the Old Testament prophecies pointing to it would have been placed on a mere probabilistic and precarious basis.

Gordon Clark, for example, says that Judas could not have chosen any other alternative than what he did choose, for God had already predetermined Judas to be the unfailing agent of the divine plan to bring Christ to the cross. Had God not predestined Judas to choose inevitably what he did choose, then Judas might have gone off to Spain with Mary Magdalene at the very time when he was needed to betray Jesus. No, Clark will not allow anything to interfere with this "necessity of infallible certainty." God had to work in and through Judas and everyone else in order to accomplish perfectly his will or plan.[29] Billy Graham holds to the notion of divine Providence and says that in the end God will get his way. But he does not like to go into detail in the way that Gordon Clark does. Only the appeal to "mystery" can keep Graham from either entering the camp of Calvinism or forsaking the camp of Evangelicalism altogether.

MAN'S FREE WILL

Billy Graham wants to give God credit for the good only and not the evil. The only way he can do this, he believes, is to bring in the mysterious notion of free will. So much hinges on this one elusive notion, and Graham uses it for all it is worth. As noted earlier, he cannot admit that God might have made men both free and yet incapable of sin. It is clear why Graham cannot admit this; for if he did, then it follows that God could have made an absolutely perfect world in which hell would not even be a possibility. In fact, Graham believes that in heaven the possibility for human beings to sin will not exist. He promises that when Christians die and go to heaven they will not have to worry about falling into sin inasmuch as all temptations have already been completely removed from the celestial abode.[30] Presumably in heaven humans will have absolute free will without the option of hell from which to choose. It pleases Graham to think that in heaven men will not be able to choose to go to hell. But it also pleases him to think that on earth men are able to choose to go to hell if they want to. Of course, the evangelical view is that in heaven God sees to it that his human creatures do not want to go to hell. And on earth he sees to it that they do want to go to hell, for that is their "natural" condition. Evangelicalism entails that God either *could* not or *would* not create earthly men with the desire to go to heaven only, with no desire to go to hell.

But Billy Graham thinks that a world without hell would lack free will and therefore would be imperfect. At the same time, however, the evangelist does not think that God himself is imperfect, even though he could not sin or go to hell. Graham's own position about God's freedom was stated centuries ago by another Baptist, John Gill: "God is a most free agent, and liberty in him is in its utmost perfection, and . . . *he has no freedom to do that which is evil* . . . his will is *determined only to that which is good*; he can do no other . . . and what he does, he does freely and yet necessarily." [31]

We recall that for Graham free will in man is so wonderful that it is worth the risk of hell itself.[32] But what Graham is reluctant to face up to is the clear conclusion that God the Father can himself possess every good quality without ever having to suffer genuine temptation. And what is more, Graham believes that *God's will is free even though God could not possibly in a billion centuries do anything evil.*

Curiously, Graham and other Evangelicals do finally come to believe that at least some portion of mankind will both be free and yet be unable to sin or go to hell. They will be like God on that point. But unfortunately this glorified state will come about only in heaven. There it will be absolutely impossible for human beings to sin. Yet they will be perfectly free. Evangelicals who believe in free will must someday face the question of why God did not or could not simply start men in heaven and thus bypass all the misery of earth and hell. If men already in heaven cannot now sin, then why could not God have made them incapable of sin to begin with? If doing so at the start would have deprived them of free will, then why does the loss of this choice in heaven not deprive them of it also? Perhaps Graham will be forced to conclude that God simply lacked sufficient power to start off with a perfect world that contained both free will and the impossibility of sin. Of course, if God could have started with heaven for men but did not, then his perfect goodness becomes suspect. Or perhaps heaven is not as great as Graham and others have claimed.

Writing in *Decision*, David Augsburger reveals the extent to which some Evangelicals are willing to go in order to affirm the doctrine of hell and relieve their God of responsibility for hell. In what would appear to many to be a peculiarly perverse article entitled "Hell," Augsburger boldly asserts that hell is actually the very greatest compliment that an individual will ever enjoy! Why? Because it is God's way of permitting the individual to endure the consequences of his own sin. It is God's way of respecting the individual's freedom. Augsburger insists further that it would be a terrible insult *not* to send people to hell whenever they reject Christianity.[33] (He thinks that rejecting Christianity is the same as choosing hell—no third option.)

In reply to this, however, it might be said that an insult might be better than hell. More pointedly, however, it could be said that the consequences ought not to be so thunderously disproportionate. The "freedom" offered is not just and fair if the consequences are ludicrously out of balance, as the consequence of everlasting torture seems to be. In rejoinder to this criticism the Evangelical says that only hell can satisfy an offense to divine honor or holiness. In the next chapter the issues of divine holiness will have to be examined very carefully.

DIVINE FOREKNOWLEDGE
AND GOODNESS

But let us now go back for a moment. Let us suppose not only that God has all power, all knowledge, and perfect goodness but also that man must face a choice which God does not have to face for himself, namely, whether or not to go to hell. Imagine God in the councils of eternity, long before the creation of mankind. He foresees that a great proportion of mankind will choose hell and another portion will choose heaven. The question is, does God really *want* some men to go to hell? Graham says no. Strict Calvinists say yes.

But the fact is that Graham admits that great hordes of men will actually be damned to everlasting torture. But how could this be if God did not so *want* it? It is now clear why Graham must invoke the notion of free will. Without it, the Evangelicals' God is going to appear to be sadistic.

But will Dr. Graham's doctrine of free will work? Probably not, for it fails to take seriously the orthodox doctrines of divine foreknowledge and omnipotence, doctrines which Dr. Graham professes to believe. It is difficult to avoid concluding that Graham's God was suffering some kind of pressure to create those who he foresaw would go to hell. Did he have to create them? By separating foreknowledge and predestination, Arminians like Graham ought to be free to say that God might very well have decided not to create everything that he foresaw. Because God is all-powerful, nothing outside him made him create this or that. Presumably God had some options. He could have been selective in what he created; he did not have to create everything that he foresaw. So it turns out that God might just as easily have created only those humans who would freely choose heaven. And a perfectly good and all-powerful God would even be expected to do just that, if he was going to create any humans at all.

Billy Graham and many other Arminians find themselves having to face the dilemma that God either *wanted* to create those who would choose hell or *was compelled* to do so. What this entails, however, is that either God's goodness is less than perfect or his power is restricted in some way—and it is not simply *self*-restriction on God's part. Graham's premises move him into this painful dilemma. But he refuses to draw a forthright conclusion. Understandably, he hides it from himself, for the dilemma is a direct threat to his orthodoxy. He therefore designates it as a "mystery."

Of course, the Calvinists are once again quite open and frank in claiming that God knew what he was about when he made hell. But Graham attempts to give the impression that the notion of human beings going to hell was only an afterthought to God, which does not square with the standard orthodox doctrine of divine omniscience, to which Dr. Graham professes to subscribe faithfully.

Actually, the Calvinists see very clearly that nothing can be an afterthought to God if he is truly omniscient. God does not engage in laboratory experiments in order to learn how things will turn out. He is supposed to know already. So Calvinism does not hide from the conclusion that God not only knew who would go to hell, he actually created them to go there.

Billy Graham denies that God wanted any human being in hell. However, the evangelist is powerless to explain why God, knowing full well that great masses of men would end in hell, nevertheless proceeded to create them anyhow. Apparently, Graham's God simply could not select in the way that an all-powerful and good God would be expected to select.

According to Calvinism, God knew what he was doing and he did it boldly! God hated some people and loved others. It is that simple. "Jacob I loved, but Esau I hated (Rom. 9:13)." Unfair? The Calvinists do not think so. It is not unfair because God is not subject to the principle of fairness. He is above it. God, says the apostle Paul, can love whomever he pleases, and no one can call him into question if he does not love everyone. God hardened Pharaoh's heart, but there is no court of appeal for Pharaoh to go to. God simply predetermined to use him, and God "hardens the heart of whomever he wills (Rom. 9:18)." B. B. Warfield states this position crisply: "The discrimination of men into saved and lost is carried back to the free counsel of God's will." [34] Billy Graham claims to find this terribly confusing—a great "mystery." It is not, however, a mystery. It is simply a failure of nerve on Graham's part, a failure to see where Evangelicalism leads him. And this failure is understandable, for the Calvinistic alternative is indeed chilling.

Chapter 8
A QUESTION OF HOLINESS

THE RESTRAINING POWER
OF DIVINE HOLINESS

"There is no limit to God," declares Evangelist Graham. "There is no limit to His wisdom. There is no limit to His power. There is no limit to His love. There is no limit to His mercy." [1] Nothing is impossible with God.[2] Graham also lists omnipotence, omniscience, and omnipresence as attributes of God.[3]

The language of devotion sometimes throws caution to the wind and forgets the limits of the object of devotion. The young man in love may in a moment of passion exclaim, "She's got *everything!*" The language of devotion seeks to cast off the limits encompassing the loved one. The admiring son may insist that his father knows everything or can do anything. Superpatriots have been known to make fantastic claims about what their country can do, and boys have been known to attribute all sorts of limitless powers to their football heroes. When Billy Graham says, "There is no limit to God," he may be understood as speaking the hyperbolic language of passion and devotion.

In a less passionate moment Graham acknowledges some of the limitations of his God. And the previous chapter indicated limitations that the evangelist does not explicitly admit but which seem to be implicit in what he says about God and his creatures.

One of the limitations on God's will which Billy Graham seems to acknowledge is the divine holiness. He refers to the biblical passage which says that God is "not willing that any should perish." [4] Yet apparently God's wish or will is thwarted. Let us simplify this somewhat and say that God is not willing that any of his creatures should go to hell, although, according to Graham, hordes of them will indeed go. Many have already gone. Even if we should grant that a free will that chooses evil is what leads men to hell, the question remains as to why this free will could not lead to at least annihilation rather than everlasting torment. Is hell the *only* final punishment that is acceptable to God? Graham's answer is yes!

Now, why could not God be satisfied with having unbelievers simply pass out of existence altogether? That would certainly be a great deprivation. The answer that Graham's theology provides is quite clear. God's holiness will not permit him to be satisfied with any punishment of unbelievers other than everlasting hell.

Nothing outside God forces him to demand endless torture for unbelievers. But there is definitely something inside him making such a demand: his holiness. "His holiness and His justice demand the penalty for a broken law." [5] In fact, God's holiness is such that nothing but infinite suffering could appease the divine wrath or holiness. God's holiness is infinite; and inasmuch as man's sin is an assault on God's holiness, this sin becomes infinite sin. Hence, only infinite punishment could compensate for this infinite sin. As E. J. Carnell reminds his readers, "hell is that place beyond which nothing more awful can be conceived." [6] Hell has to be awful because it is God's holiness that has been offended. Divine holiness is no trivial matter to be passed off casually. Only by infinite punishment of unbelievers could God get the point across to his creatures that his divine holiness has been offended. God would not be respected and properly feared if he merely annihilated unbelievers. Sin is heinous; hence, the punishment must be equal in severity if there is to be a just balancing of the scales. [7] "Because God is an infinite person, therefore, sin is an infinite evil." [8] The punishment must equal or fit the crime. God's holiness demands no less.

It would appear, on the surface at least, that God is torn between two wishes, urges, wills, or desires. On one hand, he does not wish anyone to suffer torment. On the other, he does not wish sinners to be simply annihilated. He wishes them to be punished forever, and this wish is God's holiness exerting itself, so to speak. God resolves this conflict, however, by punishing Christ instead of unbelievers, Graham is happy to announce. That is, God could forsake all plans to punish unbelievers if the unbelievers would only accept Christ's suffering as their substitute for punishment. But the fly in the ointment is that great throngs of unbelievers still choose to remain unbelievers. Graham insists that they do so willfully rather than for legitimate reasons. So God has to punish some people in hell forever. His holiness will not permit him to resort to mercy killing in order to put them out of their everlasting agony. God is merciful, Graham contends; but he is not *that* merciful—at least not merciful in that particular way.

GOD'S OBSESSION WITH MAN

Many persons know what it is like to be rejected by a recipient of their love. It is very difficult to let the former companion or friend go his or her own way. In some cases, the rejected lover becomes obsessed with either winning back the loved one or getting some sort of secret (and sometimes not-so-secret) revenge.

Evangelical theology seems inevitably to picture God as somehow obsessed with getting something from man. If God cannot obtain love, he will at least obtain some kind of recognition from man. Even those in hell will be reconditioned and reshaped by God to the point that they will have to confess that he is perfectly just in sending them to hell.[9] This obsession theme is very curious because most Evangelicals insist that in the great scheme of things God is so completely perfect that he does not need man at all. Man adds nothing to him. This is not unlike the rejected lover who says to himself, "I can do perfectly well without her; she means absolutely nothing to me." Except that despite himself he thinks about her morning and evening.

One of the giants among evangelical theologians, B. B. Warfield, insists repeatedly that the entire created universe is simply a "little speck of derived being." Comparing "the littleness of the universe" with the absolute completeness of God, Warfield says of the universe that "its providential government is scarcely an incident in the infinite fullness of His life." [10] This, then, would make mankind a mere incident within an incident.

If, as Evangelicals insist, man adds nothing to God's complete and wholly self-contained life, then it does appear odd that God becomes so upset with human unbelievers. He might at least let them pass into a permanent sleep devoid of dreams and experiences of any kind. But instead he must bother himself with them forever. And what is more, even after, say, a trillion years of knowing that unbelievers have suffered incredible agony, God's holiness is no closer to being finally satisfied than it was on the first day that hell was initiated. If Billy Graham's view on this matter is correct, then it follows that God must spend eternity venting his wrath while never enjoying a rest from anger. God is angry for the remainder of eternity. It does seem that evangelical theology pictures God as suffering some sort of "hangup" with the human species. Because of man, God the Father turned against God the Son. Graham says that "God turned his back on the Son; Jesus Christ was separated from God. . . . Jesus Christ died, and reverently speaking, went to hell, separated from God." [11] According to E. J. Carnell, man's sin generated a rift inside the Trinity itself. When Christ "became sin" for man, the heavenly Father actually bore "hatred" for God the Son. There was "guilt in the heavenly family." The bond of "fellowship" between Father and Son was broken apart. This disruption created within the Trinity was "unthinkably painful to heaven." [12] According to Graham and Evangelicals, God the Father literally forsook the Son—for a brief period, to be sure, but it was a period that somehow enveloped eternity.

It would seem that instead of taking man in stride, as the finite creature that he is, the God of Evangelicalism is portrayed as taking this finite creature to be a monstrous threat to the very gates of heaven—a cosmic threat to the Lord of the universe. And so, while he is supposed to provide no positive contribution to the wholly self-contained and self-sufficient life of the God of Evangelicals, man suddenly wells up as a terrible challenger to God, a challenger that God seems to be greatly worried about, as if the challenger is a threat to the divine position in the cosmic scheme of things. Indeed, the same Evangelicals who once pictured man as a mere speck are now picturing him as some sort of second god storming the castle of heaven. It seems a bit theatrical. (Leon Morris' *The Apostolic Preaching of the Cross* is one of the clearest presentations of the evangelical notion of atonement. Dr. Morris was a strong supporter of Graham's crusade in Australia.)

MAN'S PREOCCUPATION WITH HIS OWN FINITUDE

Perhaps in the final analysis this epiclike work of art produced by Evangelicals is really something of a grotesque self-portrait revealing man's preoccupation with himself, as if he were attempting to prove that he is not finite after all. The finite creature imagines himself to be a mighty terror to God, a terrifying figure forcing God himself to muster all his strength to overcome him. Indeed, the finite creature called man even imagines that he is important enough to generate animosity within the changeless God himself. Aristotle may have referred to God as "the Unmoved Mover," but at the other extreme Evangelicals seem determined to demonstrate that man can rock God on his heels, even if it is the sin of man that makes waves in heaven and creates the great cosmic splash, causing the Deity to react with a wrath or rage that thereafter never simmers down for all eternity.

Paradoxically, it is evangelical theology itself that warns of the sin of pride. Perhaps in some areas at least evangelical theology is but one of many examples of human pride, of man's inclination to think more grandiose thoughts of himself than are justified.

Evangelicals leave the strong impression that once God made man, the Creator was thereafter unable to remove this mortal speck from his eye. It is often a demeaning experience to be ignored or to go unnoticed. And whatever else may be said of the evangelical theatrical production, one thing is clear: Evangelical theology, despite its declarations against human pride, has made man a noticed star in the cosmic production. Man may not be God, but evangelical theology allows him to costar with the greatest Actor of them all. And that certainly beats remaining a mere creature of earth who lives his fourscore and ten and then is no more. There is something heroic and daring about evangelical theology. Something Promethean. Something wildly fanciful, even romantic. Evangelical theology turns out to be in many ways a sensational work of inventive art.

HELL AS MAN'S AGGRESSION

As Freud suggests, humans are very ambivalent creatures. They can suffer great agony from the hands of their persecutor while at the same time admiring, envying, and identifying with him. Men have often admired and even worshiped power. Strict Calvinism is a prime example of both the ambivalence toward absolute power and the worship of it.

Perhaps, after all, the doctrine of hell is a tale of man's own capacity to hate outsiders, just as heaven reflects man's hopes and dreams for insiders. The doctrine of hell is a strange stone to place around the neck of deity. Perhaps it does not belong there at all.

It is sometimes difficult for people to grasp what is entailed in the evangelical doctrine of hell. Imagine all the agony and unhappiness produced by all the atrocities, crimes, and villainous deeds done by Joseph Stalin, Adolf Hitler, and all the rest of mankind. Now compare the weight of centuries of man-made misery to the aeons of misery which God will presumably bring about in everlasting hell. The conclusion is plain. In terms of human misery and agony, the Evangelical's hell is so much more evil than all the collective evils of men as to make the comparison ridiculous. The Evangelicals thus find themselves in the awkward position of having to acknowledge that if hell is God's punishment for the grief which men have caused one another, the punishment for it far excels the crime in both horror and atrocity. The punishment, far from redeeming anyone, is simply another case of what the punishment is supposed to be punishing. Hell becomes another manifestation of wrath—a prolonged siege of rage.

So it is perhaps not farfetched to suggest that the notion of hell may be another case of finite man's smoldering revenge welling up to infinite and grandiose proportions. The fire that is said to burn forever in hell is in reality the fire of rage and revenge burning within frustrated mortal men. That is, hell is man in his worst hours, when the imaginations of his heart are filled with thoughts of hot revenge.

One evangelical theologian considers the question of how "the saints in heaven [can] have pleasure if they know there is a single human soul still in hell." The theologian answers by simply assuring the reader that in due time the saints will be able to take pleasure in the fact of hell. Otherwise, the saints would be better than God! [13] In other words, it presumably does not disturb God that certain human beings suffer forever; so why should it disturb the conscience of a mere mortal man? What this Evangelical's reply perhaps fails to consider, however, is the possibility that the imagined willingness of God to underwrite eternal hell is in reality a reflection of man's own willingness to release hostility upon his feared and despised fellowmen. And yet perhaps the thought that saints in heaven cannot, after all, receive pleasure from the realization that one of the members of their species is suffering forever is an expression of the better side of man, when mutual aggression gives way to mutual concern.

Evangelicals do not envision a future life wherein both peace and theological disagreement can happily survive simultaneously. In heaven all intelligent creatures are supposed to subscribe to all the fundamentals of Evangelicalism. If they cannot, then they will not be in heaven. Unfortunately, the only other place for them is the Cosmic Concentration Camp. No other options. But if there is life after death, then perhaps there exists more pluralism, diversity, and variety than Billy Graham and Evangelicals can imagine. Evangelicals eliminate all conflict and disagreement in the next life by segregating humanity into two groups— the orthodox and the miserable. No room is made for the unorthodox outside hell. Unorthodoxy is counted as wickedness deserving torment forever. But perhaps there will be many heavens, with varying degrees of happiness, varying life-styles, and even varying philosophies and theologies. In that way men could live in the kind of communities and environments appropriate to their special personalities. An all-powerful God could presumably keep the communities from infringing excessively on one another. And if some men should appear actually to want to suffer the misery of hell, then God may provide them with the option—although, paradoxically, Evangelicals equivocate regarding whether they think unbelievers actually *want* to be in hell. Of course, a God of power and goodness would presumably respect the freedom of his creatures sufficiently to permit those in utter misery to elect to undergo euthanasia rather than suffer outrageously forever.

In short, for all its speculative imagination about cosmic events, evangelical literature has demonstrated an ability to think only in two airtight categories—heaven and hell—rather than many. Yet even within these narrow confines Evangelicals have developed, however slightly, the notion of *degrees* of bliss in heaven and of agony in hell. With a little more imagination, the continuum of degrees—or of life-styles—could possibly be increased, so that the options would not be reduced to a heaven or a hell.

For all his talk of free will and free choice, the evangelist who created "the hour of decision" provides only two options, neither of which appeals greatly to the major portion of mankind. According to Graham, within heaven, where orthodoxy alone reigns, there will be "ranks of celestial princes" as well as "potentates" and "rulers," which suggests that there must also be subjects who are ruled.[14] But this variety is only within the Heavenly Country Club and its exclusive membership. This is fair enough, except that it will not tolerate other country clubs offering a measure of happiness in other life-styles and views. It is either Heavenly Suburbia with a fixed orthodoxy or the Cosmic Ghetto for all who cannot accept orthodoxy. Other options are not permitted. It is thought that only the orthodox can live together in peace and happiness. And there can be only one orthodoxy. There is "only one door" to happiness in the next life, and it is very narrow. There is only one way to get there.

Whenever Billy Graham and some of the Jesus People are observed holding up one finger in the air, they mean "one way"—one way *only*. While the way to exclusive happiness in the next life is narrow, the way to misery is very wide. The evangelist asks, "Have you, by faith, entered the narrow gate? Do you now walk on the narrow road that leads to eternal life? Or, are you among the masses of humanity who are on the broad road leading to destruction? What is your destination? Which road are you taking? Not every person will be found in heaven." [15]

It once troubled B. B. Warfield that his God would have to watch most of his human creatures slide off into hell. So he wrote an article entitled "Are There Few That Be Saved?" to prove that a larger percentage of people will be saved than lost. The article was written in 1915; at that time there was greater hope that the masses of men would soon "turn to Christianity." [16] Today this hope flares up only now and then as men watch the population charts. It does not seem strange to Billy Graham that God will lose most of his human creation to hell. After all, each individual will have had an ample supply of free will.

THE AGONY AND THE ECSTASY

In his book *On Aggression*, Konrad Lorenz, the renowned observer of animal behavior, writes that the close bond of friendship among animals is found only in those animals with highly developed patterns of aggression unleashed on members of their own species. Going into Lorenz' explanation of this would probably take us too far afield, but what is important to grasp is Lorenz' thesis that in animals the capacity to love develops only among those species with the strong capacity for aggression. "There is no love without aggression." And "in every case of genuine love there is such a high measure of latent aggression." [17]

It is in the evolution of man, Lorenz believes, that this capacity for both powerful love and powerful aggression toward members of one's own species reaches its earthly peak. No animal can love like man, nor can any equal his powers of hatred. His ecstasy of love is challenged only by the agony resulting from the hatred he harbors for some of his fellowmen. Despite its rejection of the theory of evolution, evangelical theology carries this amity-enmity complex into heaven itself.* Only God can excel all others in his power to love. And, as the doctrine of hell shows, only God can excel to the fullest in the power to manifest aggression. Curiously, evangelical theology even attributes to God the principle of intraspecific aggression, that is, aggression toward one's own kind. In the evangelical version of divine atonement, God the Father turns against God the Son and releases upon him the fullness of his holy wrath.

There is a deeply tragic refrain in the notion that none can love greatly without also manifesting intense hostility and aggression. Evangelicals are fond of pointing out how frequently the New Testament makes reference to Jesus' talking of hell. One writer, who does not pretend to be a believer, writes of man:

> In the same individual we find capacity for tenderness, sympathy, charity, and infinite capacity for cruelty, callousness, destruction, hate. Herbert Spencer saw it as the natural consequence of the life of social man, who must obey two codes: there is the code of amity, which he must honor in his relations with social partners, and the code of enmity, which he must honor in his relations to the outside world.[18]

It is, in short, the war between the insiders and the outsiders. And far from providing a way of somehow overcoming this tragic war, the Evangelical's Prince of Peace only perpetuates and intensifies it, and guarantees that it will never be overcome in all eternity. Indeed, the bond of grace and love for the insiders ("the elect") is strengthened by the thought that in the end the outsiders will suffer agonies beyond belief.[19] The intense love in heaven depends for its existence on the smoldering flames of intraspecific aggression that the doctrine of hell so vividly symbolizes. No hell, no heaven. That is the alpha and omega of evangelical psychology. The attribute of divine holiness in Billy Graham's religion turns out to be a mystified version of man's own propensity to hate outsiders. (Whether this propensity is innate or learned is a

---

* What does it mean to say that human aggression is instinctive? It is more fruitful to inquire into the biological and cultural conditions by which this aggression comes about.

significant issue that will be touched on in a subsequent chapter.) The only option which Billy Graham offers other than eternal hostility is absorption. Unbelievers cannot be tolerated. They must either join up with believers or become the victims of the endless wrath of God.

Freud, in his later years, came to the following chilling conclusion about man: "It is always possible to bind together a considerable number of people in love, so long as there are other people left over to receive the manifestation of their aggressiveness." [20]

Evangelical theology in effect says the same thing about God. He cannot love Jacob without hating Esau. That is the way God is. And that is why he cannot simply annihilate the outsiders. That is why he cannot somewhat mercifully put them out of their eternal misery. God *needs* them! Without them he could not love the insiders of heaven. The Evangelical's God cannot love some of his creatures unless he has others to torment. If he should resort to the mercy killing of those in hell, the saints in heaven would find themselves in utter terror, for God would then have to select from among the saints of heaven some to receive the manifestation of his aggressiveness. Only in that way could his love be sustained. The everlasting bliss of heaven is fed by the everlasting agony of hell. Let those insiders in heaven be thankful, therefore, that some of their fellowmen are suffering in hell; for if they were not now in hell, then the saints themselves would have reason to fear the worst. And that fear would itself be another hell.

In an address entitled "The Predicament of Man," Arthur Koestler finds man's predicament to lie in the power of love to generate hostility and cruelty.[21] Billy Graham is constantly preaching that the only hope for peace lies in total surrender to the Evangelicals' God. However, the example which Graham's Deity sets for all is nothing different from what is found every day among men. It is very simple: "You agree with me and accept my terms; then we will have peace together." Hitler offered Czechoslovakia the same deal. Marxism makes the offer to anyone, and Arthur Koestler once applied for it. He stated his "readiness to serve the cause in whatever capacity the Party decided." [22] He even became a preacher of the Marxist gospel. But against the warnings of his comrades in the Communist party, he began to think seriously about writings critical of his faith and to converse with sinners and publicans and the bourgeoisie. For a while his faith was strong. Later he wrote of this kind of all-out commitment: "Faith is a wondrous thing; it is not only capable of moving mountains, but also of making you believe that a herring is a race horse." [23]

To make a complex and involved story short, Koestler's faith in Marxism began to waver and eventually to come apart at the seams. In an article in a book entitled *The God That Failed*, he tells how the atrocities which Marxism had perpetrated kept weighing on his mind. His long love affair with Marxism had to come to an end. Similarly, many former Evangelicals and fundamentalists have found the atrocities attributed to God to be more than they could in good faith live with. They too have had to walk away from at least one version of "the God that failed." God seemed to them to be made in the image of the ignoble, aggressive dimension of mortal man. Some aspects of their evangelical faith were very meaningful to them, but they discovered that most of these meaningful and valuable aspects could be found elsewhere without all the meaningless aspects.

Chapter 9
THE INNER SELF AND THE CIRCUMSTANCES OF LIFE

A CHANGE FROM WITHIN

In the debate about environmentalism, Billy Graham is aligned on the side of those who say that the culture and society cannot be reformed until the individual is first changed from within. In a recent book the evangelist writes: "Idealists in many generations have tried to shape a better world through education, humanitarianism, science, and giveaway poverty programs. All have failed. The individual must be changed." [1] Characteristically, the evangelist does not say to what degree they have failed. In one of his earlier books he makes another categorical and blanket statement: "Humanism has failed." [2] No qualifications are offered.

At root, says the evangelist, the trouble is that inside every individual person is a disease called sin, a plague that causes all the troubles and difficulties in the world. This inner sin does not cause merely *some* of mankind's troubles. "It causes all the troubles, confusions, and disillusionments in your life." [3] So if things are ever going to be better, a change has to come from within.[4] As noted earlier, Graham in his less cautious moments promises that if you will, by faith, change from within, then "your conflicts will disappear and your inner tensions will vanish into thin air." [5] In short, a "conversion to Christ" is both a necessary and a sufficient condition for finding oneself free of all inner tensions and conflicts. In his less sensational moments, however, the evangelist simply warns that this conversion is a necessary condition. Which is to say, if a person is not "converted to Christ" he will not have peace —or at least not true peace and true happiness. Graham seems vaguely aware that there are other variables that still may prevent the arrival of peace.

Time and events have toned down Billy Graham's promises slightly, although even in the 1970's he will still now and then promise instant cures. But just as *Mad* magazine stole Al Capp's thunder, so some of the "turned-on generation" stole Billy Graham's thunder by promising instant transportation to higher realms beyond the empirical world. In a book written in 1966, Dr. Graham, still making fantastic promises and offering superb bonuses, nevertheless introduces a note of caution. He says:

> If the human race should suddenly turn to Christ, we would have immediately the possibility of a new Christian order. We could approach our problems in the framework of Christian understanding and brotherhood. To be sure, the problems would remain, but the atmosphere for their solution would be completely changed.[6]

Notable in this passage is that while the evangelist still invokes the word immediately and says the atmosphere would be "completely changed," he hedges. A new Christian order is not now promised but only "the possibility" of it, even if everyone is converted. Furthermore, the problems remain, although a new "atmosphere" for their solution is postulated. Even the use of the word atmosphere seems to be a slight concession to the importance of a favorable external environment for coming to terms with human problems.

But promise-making, once begun at a very high pitch, is not always easy to control. Hence, in the same book from which the above quotation is taken, Graham promises "the one thing that will solve the problems of our world—changed men. Man's basic problem is spiritual, not social. Man needs a complete change from within." [7] But this change takes place if and only if a person "can come to Christ by faith and emerge a new man." [8] "The new man is Christ formed in us." [9]

If it is greatly desirable that an individual be changed in some sense, then presumably something is wrong with him as he is. A program designed to change an individual ought to spell out what the problem is and what evidence exists for thinking that the problem is a real one. A person who is not a Hindu may not think that he has a problem simply because he does not wish to become a Hindu. So also with his not wishing to become a Christian. Assuming that there is some genuine problem and that the individual needs changing, it does not follow that just any change will do. Attempts ought to be made to give some reasonably clear notion as to how the new situation will in fact meet the problem. And then some of the important specific procedures for making the appropriate change ought to be spelled out. Graham's "Plan of Salvation" is a step in this direction. A good plan will specify definite procedures that can be executed, checked, and compared with specific steps of other plans. A plan is more than a promise.

The following paraphrase of Dr. Graham is offered in order to show that promise-making is an easy practice to fall into no matter what is promised: If the human race should suddenly turn to the compassionate Buddha, we would have immediately the possibility of a new Buddhist order. We could approach our problems in the framework of Buddhism and brotherhood. To be sure, the problems would remain, but the atmosphere for their solution would be completely changed.

Naturally, there are always those who pretend to be good Buddhists. But let us talk only of "genuine Buddhists."

The above quotation could be read in a slightly revised way: If the human race should suddenly turn to the scientific method, we would have immediately the possibility of a new scientific order. We could approach our problems in the framework of scientific understanding and brotherhood. To be sure, the problems would remain, but the atmosphere for their solution would be completely changed.

Perhaps it could be said that Buddhism has not failed; it simply has never been fully tried. Billy Graham says the same about Christianity,[10] whereas B. F. Skinner insists that while science in nonhuman areas has had enormous success, much of the trouble today is the failure to use the methods of science to understand man. Physics alone can do only so much, and in fact can do enormous harm, Skinner believes, unless it is accompanied by psychology and the various branches of behavioral or social science, as well as biology and medicine. In short, the trouble is not too much science but rather too little in an area frequently dominated by superstitious notions, which prevent the advance of more satisfactory resolutions of significant human problems.[11]

What this boils down to is this: Buddhism, Evangelicalism, behavioral science, and various other approaches to human problems have been tested to some degree. But the testing has not been under ideal conditions for the simple reason that one of the goals of each approach is to create what it regards as ideal conditions for itself. It is important, therefore, to draw out from every approach precisely what it is attempting to do, what promises it makes, what demonstrated successes it has to offer, and what procedures it has used.

It cannot be denied that most approaches seem to have enjoyed some success and some failure. There is no easy comprehensive conclusion that can be reached on this issue. Perhaps the most hopeful sign is found in the fact that many of the various approaches, despite their great differences, do in fact seem to converge on some common procedures for solving various common problems. For example, while there is room for genuine debate regarding what are said to be scientific conclusions, hypotheses, and theories, it cannot be denied that a broad scientific method has increasingly established itself among men of almost all camps. For example, those who examine manuscripts of the Bible in order to determine which ones more fully approximate the original autographs could not do their work unless they were scientifically trained in this particular field. Faith does not dictate which manuscripts are more reliable. Evidence and logic are the combined authority for making judgments on the matter.

The more or less piecemeal progress of the scientific method or approach is not sensational, but it does seem to have a certain cumulative stability to it. The scientific community doubtless needs to develop a greater toleration of unorthodoxy without sacrificing its rigorous and critical demands of unorthodoxy as well as orthodoxy. This toleration in science will probably come, not because scientists are innately more moral than others, but because the human activity of science would dry up without it. A seventeenth-century Calvinist and Baptist, Roger Williams, expressed much of the model scientific spirit when he called himself "a seeker." It is no accident that Williams was one of the foremost apostles of religious liberty in a day when unorthodoxy was sometimes considered a crime against the state.

THE INNER SELF AND
THE OUTER SELF

Billy Graham sometimes pictures the human individual as divided into two or three selves, depending on the context in which the evangelist is speaking. In most cases he favors a kind of duality—an inner self and an outer self.[12] The inner self is regarded as the true self in the sense of being truly valuable and enduring. It is the "soul," the "heart," the "spirit." [13] The outer self is likewise called by many names: "self," "the flesh," "the old man," "the natural man." [14] Loving this external self is thought to be evil "self-indulgences, such as self-love, self-will, self-seeking, self-pride." [15] It would be a mistake, however, to regard this inner and outer dichotomy to be that of the intellect, on one hand, and some nonintellectual self, on the other; for pride of intellect is on the side of the flesh and self-seeking.[16]

This distinction that Graham presupposes may seem very confusing at first, until it is realized that sometimes the inner self is understood to be primarily that portion of a person's repertoire which responds in terms of proper evangelical Christian practices. These include confession of faith in Christ as the atoning Son of God, the Bible as perfect revelation, and the Trinity; prayers and deeds that are in accord with the ten commandments and certain other prescriptions; favorable responses to fundamental doctrines, such as the miracles and prophecies of the Bible regarding the Second Coming; singing Christian hymns; witnessing; attending worship; and other such activities. This collection of behavior is "spiritual" behavior—by definition. That is what being spiritual or "leading a spiritual life" *means*.

The inner self is, then, either (1) all these activities taken collectively, (2) the agent which does these activities, or (3) both the agent and the activities. A leading evangelical theologian of the Arminian school, E. Y. Mullins, divides the human self into three: "the material me," "the social me," and "the spiritual me." "The various selves clash with each other." But Mullins also divides the individual into "the natural consciousness" and the "regenerate consciousness." He further finds in the individual a threefold distinction, namely, "will, intellect, and emotions." [17]

According to Evangelicalism, the outer man is naturally not predisposed to behave in the spiritual way, that is, to execute the particular spiritual activities listed above. Infants are not born disposed toward being Evangelicals. And that is why it has been said that the natural man is unspiritual and sinful. Man is "born into sin." "We are," says Graham, "sinners both by heredity and environment; both by nature and by nurture; both by instinct and by practice." [18]

Usually when Graham says "human nature," he means this outer self, which he says cannot be changed until the inner self is changed.[19] Unfortunately, this borders on being a mere circular statement. In some contexts it appears to mean little more than this: If the practices which comprise the outer self do not become the practices which comprise the inner self, then the outer self will never be the inner self. Which is true. But who contests this statement? It is like saying that if an artist does not become a plumber, he will never be a plumber. And that is true too. Again, who contests it? And who says that an artist *ought* to become a plumber, or an outer self an inner self? On what grounds is it said?

Billy Graham does not always have in mind so trivial a point when he talks about changing the self. It becomes more complicated than that. The apostle Paul tried to make sense of this division of the inner and outer self, and succeeded in showing how very difficult the task is, although he did make some progress in explicating the matter. The following quotation from one of Paul's letters has had considerable influence on Christian thinkers, and a close reading of it will demonstrate that Paul was taking on the painfully difficult job of attempting to give a coherent account of what has often been referred to as man's dual nature. Writing vividly of two warring selves, "the inmost self" and "the flesh," Paul says:

> For I delight in the law of God, in my inmost self, but I see in my members another law at war with the law of my mind and making me captive to the law of sin which dwells in my members. Wretched man that I am! Who will deliver me from this body of death? Thanks be to God through Jesus Christ our Lord! So then, I of myself serve the law of God with my mind, but with my flesh I serve the law of sin.

> —Romans 7:22–25

It is worth attempting to unravel this passage. First, the inmost self is seen to be identified with the mind, which delights in God's law. Second, the flesh is that "body of death" which apparently delights in sin. "My members" seems to be another designation by Paul for the flesh or the body of death. Elsewhere he identifies "the flesh" as "our sinful passions (Rom. 7:5)."

In the following passage, the apostle writes further of this war of himself with himself, and the very style of writing in this passage suggests a man on a seesaw of confusion about his identity:

I do not understand my own actions. For I [the outer self] do not what I [the inmost self] want, but I [the outer self] do the very thing I [the inmost self] hate. Now if I [the outer self] do what I [the inmost self] do not want, I [the inmost self?] agree that the law is good. So then it is no longer I [the inmost self] that do it, but sin which dwells within me [the outer self]. For I [the inmost self?] know that nothing good dwells within me [the outer self], that is, in my flesh. I [the inmost self] can will what is right, but I [the outer self?] cannot do it.

—Romans 7:15–18

Before Paul, the philosopher Plato had attempted to see man as a division of soul and body. This traditional distinction is very old and it has been variously revised.

HAPPINESS AND
THE CIRCUMSTANCES OF LIFE

Before the rise of Christianity, the Greek philosopher Zeno developed a school of thought known as Stoicism. The influence of Stoicism on various branches of Christianity is still a matter of debate, although there are at least some parallels between Zeno's Stoicism and Billy Graham's version of Christianity. According to the way of Stoicism, "happiness is not found in anything that the outer world can give," for "mingling with the world and becoming involved in its activities leads only to disillusionment and despair." [20] Some Stoics went so far as to deny that the outward circumstances of life contribute anything to happiness and contentment. The true man is the inner man, which presumably is not dependent upon the outer world.

Billy Graham often gives the impression of preaching a version of Stoicism. "Get a pure heart," he declares, "and you can be supremely happy—*no matter what the circumstances.*" [21] Whether or not this cuts across the grain of the Christian and Hebrew doctrine of man as belonging to the order of finite creation is an interesting question. In another passage the evangelist promises that "a peace can be imparted to the soul that is *not dependent on outward circumstances.*" [22] The soul, says the evangelist, has many characteristics or activities, and if his doctrine of the soul's (or heart's) independence of external circumstances is correct, then the activities of the soul should be able to carry on without external support.

But what exactly are the activities or characteristics of the soul? According to Graham, they are "personality, intelligence, conscience, and memory." [23] In contrast to this psychological theory, however, most people would probably hold that these characteristics which Graham says belong to the soul can in thousands of ways be greatly affected and shaped by outward circumstances. For example, the soul's memory cannot function well if the body loses an excessive amount of sleep. And without a reasonably functioning memory, the conscience—which is supposed to be another characteristic of the soul—cannot function adequately. Indeed, if, as Billy Graham says, the soul is characterized as having a "personality," then even this personality can be drastically altered by a change in the external conditions affecting the body. This is true of Christian and non-Christian alike.

"Peace of mind" is itself very difficult to gain and hold if one's body is in great pain or is forced to lose sleep for great periods of time. Because of severe and prolonged insomnia, the noted evangelical spokesman E. J. Carnell was deprived of considerable peace of mind during much of his lifetime. In a very frank passage written ten years before his early death, Carnell describes a particularly excruciating experience: "One Friday afternoon . . . I emotionally exploded. Having lost sleep with such regularity, I lacked courage for the future. My mind was like a mass of live rubber: continually expanding, it threatened to divide down the center." He goes on to tell of the time when the thought of "suicide took on a certain attractiveness." Describing himself further, he writes:

> An extended loss of sleep radically alters my outlook. My will-to-live decays; I become mordacious toward others. I experience *Weltschmerz* [i.e., pessimism, weariness of life]. But after a powerful sedative, I see things in a different light. The harmony of nature is restored; I am patient with others; the zest for creative living revives. . . . An imbalance in the neurophysical life will be reflected in the moral-spiritual life.[24]

For his own happiness and well-being, Billy Graham has been known to give considerable attention to the "outward circumstances of life." He eats excellent food, has always dressed exceptionally well, has traveling money, receives outstanding medical care, and certainly will never have to worry about being poor when he is old. For a man who advises all his fellowmen to "be content in whatever state they find themselves," [25] the evangelist does quite well materially in this world. Claiming that Jesus' happiness was not "dependent on outward circumstances," Graham wants others to see that they too can enjoy this same independent happiness. Jesus was "above the circumstances of life," and so can everyone be who is in Christ.[26] Some Christians would challenge this claim that Jesus was somehow above it all. He had to work for a living and held a good job, which apparently Joseph left him; also Jesus depended on food and drink, needed friends, and like every other human being he had to have his sleep—sometimes in a boat or on a hillside. Fortunately, Jesus had friends to entertain him at night when he was traveling about, and a rich man is said to have given him a place where he could be buried.

Carnell had to have a sedative to change his personality for the better. From Billy Graham's frame of reference, Carnell was certainly "in Christ," but apparently that was not sufficient for Carnell's peace of mind. Owing to bitter attacks which some of the right-wing fundamentalists made on Carnell when he was president of the Charles Fuller Theological Seminary, he found himself in need of psychotherapy in order to gain some peace of mind. The attackers attempted to persuade Fuller to fire Carnell from his job at the seminary. Bernard Ramm, another evangelical spokesman, knew of Carnell's suffering and was himself often in great despair because of the illness of his friend Carnell. Billy Graham has had to receive medication in order to help him deal with the weakness of the body. In short, Evangelicals, like their fellowmen, are finite creatures dependent at every moment of their lives upon "outward circumstances," whether they acknowledge it or not.

Graham promises that "a peace can be imparted to the soul that is not dependent on outward circumstances." [27] But there is no evidence to show that what Graham calls the soul is so unrelated to either the body or the wider physical environment. It is easy for a man like Graham to take his favored circumstances for granted. He talks freely of being above these external conditions of life. And he can afford to talk in this way; a man who can pay his dental bills, easily get rid of whatever rats may enter his bedroom and kitchen, make long-distance phone calls to exert influence or to talk to friends, play golf in Florida, and enjoy great fame and success in his business—that man has some means and circumstances for being happy and content. True, these means do not guarantee happiness, but they can increase the probability for it.

Evangelist Graham insists that the external circumstances produce only "superficial happiness."[28] But this seems to be a rather immoderate statement. His wife is in some sense external to him, and yet his happiness presumably depends considerably upon her. It is doubtful that he would want to designate this happiness as mere superficial happiness.

Sometimes it is difficult for us to determine what is internal and what is external to a person. In fact, the very same entity may be viewed as either external or internal. For example, the cortex of the brain may be viewed as environment vis-à-vis the thumb, or vice versa. Inside the skin of an individual are various bodily organs that are internal to the total organism and yet external to each other. Turning this around, we might say that if one aspect of the human individual may be regarded as external to every other aspect, then perhaps *together* the various aspects are integral (internal) to one another. But what can be said of the soul? Is it internal or external to the body? Is it an invisible and undetectable organ of the body? Billy Graham may not want to accept explicitly such a notion.

He does sometimes picture the soul as dwelling inside the body, as if the body were a house while the soul is a resident roaming about inside. On the other hand, upon leaving the body at death the soul presumably becomes external to the body. Graham sometimes talks of an individual human being as if he were two or three persons forming a kind of committee. Sometimes these members get along rather well, while at other times they fight and feud with one another. For Graham, only one of these committee members is the "real" person, whereas the temporal body (which is a kind of second-class person) is regarded as more or less the servant of the "real" person or "soul" or "spirit."

Sometimes it makes sense to regard what is internal to a person to be his own desires and wants and perhaps also the expressions of those desires and wants. What is external to him, then, is anything that is not directly an expression of his desires or wants. Sometimes we do not know whether to classify as internal what once was external but is now a satisfaction of our desires. Furthermore, men have conflicting wants. And sometimes Graham seems to think of the inner self of the Christian man as the wants and desires which are in accord with evangelical religion and morality. The desire for evil things, then, may still be a part of the Christian person, but this desire is not *from the heart.* That is, the Christian man does not have in his heart lust and other evil desires, which is to say that he cannot satisfy these desires without feeling great guilt. Such desires belong to the "old man," which is perhaps a way of saying that the "old man" is nothing other than these evil desires.

It is not at all clear what Graham means by "the soul" when he claims that the soul can somehow function apart from external circumstances. Despite talk of this independent soul, Graham finds it very difficult to think of a human person as pure soul. Even in heaven a human without a body is nobody. So Graham settles on a compromise by affirming that in heaven the human individual will not be pure spirit after all but will have (or *be*) a "spiritual body." It may or may not be true that in the next life there could exist a soul without a body, but we must conclude that on earth the supply of blood and oxygen in the body seems to be absolutely essential to any form of human life and happiness, whether the person is an Evangelical or a humanist. Indeed, a person's intelligence, memory, and personality are greatly affected by the many variables of the blood supply alone. And of course the blood depends upon diet, work habits, and other ingredients known as external circumstances.[29]

Like Norman Vincent Peale, Billy Graham sometimes takes for granted the social, linguistic, educational, economic, and material environment which has been so hard-won and which is not always appropriately available to everyone. Peale and Graham share this forgetfulness with many sons and daughters of affluence, which is not to condemn affluence but rather to indicate how very useful it is in supporting human happiness and long life. Graham claims that "the Christian life is the only genuinely happy life, for the happiness and joy of the Christian does not depend upon circumstances." [30] Unfortunately, in making the claim, Graham is riding roughshod over very obvious empirical factors which many adults and unaffluent youths must face constantly in their day-to-day living. Doubtless the id (or whatever we call that aspect of the individual representing uncontrolled wish-fulfillment) is disposed to kick aside the finite limits and to fancy itself free of the encroaching environment. But this dream of absolute freedom is rudely interrupted by so mundane a reality as a toothache or the flu.

Too often Billy Graham thinks of Christ in the very way that some youths think of love. "If you just have love, you don't need anything else. You have it all." Unfortunately, even love—or especially love—cannot be effective without a considerable amount of favorable external conditions for moving it into operation. Love without concrete ways and means is mere sentimentalism at best. Similarly, living in Christ without the means for living in the world is usually not much of a living.

A mother once wrote to Billy Graham regarding a very serious problem. She and her husband were doing well in raising their three normal and healthy children. But their fourth child was a mongoloid. The family physician had recommended that the afflicted child be placed in a home specially designed for caring for such children. "What do you think?" the mother asked the evangelist.

Graham's answer, in opposition to the family physician's recommendation, was that the mother should not place the child in the home. Graham explained to her that the mongoloid child could "with proper understanding and much love" be "habilitated to society." If the mother was not feeling guilty before writing Graham and before making the heartrending decision about her child, Dr. Graham's following words to her suggest very subtly but effectively that she *ought* to begin feeling guilty: "The tendency today is to seek the easy, convenient way out of difficult situations. You must remember that you must live with yourself, and if the guilt feelings you experience outweigh the release from caring for the needing child, it would seem to be an unwise move to send him to a special home." Graham went on to explain that "this abnormal child needs your love as much or more than your other children." He even indicated that God might have sent the child for "a special reason known only at the moment by God." [31]

The evangelist did not even hint that the mother's decision would have to depend on the special circumstances and conditions of her family. In some circumstances it would be better to keep a mongoloid at home; in other circumstances it would not. But evangelist Graham totally ignored the role of circumstances. The fact that this mother might have to devote anywhere from ten to forty years of her private and personal life to watching after the mongoloid seems not to have dawned on the evangelist. The circumstances and conditions involved were oblivious to him. Dr. Graham devoted little of his own personal time and energy to raising his children, and he does not seem to feel that he was wrong in this choice. Fortunately, he had someone who could do the job for him. Yet he warns the mother of the mongoloid that she may know guilt if she in effect employs someone else specially qualified to care for her child.

Graham's apparent insensitivity to the external circumstances under which other people have to live makes much of his "come-on preaching" greatly irrelevant to many people. If evangelical Christianity had to travel on the promises of such preachers as Billy Graham, it would have stalled long ago. The truth is that great sums of money, time, and energy, as well as all sorts of concrete programs for modifying the circumstances of the convert's life, are essential if the convert is to be changed and remain changed. The conversion experience itself is nothing without a new and supportive environment.

Billy Graham preaches that God radically changes the individual from within. The evangelist even gives the clear and distinct impression that the external conditions have nothing to do with this inner change. But in many ways he knows better than this, and his actions outside the pulpit show that he does know better. When he is not giving his hard-sell come-on, his sermons sometimes demonstrate clearly how seriously he takes the outward circumstances of life. If the soul could, as Graham says, have peace and happiness without depending on the external circumstances and conditions, then why should the evangelist greatly concern himself about pornography, nude films, and other external matters? Could it be that he thinks that even the inner self can be changed and shaped by the environment? Apparently so. Indeed, one reason for his having a home built in the mountains of North Carolina was to provide his children with an external environment free of a parade of autograph-seekers and free of constant exposure to a big-city environment.

In the Spring 1972 issue of the *Saturday Evening Post* the evangelist says that much of the happiness of his own children has been "because of the place [where] we live" "in the mountains." Of his children, Graham acknowledges that his wife "reared them like mountain children." In fact, his children were blessed with both the environment of mountain living and the material advantages that many mountain children lack. In other words, Graham's children enjoyed both the affluence of suburban children and the gentle protective surroundings of the small mountain village. The evangelist and his wife deliberately chose to avoid rearing their children in a big-city environment because they were aware that such an environment is not conducive to the evangelical life-style. Graham's decisions about his life and that of his family show clearly that he knows that a person is shaped by his environment—the evangelist's sermons notwithstanding.

MAN AND SOCIETY

It would be a mistake to think that Graham's come-on is somehow a product of a cynical manipulation of his audience. It would be a mistake to think that he does not believe in what he preaches. The point is that he believes in his come-on, and he also believes in something that does not fit with it. In short, like most of us, Billy Graham has not developed even the major aspects of his outlook into a coherent view. He has yet to develop a coherent theory of the relationship between the individual and society. Sometimes he takes the view that individuals are somehow outside society, while at other times he holds that individuals are greatly shaped by their society. The most persistent view of the evangelist, however, may be outlined as follows:

The individual is to a great degree affected and shaped by his culture and society. But there is one thing that is absolutely fixed and over which society has no influence. It is human nature.[32] Individuals are simply *born* sinners. To be sure, society corrupts them even further after birth, but the "instinct" for evil was already there from the start.[33] That is what is meant when Graham says, "Many leaders are beginning to agree that the prime problem is man, not society." [34]

Graham seems, at times at least, to take a position opposite to what has been attributed to Rousseau, who is said to have believed that the individual is born an innocent "noble savage" whom society corrupts. For Graham, it is the other way around. The individuals are born corrupt, and society reflects this corruption. The fault is not in our stars or society or environment, but in ourselves. So Graham's advice is for men to "freely acknowledge that there is a defect in human nature, a built-in waywardness that comes from man's natural rebellion against God." [35] Hence "man's basic problem is spiritual, not social. Man needs a complete change from within." [36]

PROCEDURE FOR PROGRESS

When Graham says, as he often does, that change for the good in society cannot come until men are changed from within, he is not as clear as we might hope he would be. One reason for this, as we saw earlier, is that as a matter of empirical observation people can be changed for the better by changing their environment. One noted defender of evangelical theology, E. J. Carnell, said very frankly in his book *Christian Commitment*—which he himself regarded as his best book—that he was made a better person by a "powerful sedative." And, as he says, "an imbalance in the neurophysical life will be reflected in the moral-spiritual life," [37] which is another way of saying that a person's morality and his religion can be modified by chemistry and biology.

Carnell had no intention of giving any support to the naive drug cult when he mentioned the sedative that so affected his life for good. The point is that man is a finite creature in an environment of all sorts of variables that can shape and influence him. The implication of Carnell's open and frank confession is very simply this: Even the so-called inner man is affected by the temporal circumstances of life—both for good and ill.

Graham is extremely ambivalent about people who seem to have peace and happiness and seem to be moral even though they are not evangelical Christians. Early in his ministry he would say something to the effect that when a person is "converted to Christ," then "contentment, peace, and happiness come into your soul *for the first time*." He would even say, "I have searched the world over in my travels for contented and happy men. I have found such men *only* where Christ has been personally and decisively received." [38]

Of course, if contentment and happiness are defined in such a way as to include acceptance of the evangelical "fundamentals," then Graham is once again not establishing a point so much as defining a word. If, however, he is purporting to be making an empirical generalization, then he reveals that in his travels he either did not observe very carefully or went to the wrong places or went at the wrong time.

What has apparently never seriously dawned upon Billy Graham is the genuine possibility that man is always and wholly shaped and molded by the multicolored environment that is both inside and outside his skin. A person does not simply change from within by some "inner willpower." If a person wants to give up being an alcoholic, let us say, he does not simply sit down and call upon willpower to solve the problem for him. Rather, he may be urged by friends (who are a part of his external social environment) to go with them to AA or to the hospital. Indeed, an alcoholic will have to find himself living in a considerably new environment before his drinking behavior can be significantly changed. Graham likes to tell how God converts this or that drunkard. But what is often obscured is the fact that the drunkard's behavior was modified because his environment was changed. He was encouraged to go, or was even taken, to church instead of to the bar. He was given new material to read and new duties; he was urged to keep busy witnessing and associating with new friends. In short, the external circumstances were drastically changed in order to reshape the drunkard's behavior until new patterns were established. One reason for the phenomenal success of Weight Watchers is that it is composed of a "community" of like-minded (or like-bodied) individuals who know that they need the support of one another to solve a common problem. This community becomes a significant part of their environment. Members of Weight Watchers are making progress because, like members of one church in the Bible, they are "not neglecting to meet together" and are "encouraging one another (Heb. 10:25)." Or to use the language of psychologist B. F. Skinner, Weight Watchers assemble in order to give one another "positive reinforcement" when they lose weight. Victory over fat is like victory over sin—each success reinforces another success. It is the function of the church or Weight Watchers to oil the wheels of successful triumph over sin or excess weight.

So putting off the "old man" and putting on the new is not an exchange that takes place by hocus-pocus. Even the moment of conversion is a symbolic moment representing a long train of events leading up to the more dramatic moment. The conversion moment did not occur in a vacuum or without a history. Thus when Billy Graham announces that there is only "one thing that will solve the problems of our world—changed men," he is not being very informative. What needs to be specified are the exact changes in the polyphased environment which bring about the desired change in the individual. It would appear that, despite what Graham says, often social, biological, economic, and physical changes in the environment precede the changes in the individual. Indeed, Graham himself functions as a part of the external conditions, exerting some influence and control on those who hear him. He knows this in some sense. Even when he says that it is really the Holy Spirit who does the moving and changing in the inner self, Graham still seems to hold that the Holy Spirit works through the evangelist and his team. Hence, the external environment in its numerous facets shapes the individual.

In fact, Graham frankly says that the individual is helpless to change himself. That is what the notion of grace is about. Help must come from without. "The Bible teaches," says Graham, "that the new birth is an infusion of divine life into the human soul. . . . Christ, through the Holy Spirit, takes up residence in your heart." [39] "Thus the Bible teaches that man can undergo a radical spiritual and moral change that is brought about by God Himself." [40]

Graham believes that isolated in himself alone, the individual can do nothing. God has to enter from outside the individual into "the center of his being, the heart, directing the will to new motives and new conduct and new ideals." [41] "The transformation in him came, not by his personal efforts, but by the power of the indwelling Holy Spirit." [42] What Graham is saying in effect is this: Outside the natural man is God. Inside is the principle of evil at work. Also inside is the longing for God to come in. Thanks to the influence of such external factors as preachers and Christians' witnessing, the inner heart is stimulated to open up. And when it does open, God comes in and sets up a permanent source of stimulation or influence.[43] However, not even this seems sufficient, for if this "new man" inside is not stimulated by outside conditions, then he is starved. To function properly, the new man has to be nourished "by reading his Bible, by praying, and by going to church." [44] This threefold program is apparently very essential if the new behavior patterns inside and outside are to become and remain established.

Now, it cannot be denied that, like the Ptolemaic theory of the heavens, this psychology of Graham's—with its inner and outer self, as well as the Holy Spirit and the old Adam—is very knotty. What is clear, however, is that the external environment is very essential to shaping a person to be what he is. To be sure, the environment is much more complex—more riddled with variables—than utopians and evangelists have tended to recognize. Nevertheless, the fact is that men as individuals are what their vastly complex and complicated environment shapes them into being. And this is precisely why anyone interested in changing human beings has invariably been interested in what their environment is like.

Billy Graham rebukes preachers who get off on social issues. In Graham's opinion, "the changing of men is the primary mission of the church." [45] Apparently, when he made this statement he genuinely believed that those preachers whom he was criticizing are in total disagreement with him. But they are not, for they too wish to change men. So it turns out that the difference has to do with the *method* for changing men. Hence, Graham adds, "The only way to change men is to get them converted to Jesus Christ. Then they will have the capacity to live up to the Christian commandment to 'Love thy neighbor.' " [46]

Unfortunately, the debate is not closed so easily, for there are many who *define* conversion to Jesus Christ in terms of loving one's neighbor —at least that is one of the defining characteristics. Still others, however, hold that loving one's neighbor comes only after the development of prior factors in a person's life, although those prior factors do not necessarily include a belief in a virgin birth, the substitutionary atonement, the literal Second Coming, or the other "fundamentals." Despite the fact that the Bible makes no explicit statement as to either the theological meaning or the moral significance of the virgin birth, Billy Graham insisted that the virgin birth of Christ was a foundation stone of Christian faith.[47] Of course, if one does accept the infallibility of the Bible as a major premise, as Graham does, then presumably anything mentioned in the Bible may be taken as "one of the foundation stones of our Christian faith"—anything from the virgin birth to the floating ax head or the dialogue between Balaam and his ass. But what if some of the "miracles" are to be regarded as merely contingent, while others are necessary? This is a distinction that proves to be difficult to make for someone accepting the "miracle" of an infallible Bible. (Whether or not the last-mentioned "miracle" is contingent is an interesting question.)

This entire issue as to what it means to be a Christian—or to be influenced by Christianity—in contemporary times is often subject to very heated debate. There are many groups professing to embody or to know the "essence of Christianity." It is a debate paralleled in some ways by those who claim that they are the "true Marxists," or the "true Freudians." Do the "true Freudians" continue the precise metapsychology of Freud himself, or do they carry on his spirit of inquiry? Do the "true Christians" continue Jesus' belief in demons and hell, or do they carry on his spirit? There is no simple way of answering such knotty questions. It might help if the purpose of asking them is clearly explored. That is, it is important to understand what the point of such questions is. What difference does it make whether one is a true follower of Marx, Adam Smith, or Freud? For Graham, only the true followers of Jesus will go to heaven and will have freedom and happiness on earth.[48] Those who are not the true followers will go to hell.

TOWARD A
PRACTICAL CONCLUSION

It seems that Billy Graham very slowly is becoming aware of the impact of the complex environment on the individual human being. Despite his simplistic claim that social, economic, institutional, and political reforms come through "conversion of the heart to Christ," the fact remains that great numbers of Evangelicals have been converted to Christ for years but are still racists, war hawks, hostile to the poor, and by and large not concerned to do much more than promote the narrow interests of their own class. Apparently, "knowing Jesus" did not change the social outlook of men like Billy Graham's own pastor, W. A. Criswell, who had "known Jesus" for a third of a century before his social outlook altered in any noteworthy way.

It was the improved attitudes and values of the cultural and social environment that induced social reform in men like Criswell. Far from exerting moral leadership in institutional and social reform, many evangelical spokesmen have dawdled and procrastinated and have hidden behind the excuse that "original sin" will make waste every social reform anyhow. Fortunately, they have not taken this attitude in medicine and have declined to conclude that medical improvement is all vanity because we shall all eventually die anyhow. There are some hopeful signs that if some progress can be made in improving the wider circumstances and conditions of human life, then contemporary Evangelicals will at least not turn away from it.

Billy Graham has sometimes attempted to make evangelical Christians appear to be the major source of humaneness in the world. But this seems a bit difficult to support in the face of their conspicuous reluctance, and sometimes resentment, in encountering the challenge to contribute to the social and material improvement of the conditions of the down-and-out. Thanksgiving baskets and other spotty, short-term, and unreliable methods have not made evangelical Christianity appear as the great moral force Graham claims it to be. Embracing a quasi Stoicism as if it were a Christian psychology, some Evangelicals have often used the term spiritual to disguise their tendency to shelve and table certain improvements in the social, legal, and general institutional life of men of all classes.

This is not to say, however, that evangelical Christianity is a superevil force in the world. It is simply to say that it is a movement that does some great good in certain areas and some great harm in other areas. Either attacking or defending evangelical Christianity as a whole would seem to be fruitless. It is better to focus on specific presuppositions, practices, doctrines, and attitudes with a view toward stimulating some definite revisions, reforms, and improvements. Some persons, however, insist on going the whole hog, so to speak. In some situations an all-or-nothing response may be appropriate. Billy Graham thinks it is definitely appropriate with regard to the evangelical Christian way. He calls this stance a "total commitment to Christ." This may be translated as a total commitment to a program of living that includes a refusal to question certain doctrines and prescriptions which God is thought to have revealed in propositional and infallible form. Needless to say, there are many other kinds of Christians, as well as non-Christians, who cannot in good faith agree with this program.

In practice, Evangelicalism will probably be making adjustments and revisions here and there. To be sure, sacred words and formulas will doubtless continue, but some of the meaning and substance behind the words will change—sometimes for good, sometimes for ill. The changing times, for example, have already greatly modified the practical way that evangelical Christians understand the commandment to observe the sabbath. What they do now on Sunday would have been regarded by many nineteenth-century Christians as breaking one of the ten commandments or laws of God. Professional football as a business and a game has never drawn criticism from Billy Graham, even though the games are played on "the Lord's day." Coach Tom Landry even served as head of the committee for promoting Dallas' Billy Graham Evangelistic Crusade. In fact, Coach Landry gave a public testimony in September 1971 at one of the Graham meetings, and many people saw and heard the big-name coach give his testimony on TV. In short, Graham has given encouragement to what many Christians a generation or two ago would have called "sabbath-breaking." And in James 2:10 the Bible says: "For whoever keeps the whole law but fails in one point has become guilty of all of it."

Probably one of the great weaknesses of recent evangelical Christianity has been its failure to take seriously this temporal, finite world. Or to be more precise, in the United States at least, numerous middle-class Evangelicals seem to take this life seriously for themselves but not for those who do not enjoy at least middle-class living standards. The poor, the neglected, and those discriminated against are urged to think about the next life and to focus on the spiritual realm here and now. As Billy Graham says, the spiritual problems are the basic problems. A passage such as "But seek ye first the kingdom of God, and his righteousness; and all these [material] things shall be added unto you (Matt. 6:33, KJV)," is freely quoted to the deprived and neglected. And there is even a tendency for many middle- and upper-class Evangelicals to assume that if a person is not doing reasonably well materially in this world, he must not be very spiritual. He must not have sought the kingdom and righteousness of God. After all, the Bible promises to "supply all your need according to his riches in glory by Christ Jesus (Phil. 4:19, KJV)."

Some of the early Christians could imagine a better environment, all right. But not a better earthly, temporal environment. They longed for the new celestial environment. And that is one of the weaknesses of much of Christianity today. It even drains off interest in improving the environment of the temporal world for the deprived people. Practical programs to improve the environment of the needy are very spotty and meager. The apostle Paul says, "As we have therefore opportunity, let us do good unto all men, especially unto them who are of the household of faith (Gal. 6:10, KJV)." Unfortunately, suburban Evangelicals in the United States seldom have opportunity to do sustained good for the needy, for they rarely see the needy. And those of the "household of faith" are probably solid middle-class Americans anyhow—"insiders," that is.

Contemporary evangelical Christians in the United States have been most reluctant to join non-Evangelicals in seeking to make a somewhat improved earthly environment. It is as if Evangelicals are saying, "Unless we receive at least the major credit for the improvements, we will not cooperate!" "The uneasy conscience of the Evangelical," to use Carl Henry's phrase, has not been all that uneasy. It is, however, too simple to blame Christianity for the ecological crisis, as some writers have done, although it is true that at least some versions of Christianity have not taken seriously the wider temporal environment.

Sherwood Wirt, editor of *Decision*, has written a penetrating and perceptive book, *The Social Conscience of the Evangelical*, in which he treats 1960 as a turning point for Evangelicals.[49] He sees signs that many evangelical leaders are coming out of their shells, and he argues that there is biblical justification for a revised evangelical social ethic.

One of the stones around the Evangelical's neck has been his holdout principle, which demands that reform not be encouraged until the proper belief in the "fundamentals" be ascribed to first. Sherwood Wirt offers his fellow Evangelicals a direct way of coming to terms with this issue of priorities. He writes: "The issue cannot in any case be settled by argument; and the people of the Book would look far better if they simply left the question of priorities to work itself out, and they in turn got about the King's business." [50] And for Wirt, "the King's business" includes social and institutional reform.

Where there is need for such reforms, then Evangelicals ought to do their part to work with others on specific plans and programs held in common by men of various faiths and philosophies. And if the evangelical program of "accepting Christ" is relevant to these reforms, then such relevancy will doubtless reveal itself in due course. This point of relevancy may be made about any other approach or way of life. The self-righteous elitism of any group does not offer a constructive approach to a particular program but is, rather, an attitude that children show on the playground whenever they cannot always get their own way. Wirt's criticism of his own Evangelicals is a good criticism of any other group demanding whole-hog commitment from others before cooperating with them to help control some of the major social ills.

Before a congressional hearing in 1967 Billy Graham set a precedent for Evangelicals by testifying in behalf of antipoverty legislation. This may be judged as Graham's rather late attempt to climb on a bandwagon. Or it may be regarded as his profound way of coming to terms with the problem of priorities that has plagued his thinking for a long time. Whatever interpretation is made as to his motives, the practical point not to be lost is that the evangelist did in fact lend his significant voice in a cause which cannot do well without the support of men like Billy Graham. If the apostle Paul could rejoice over the fact that the gospel was preached even by men of mixed motives, then perhaps Christians and non-Christians of all shades can rejoice whenever social improvements are brought about even by men of mixed motives. Let Evangelicals worry less about whether or not they will receive major credit for reform, for one thing is clear—without their activity in social reforms, many of the reforms will never see the light of day.

One area of social reconstruction in which Evangelist Graham may be regarded as a leader rather than a follower has to do with reducing the great number of deaths and injuries resulting from highway accidents. This concern fits to some extent with his attitude toward drinking. Driving while drinking is by and large a middle-class problem, and Billy Graham cannot be said to have simply joined the middle class on that very important social and public issue. Those who criticize Graham for recommending specific programs of reform and legislation fail to realize that there is a great demand for creative and fruitful ideas and programs, and if Graham or anyone else can contribute to the developing of workable programs, then so much the better. The test of a plan lies in its results, not its source. Evangelicals, humanists, personalists, and all varieties of people could serve themselves well by remaining open to programs that seem workable, no matter what particular group proposes it.

Perhaps Evangelicals will forgive the following statement because it is meant more as a forthright challenge to them than a criticism: If some of the same imagination that goes into defending evangelical theology could be utilized for developing imaginative models and programs of social betterment, then society as a whole might greatly benefit. This includes letting what is offered speak for itself and stand on its own merits, rather than presenting it as if it has just come hot off the altar of God.

Graham thinks it is perfectly right when "the church speaks as a church" on "a moral or spiritual problem," but he thinks the church ought to restrain itself more on social and political issues.[51] However, even in Graham's mind the realm of the spiritual is not always consistently defined. We might ask, "Is the problem of highway safety a spiritual, moral, social, or political problem?" Graham himself says that it is at least a spiritual problem, and in 1955 he preached a sermon entitled "Highway Safety—A Spiritual Problem." However, it is not clear why highway safety should be a spiritual problem, while such matters as better working conditions, welfare reform, women's employment opportunities, adequate day-care centers, medicare, social security increases, and the war in Southeast Asia are social and political in nature rather than spiritual. When Graham joins the moral and the spiritual issues together in one class, and social and political issues in another, the question is raised whether the moral and the spiritual realms are purely individual or private matters. Some of Graham's preaching suggests this, but there are many other indications that he is not wholly content with this restricted meaning. In short, despite himself, the evangelist seems to be in process of redefining somewhat the meanings of the terms spiritual and moral.

He says that while clergymen as individual private citizens may properly speak out on social and political matters, the church as a church ought to say little, "especially when the issue settled either way is not a moral or spiritual problem." [52] What Graham fails to realize, however, is that some clergymen, because of their position or status, cannot easily be taken as simply giving their own personal view. Billy Graham is usually not merely a spokesman for himself. This fact may be unfortunate, but it must not be ignored. In many ways Evangelist Graham is unofficially but very clearly the voice of at least institutional evangelical revivalism. No matter how much he may say that he is giving only his own private opinion, he almost invariably will be taken as a powerful representative of a major spiritual force in America.

This is not to say that he should muzzle himself. Rather, he should admit that he does in fact carry this weight and does utilize it very effectively. In the controversies over the external circumstances and environment Billy Graham has taken sides often and will doubtless continue to do so. By hiding behind the word spiritual he cannot expect to find immunity for himself. His presumption that he, like God, is somehow above the controversies is often an admission that what the controversies are about in their complex details is really beyond his grasp. His opinions and programs, therefore, need to be both considered and scrutinized on their own merit or demerit. Perhaps he does himself a disservice by being dubbed "God's man with God's message," for the woods are full of all sorts of preachers and groups making this rather sweeping claim.

Nevertheless, in the final analysis those who would like to ignore Evangelicalism and pretend that it is not an important part of the American scene fail to appreciate the fact that social and political reform in any democracy, of whatever degree and sort, must depend on groups finding common values despite some strong disagreements. And it must be remembered that evangelical Christianity has great resources for good at its disposal—a ready audience, institutional patterns, numbers, tradition, money, and influence. For good or ill, Evangelicals are definitely in the world and considerably of the world also. Indeed, they possess much of this world's external goods.

Chapter 10
THE NATURAL AND
THE SUPERNATURAL

THE NATURAL VARIABLES

Religious spokesmen sometimes testify to the "power of prayer" in the lives of people. Prayer has been recommended as a source of tranquillity and peace in the home. Sometimes *calcium* has been recommended as a means of introducing agreeableness and kindness into family relationships.

Dramatic and remarkable cures have followed prayers or other religious activities. Adelle Davis tells of a young woman whose physician had told her that because of a painful swelling in her leg, she would never again be able to play tennis. But thanks to heavy doses of two specified vitamins, the young woman was remarkably restored to her health and she resumed her tennis playing.[1]

Were the cures by prayer supernatural, whereas the cure by vitamins was natural? Or were they one and all supernatural? Perhaps they were all natural cures.

There are, of course, homes in which graciousness and a measure of tranquillity are enjoyed without prayer. Whether this is the case in homes with very little calcium will have to be determined by a trained observer. The point to be raised and explored here has to do with the natural means and the supernatural means to human happiness. It will be very useful to begin with at least a rough descriptive definition of the term *natural*; otherwise, the more difficult meaning of *supernatural* may remain floating in a night of obscurity. The natural realm pertains to phenomena whose manifestations can be observed either directly or by means of instruments. Furthermore, these phenomena are functionally related to one another, which means that patterns of relationship among them may be detected and related to other patterns of relationship.

A natural explanation must not be confused with the usual explanation, however. To give a natural explanation is to give one that is based on observable data which can be checked by other people. Furthermore, the propositions expressing the explanation must cohere with one another. Of course, this two-pronged criterion of empirical data, on the one hand, and coherence, on the other hand, may not be fully measured up to. And when it is not, then to that extent the explanation offered is incomplete.

The observing of a pattern of relationship may begin as follows: A mother observes that her child breaks out with rash whenever he drinks more than one glass of orange juice in one day, provided the child is also allowed to eat a sandwich having tomatoes in it on the same day. This happens over a period of two months. Or Betty may observe that when her father comes home early he is in a happy mood, whereas when he comes home after seven o'clock he is always in a pensive mood. A pattern is detected. Or young Tony observes his own behavior carefully enough to note what appears to be a pattern. Every time he comes in from playing at Johnny's house up the block, he sneezes a lot. Tony does not know why, however. That is, he cannot detect any other relevant pattern and functional relationship. But the allergist, after testing him, finds that Tony is allergic to ragweed. Upon being shown a picture of ragweed, Tony's eyes brighten and he exclaims, "There's a lot of that stuff in the lot next to Johnny's house. We play there all the time!" So another connection is made. A pattern is beginning to be established.

Whenever such patterns are established on an extremely wide scale, the relationship begins to be thought of as a scientific law. But that is a long way from the simple observation of a few patterns. Nevertheless, humans could not live without these observed patterns, for on the basis of them people plan their lives and make predictions. Knowledge of scientific laws is useful for predicting, and therefore controlling, the behavior of nature and man in varying ways and degrees.

Needless to say, the above version of the natural (in contrast to the supernatural) would need refining if we were to attempt a more exacting level of analysis. But this one is useful enough for the present. Those who reject this preliminary definition may create their own, although the advantage of the one above is that it is in accord with that of a large number of specialists writing on the subject. The important point here is, not so much to prove that the above definition is the best one, but simply to reveal how the word natural will be understood in the remainder of this chapter. This is a point of clear communication rather than intensive argument or proof that the above definition is inescapable. (*The Encyclopedia of Philosophy* offers a more sophisticated treatment of the notions of natural and law of nature.)

The interesting thing about finite man is that, like other members and offspring of nature, he is not exempt from the patterns and regularities of nature. He lives with them or plans around them and even exemplifies some of them, but he cannot simply wave a magic wand to dispose of them. Not even free will can do that. At every second of his life man is subject to variables. To some persons this may seem humiliating or deflating, but that seems to be the way things are. The finite creature who is a "little lower than the angels" is encompassed by a host of variables or factors that shape and reshape him from moment to moment. Water is just one of these numerous variables essential to his very survival. Other variables or factors of the complex environment are not essential to an individual's survival as such, but without them his life would be greatly different, which is to say that *he* would be greatly different.

EVANGELISTIC CRUSADES AND THE VARIABLES

One of the most awkward things that happens to supernatural faith is that the realm of mystery keeps turning out to be observable variables in recognizable patterns. Supernatural phenomena seem to be translated into natural phenomena. A Baptist weekly relates the story of a child, Maria Garcia, whose long periods of suffering "had caused her father to pass her off as a 'demoniac.' " [2] But a physician discovered that the child had a brain cyst. No demon was observed. However, perhaps the father had no intention of explaining what caused his daughter's strange behavior. By using the term demoniac he may simply have been more or less describing or classifying her behavior in order to distinguish it from more normal behavior. Whatever the case, he certainly had no way of knowing that there was a connection (pattern of functional analysis) between his daughter's strange behavior and a small growth inside her skull. If he was in fact attempting to find a cause, he apparently had to fall back on the notion of some supernatural phenomenon such as a demon, which was vague enough to escape critical analysis yet sufficiently imaginable to satisfy his mind.

A child with a brain cyst ought not to be treated as one possessed by an evil being. In contrast to supernatural explanations, natural explanations of what is going on allow us often to focus on the relevant variables, in order, if possible, to change them in the interest of reducing human suffering or increasing happiness.

Revivals and crusades are today made into a more precise and exacting practice in the interest of obtaining desired results. If testimonials from football players or beauty-contest winners will serve as useful variables in influencing some of the audience to move down to the front to "accept Christ," then Evangelist Graham will use such testimonials. In fact, one disturbed group of Christians raised the question of whether big names from sports and show business block the way of the Holy Spirit in the evangelistic rallies. Billy Graham has, of course, been using big-name testimonials for decades. He still drops the names of celebrities freely, apparently for the purpose of influencing his audience to be more Christian. The debate, then, is the practical one of judging how effective the big-name variable is in winning converts and decisions.

In this controversy, one Baptist leader and editor of *The Baptist Standard*, T. A. Patterson (himself a big name among Texas Baptists in particular), said that "the tendency to exclusively use show business or sports personalities [in testimonials] could leave the impression on youth that these are [the] only occupations worthy of their consideration. It would be well to use scientists, housewives, farmers and business executives." Patterson went on to insist that these popular personalities not be used to draw people to the services and to conversion. "Only the Holy Spirit can do that," Patterson reminded his audience.[3] This seemingly comes close to regarding the Holy Spirit as one of the variables, in this case the most significant one, like calcium or something more essential in the diet. However, to regard the Holy Spirit as a variable would appear to be regarding him as belonging to the natural realm rather than the supernatural, and Patterson would not want to go that far.

The use of celebrities in religious rallies is increasing in Patterson's Texas at least, perhaps because the practice is believed to be working well. In order to determine more certainly that this variable is highly significant, the evangelists would have to agree to use celebrities at certain times and not use them at other times. Of course, other significant variables will have to remain more or less constant if the experiment is to be successful.

An evangelistic crusade is not created by magic. Many variables go into its making. God is sometimes given the ultimate credit as a significant variable among others, or at other times as the variable underwriting all the others. In order to understand better how Billy Graham and his team of associates look upon the coming of a revival, we may compare it to the way people look at the coming of rain. Some hold that rain comes strictly according to divine pleasure, regardless of what human beings do. Similarly, some Christians hold that revivals happen only by the good pleasure of the Almighty and without the useless activities and "rain dances" of mortal Christians. Hard-line Calvinists sometimes take this position. Just as the farmer has no control over the rain shower, so the evangelist and the church workers have no control over God's outpouring of the Spirit or over the "showers of blessings." In 1792 William Carey, the father of the modern Christian mission movement, spoke to a group of Christian ministers at a meeting in Nottingham in order to propose a plan for evangelizing the heathen nations. But he hit a stone wall, was called a "hare-brained enthusiast," and was silenced by the moderator in the following words: "Young man, sit down. When God pleases to convert the heathen, He will do it without your aid or mine." [4]

The early American Calvinist preacher Jonathan Edwards looked upon a revival as a spontaneous happening, without human planning—a "surprising work of God" coming without warning and without conscious human preparation. From first to last it was God's direct doing. But a hundred years after Edwards' time another American wrote that a revival "is not a miracle, or dependent on a miracle in any sense. It is a purely philosophical [i.e., scientific] result of the right use of the constituted means." * The man making this cool statement was not the atheist Robert Ingersoll or some agnostic. Rather, it was one of America's most successful and effective evangelists—Charles G. Finney, who claimed to have experienced in his own life numerous vivid and personal encounters with both God and the devil.[5] Evangelist D. L. Moody, who bor-

---

* Charles G. Finney in W. G. McLoughlin, Jr., *Modern Revivalism: Charles Grandison Finney to Billy Graham* (New York: Ronald Press, 1959), p. 11. Used by permission.

rowed somewhat from the methods of American big-business practices, once criticized those who "think that revivals come like famines and like hurricanes." [6]

Finney and Moody, as well as John Wesley, would do something to make revivals come, rather than wait to see if they might happen. Revivals can be worked up, planned, and now even institutionalized. The element of old-style surprise and unpredictability is trimmed back to a small corner of the cloth, and some of the results of evangelistic crusades are becoming more predictable. Although Jimmy the Greek has not moved into the business of predicting revival scorings, this is not inconceivable, no matter what may be the virtues or lack thereof in such a practice.

Predicting and controlling both rain and revivals may become more exact in years to come. Prayer has been thought of as a triggering variable in bringing rain, although the number of failures in this experiment with prayer is perhaps in excess of the number of successes. Evangelist John R. Rice tells of his experience of praying for a rain in barren west Texas. He and his group asked for rain within twenty-four hours and got a mighty storm rushing in "from nowhere." That was a rare incident. It happened in 1931, and Rice was still telling of it in 1942.[7] In 1971 west Texas needed rain badly, but neither prayer nor anything else seemed to work very well.

When it comes to accounting for mighty revivals sweeping in upon a town, Billy Graham and his associates seem to have a way of offering a compromise in explaining its arrival: (1) God brought it; (2) revival-makers (i.e., ad men, visitations, church workers, newspaper contacts, and the like) were used as God's agents; and (3) prayers and supplications also were effective. In this way both God and man receive credit, although God receives the most credit. Without him none of the others could have carried on. Phone calls, public relations, TV spots, radio plugs, and other natural and supernatural phenomena are all acknowledged to be variables by which the revival is thought to come about. Hence, the revival tends to be regarded both as a miracle and as the result of loyal mortals appropriating natural means for supernatural ends.

Referring to the "conversions" and "decisions" at the September 1950 Rose Bowl rally, an editor of *Christianity Today*, Carl F. H. Henry, remarks, "What were these but mid-century reminders that the *miracle* of grace still *happens,* and that God's hand is not yet short-ened." [8]

But as Henry shows, this rally did not take place without the diligent labor and planning of a virtual beehive of workers. He points out how visiting specialists were brought in to help make the rally a success.

> For the week beginning with Billy Graham's arrival, the promotional effort of the committee was aided inestimably by one of the ablest evangelical publicists in the Southland, Lloyd Doctor, former Salvation Army captain, who had learned in his early years in Kansas City that the press could "make or break" a community event.[9]

Lloyd Doctor utilized his influence with "bosses on the city desks" as well as with religious editors. Graham's reputation had been skyrocketed by sympathetic Hearst newspapers, and his aides were taking no chances with such variables as newspapers. The favor of the newspapers was openly courted, and enough of them responded to help make the rally a huge success. Indeed, even Graham's arrival at the Los Angeles airport "was scheduled so as to take advantage of maximum press coverage." [10] It is fair to say that Jonathan Edwards' notion of "a surprising work" has been greatly modified by the Billy Graham crusades.

On and behind the scenes of the Billy Graham evangelistic crusades is an enormous amount of hard work and a highly professional organization. It is reasonable to assume that without much of this work and technical planning, the revivals would not come about, which suggests that Jonathan Edwards simply was unaware of the natural relevant variables or means which at least assisted the coming of his own revivals. Graham expresses surprise that God continues to use Billy Graham for so many years when other evangelists before him had comparatively short periods of revival success on a wide scale. Perhaps it would remain for one of his team associates to say that Graham's expert organization makes it possible for God to work more efficiently and over a longer period of time "to bring men to Christ." Some might even say that when God called Billy Graham, he foreknew that the evangelist would develop an efficient organization. So God simply called the organization into the evangelistic ministry also.

J. P. Morgan served as treasurer of D. L. Moody's "Guaranty Fund" in New York, and Moody sought to utilize some of Morgan's business-like efficiency in winning souls. He told businessmen that their support of his evangelistic ministry was a good investment for their status in heaven. In addition, Moody preached a socially conservative message that was considered to be good for business.

Extremely influential in bringing Billy Graham to Madison Square Garden in 1969 were some "pillars of America's business establishment." The wicked city was said to be suffering from poverty—spiritual poverty, that is—and Graham was regarded as the troubleshooter who could do the job if anyone could, with the help of God. Roger Hull, chairman of the board of Mutual Life Insurance Company of New York, observing that "society is becoming too materialistic," decided to invite other business and ecclesiastical leaders in New York to help them. George Champion, then chairman of the board at Chase Manhattan Bank, joined Elmer W. Engstrom, then president of RCA, in heading up an executive committee for Billy Graham's New York crusade. Multimillionaire W. Maxey Jarman, head of Genesco, Inc., was persuaded to serve as treasurer.

What these men of material means seemed to want Graham to do was not altogether clear. There was some talk of his helping to develop a religious "environment," somewhat like that found in the home towns where these men of wealth grew up as boys. Champion remembered Normal, Illinois, and is quoted as saying that Normal was where "there was the highest of moral principles. Everybody knew each other, everybody went to church, everybody's life was an open book." Hull remembered Mississippi, where he, like Graham, was converted under the preaching of an itinerant evangelist.[11]

New York City was, for these men, not a place to live but a place to work. They apparently wanted Graham to make New York City a place for their kind of people—less the big city and more the tribal village. Of course, there are considerable advantages on the tribal end of the continuum, and also some serious disadvantages, one of which is loss of pluralism and variety. In any case, these influential men of means were very important variables in the success of the crusade in Madison Square Garden.

At the end of Billy Graham's crusade sermons, the hymn "Just as I Am" is usually sung while people walk to the front to make decisions. The Lord cannot work well in confusion, the crusade team believes, which is why trained "counselors" assist the prospects in making their decisions. Having memorized a few passages of the Bible as well as the "Plan of Salvation," the counselors seek to catch the fish or to bring in the sheaves as efficiently as possible. Because poor counselors could be offensive at worst and ineffective at best, each counselor is required to undergo a few days' special training for their very important task.

If a particular case becomes too difficult for a counselor (although the existence of real, honest intellectual doubt is not readily acknowledged by Graham and team), the unsuccessful counselor, by merely raising his hand, signals that he needs help from someone more thoroughly trained than he. This keeps down controversy, for it is very disconcerting to have a counselor who himself begins to show doubt and lack of confidence. When the better-trained counselor comes to the rescue, the original one unobtrusively slips away to do the work that he is equipped to do. Furthermore, certain monitoring counselors roam about looking for tenderfoot counselors in trouble. If the tenderfoot is tapped on the shoulder by the monitor, he is supposed to pull away in order to permit the monitor to take over.

When a dispassionate observer realizes how easily the whole scene down front could fall into pandemonium (in a figurative sense), the counselors' training program must be acknowledged to be a very central part of the crusade's success. Having no such an organization at his disposal, Jonathan Edwards had people from his audience passing out in the aisles, barking like dogs, and undergoing all sorts of contortions of the body. But then Edwards' time was perhaps a bit more tolerant of overt bodily manifestations.

Very sensitive to the charge of "Save 'em and drop 'em," Graham's team has a follow-up program designed to guide the new convert or the revitalized Christian into an active church. The counselor is supposed to phone or visit him within two days after the "decision" and, if possible, "lead" him to mail in a card which will eventually "lead" to an invitation to take a correspondence course, as well as receipt of a free one-year subscription to *Decision*. This magazine contains Graham's sermons, Bible studies, and other material designed to reinforce the new convert in "the way."

At the same time, a pastor in the town of the new convert is provided information about the convert. Little is left to chance. And some of the Evangelicals who are very critical of Billy Graham's superefficient organization say that little is left to the Holy Spirit. In any case, the Graham machine works like a well-tuned automobile. And without the numerous typists and secretaries doing their work, the machine would be running on only three cylinders at best. The apostle Paul, after observing the Graham team, might today say that the Lord calls not only pastors, teachers, and evangelists, but also typists and secretaries.

The work of the Billy Graham Evangelistic Association headquarters in Minneapolis is a marvel of human-computer cooperativeness and efficiency. The faith of Billy Graham may or may not be as simple as he claims, but his Minneapolis headquarters is far from simple. Evangelistic crusades often have to be planned five years in advance. One way of insuring that people will attend the evangelistic meetings is to recruit recruiters. Pastors and churches are approached and involved in the coming crusade. Each cooperating church is given an attendance quota which it is asked to meet, and sometimes free tickets are donated to the members of the church's "delegation." D. L. Moody used to instruct church people to stay away from his revival meetings so that the sinners, the unchurched, and the lower classes could find seats. But his instruction was disregarded, and most of those attending his meetings were already converted.

The members of Graham's team, however, do not even attempt to follow Moody's example. They want everyone to come. Empty seats are adverse psychology, as if the Spirit could not work so effectively if there are too many empty seats. And this is obviously true for those who believe that because the Spirit is working in extraordinary ways at Graham's meetings, he therefore must have great numbers of people for this work. In New York in 1957 Graham and his team arranged to black out the TV broadcast for the entire metropolitan area in order to assure capacity attendance. It is a very long way from Pentecost and Jonathan Edwards to Billy Graham's highly organized, highly publicized crusades. The team members do not wait for the Holy Spirit to work directly on newspaper editors; rather, the Spirit is believed to prefer to work through Christians, who in turn work on editors and the like. Henry writes: "When newspapers did not use our copy at all, we were usually right in inferring that *personal contacts* had not been made." [12]

The Lord may work in mysterious ways, but the work of Billy Graham's organization, with its host of unpaid helpers, is not mysterious at all. It is a matter of long, hard, patient hours, careful preparation, attention to minute details, persistence, contacting VIPs, raising money, checking and double-checking, and, in short, pouring out great human and machine energy into manipulating the relevant variables. The many workers—both paid and unpaid—put their hearts into their work, for they passionately long for the "showers of blessings" that will fall upon them when Billy Graham comes to town.

TRANSLATING THE SUPERNATURAL
INTO THE NATURAL

Despite the conspicuously natural means used by Graham and his organization, the evangelist himself still insists that the crusades are supernatural miracles. God works through humans and machines, Graham agrees, but there are also gaps which God is thought to fill in directly. Some things God cannot leave for others to do. But Graham will not agree that in the history of evangelism these gaps have been steadily closing, or steadily acknowledged as being closed. He cannot agree that God's work seems to become increasingly *indirect*, as if he were delegating more and more of his work to others.

Ironically, however, there is a kind of "death of God" trend in evangelism. To be much more precise, Christ's direct work in revivals seems to be giving way to his indirect work. The supernatural is found more and more to be manifested in the natural. Christ's work is carried on, as it were, by remote control. Christ remains behind the scenes and works either mostly or exclusively through various agents and means.

What seems genuinely to frighten some of those who resist Graham's highly organized approach to evangelism is the thought that Christ will eventually be seen as simply a name for all the relevant natural factors and variables that go into making up a revival. The supernatural element becomes, then, a will-o'-the-wisp at best, a ghost in the machine. Consider the following analogy. A man who has never seen a university is brought to a campus and promised that he will be shown a university. He is then taken around and shown the classrooms, the offices, the library, the administration building, the student union and mail room, the dormitories and gymnasium, and the other buildings, as well as the faculty, students, and others working for the university. Finally, after observing all these, the visitor comments, "It's all very interesting, but *now I want to see the university.* You promised to show it to me. Where is it?"

The university is found to be nothing except all these various aspects combined together in their special way. They *are* the university. And some Christians seem to be in dread of the thought that *the "workings of Christ" in the revival will turn out to be nothing other than the organizations, prayers, personal decisions, computers, and the numerous other factors said to constitute the revival,* with Christ himself being left out of the picture altogether. The fear is that the remaining gaps which God is supposed to fill in directly are really filled in by natural, observable phenomena. It is feared that the crusades are human crusades only, composed of no supernatural ingredients, no supernatural variables. Hence, what is presently understood only partially about the Billy Graham crusades may in the future become more clearly understood, not because a supernatural "mystery" will be revealed, but because some of the remaining undetected natural variables and patterns will be more thoroughly studied.

If this conclusion should be accepted, it would not follow, however, that the crusades are wholly human, for no activity can be wholly human, inasmuch as *nature is the necessary condition of all human activity.* Finite man's failure to see this clearly and steadily has generated considerable ecological and other kinds of problems. Perhaps it is time for theology to take nature more seriously, for it may be that nature in all its richness and complexity *is* the activity of God. If so, then man's dependence on nature is dependence on God, which suggests that knowledge of the patterns and laws of nature is the touchstone of theology.[13]

CONVERSION TO CHRIST

Billy Graham holds that conversion is a supernatural phenomenon that cannot be fully accounted for by natural variables. It is a miracle, a mystery, a transcendent reality to be accepted by faith.

Supernaturalism has had a long tradition of backtracking and steadily losing ground. One Southern Baptist, Wayne Oates, notes that science has naturalized one area of religion after another. This does not mean, however, that religion has been, or ought to be, eliminated. Rather, religion has been increasingly understood in a more naturalistic and personalistic frame of reference. Oates writes that science "always pushes religion to a deeper analysis of its reason for being. The sciences of cosmology—astronomy, physics, geography, and so on—were originally the domain of religious interpretation." [14] In this steady process of naturalizing the supernatural, the domain of science has continued both to expand its borders and consequently to enrich itself.

Few people today hold that the stars and planets are really supernatural beings. The heavens are natural phenomena, not deities or angels. Yet in times past men who regarded the stars as natural bodies were sometimes persecuted. Over four hundred years before Christ the philosopher Anaxagoras was expelled from Athens because he taught that the stars were a part of the natural order. Today science, having shown that the heavenly bodies are natural bodies, is now showing that *religious experiences and conversions are natural rather than supernatural phenomena,* and this is very threatening to Billy Graham and Evangelicalism.

For some people this expansion of science into the realms of religion and of human experience means that religious experience of every kind is doomed. But the naturalistic understanding of religion no more eliminates all religious experience than the naturalistic understanding of the stars eliminates the stars. What changes is the way religious experience is taken and explained. To be sure, many stupendous claims about what religious experience and conversion can do have already been exposed as empty claims. On the other hand, however, the careful, relentless scientific study of religious experience has revealed some conclusions which are surprising to some who previously regarded all religious experience as nothing but a form of neurosis.

The nature of science is to seek reliable conclusions impartially. And the drift of scientific research seems to be that, at least for some people, religious experiences of certain kinds and settings are integrating to the personality. In his article "Behavioral Science, Religion, and Mental Health" psychologist Gordon W. Allport discusses the fact that religion often can "knit fragments together" in a person's life.[15] But, Allport also warns, "in some forms, religion instills an abnormal degree of terror, injurious especially to sensitive children; it may arouse pathological feelings of guilt; it may inculcate superstition."[16]

Billy Graham likes to point out that his own preaching of forgiveness is therapeutic and a source of mental health. In a March 13, 1972, TV sermon he stated that considerable mental illness and insanity result from guilt, and he then proudly announced that on behalf of God he was offering forgiveness to people. In fact, sometimes when Graham says "Accept Christ!" he means, "Avail yourself of this forgiveness!" Sometimes this is what he means by "conversion": "Recognize your guilt and accept God's forgiveness."

However, two points need to be considered in this connection. First,

Graham's preaching not only offers forgiveness, but also generates certain unnecessary and irrational guilt. But given his theological frame of reference, he could not consistently do otherwise. As noted earlier, the sin at the top of the evangelist's list is the failure to confess Jesus as the preexisting Son of God who died as a sacrificial lamb. If rejecting this is a sin, then Jews and most members of the human race live and die totally outside the circle of forgiveness.

The second point about Graham's offer of forgiveness is that it demands considerable theological agreement with himself. Let us suppose that a man has cheated another man out of a large sum of money. Is there forgiveness for him? If the thief repents and seeks to restore the money to his victim, can he be forgiven? To be sure, restoring the money is not a means of purchasing forgiveness in the sense of making total restitution, for the foul deed done has had all sorts of personal and social implications that simply cannot be undone. The irreversibility of time would seem to render impossible any perfect restitution and atonement, regardless of what form it takes. But the repayment that is offered by the thief to his victim can at least serve as a token or sign of the repentant man's sincerity and repentance. Moreover, the victim may simply need the money stolen from him; having it returned would certainly do him some good.

However, Graham holds that God is in the picture and wants for himself *full* payment from the thief, inasmuch as God's law was violated. And because no mere man could possibly recompense God for whatever loss God might have suffered personally, the only remaining course for the sinner is to accept God's offer to make full restitution on the thief's behalf. How does God make this restitution? By taking out his wrath on Christ the Son and thus satisfying his own demand for payment. In short, says Graham, "Jesus paid it all" by allowing himself to be executed by the Father through the hands of Judas, Pilate, and the others. Of course, Graham still thinks that the thief ought to restore the money and give some sign of his sincere repentance.

Now, what this entails is that before forgiveness can be enjoyed, a particular theological theory of atonement must be at least implicitly believed and accepted by the person seeking forgiveness. Unfortunately, Graham's view of the atonement—which is a mixture of penal, substitutionary, and moral influence theories—is not the most coherent conglomeration of theology that Evangelicalism has pieced together. Consequently, for many people it is intellectually unworthy of acceptance. Graham, of course, insists that those who reject it do so, not on intellectual grounds, but because they are immoral. And one reason that he calls them immoral is that he observes that they do not accept his theory of the atonement.

There are some people who insist that Graham's theory of the atonement is itself immoral and regard it as an expression of the human preoccupation with blood, vengeance, and violence. In a sermon entitled "The Life in the Blood" the evangelist reveals in his thinking what can only be described as a magical attitude toward blood. "The most mysterious substance in the human body," he says, "is the blood." [17] He reveals that in college he wrote a paper on "the subject of blood as it is found in the various religions." He points out how around "the world blood occupies a prominent position," just as it does in the mind of Billy Graham. He notes that the Aztecs slaughtered more than twenty thousand human beings annually on altars built to their gods. He further calls attention to the fact that the Red Guards were marching in the streets of Peking and chanting, "Without the shedding of blood, there will be no revolution." [18]

Does Billy Graham offer a religion that somehow transcends this human obsession with blood and violence? On the contrary, he insists that God himself demands blood, for "without shedding of blood [there] is no remission (Heb. 9:22, KJV)." In short, God will not forgive unless somebody's blood is spilled. Apparently, in Graham's mind at least, there is something magical about blood. The trouble with the world, he insists, is that ever since Adam and Eve ate the forbidden fruit, mankind has suffered blood poisoning. The bloodstream of the human race has been polluted—thanks to that thoughtless first couple in the Garden of Eden.[19]

So God will not accept bad blood, which means that, according to the evangelist's theology or alchemy of the blood, God can gain his satisfaction only if good blood is spilled. This is where the Son comes in. God the Father arranged for the divine Son to be born of good and pure blood so that the Son could spill it on behalf of sinners. After the bloody sacrifice of the Son to the Father is made, then God is free to accept sinners. For Graham, the blood of Jesus somehow washes and purifies those who repent. It makes them as if they were the purist virgins.[20] What a psychoanalyst would make of this strange talk of blood and virgin purity is something that might prove fruitful to pursue but is too involved for this book. In *Atonement and Psychotherapy*, Don S. Browning has made an interesting beginning in developing a more coherent notion of atonement.[21]

The conclusion to be drawn here is that once supernatural explanations and speculations are cut loose from their root in the systematic study of natural phenomena, they tend to veer off into magic. Nature is certainly more variegated and is far richer than some naturalists have thought, but Graham's version of atonement has turned religion into crude magic. Christ becomes the magic word that makes all evils disappear and all problems vanish into thin air. Most children have fantasies of magical executions,[22] and in the infancy of the human race belief in magic was widespread. Graham's magical notion of what may be called the "Christ: Presto!" gospel fills a considerable part of his preaching. However, in his recent book *The Jesus Generation* he seems to have become more critical of the "instant cure" gospel of naive youths, although not of himself.

Theists who reject the evangelical framework of forgiveness need to explore the theme of forgiveness in a broadly naturalistic and personalistic context. The fact that Evangelicalism has pretty well botched the theme is no excuse for theistic naturalists and personalists to ignore this very important dimension of interpersonal relationships. Neither sentimentalism nor pseudorighteousness provides fruitful soil in which to cultivate forgiveness. In fact, it is very possible for the natural variables of forgiveness to be more thoroughly observed, analyzed, and studied both historically and experimentally. Men often need conversion, not just one conversion, but a number of conversions in their lifetimes—conversions of various sorts and degrees. Many human lives need interpersonal help if they are to be changed from patterns of destruction, abulia, boredom, fanaticism, resentment, and general unfreedom. Billy Graham seeks to offer this interpersonal help and has been somewhat successful in it for some people, but some of his theological barbed wire has both directly and indirectly caused serious and unnecessary injury to many persons.

Most religions have offered some sort of initiation rite, some symbolic expression of passage from one life to another, or, as we today might say, passage from one life-style to another.[23] Young people today are often put through the painful ordeal of falling out of love without anything constructive to turn to. They also suffer powerful disillusionments on every hand and sometimes have little help in recovering from this "death." Indeed, this dying and rebirth is a contemporary natural phenomenon that the young, the middle-aged, and the old seem to be experiencing in varying degrees of success in this day of "future shock." The crucial need, therefore, is to develop sympathetic, naturalistic, and humane modes of conversion and transition from the death of disillusionment to a new future that is not what Freud calls "the future of illusion."

Billy Graham is a major contemporary figure in the attempt to help people in their transition from the old man to the new; but, unfortunately, his frame of reference greatly thwarts his efforts to be of considerable help to great numbers of people. Furthermore, he is so busy selling the one and only "true way" that he greatly limits the possibility of individuals' exploring and analyzing life more profoundly than Graham's Evangelicalism can tolerate.

CHANGING MEN BY CHANGING THEIR ENVIRONMENT

As was pointed out above, for Billy Graham the expression "Accept Christ!" sometimes means simply "Avail yourself of forgiveness!" But at other times "Accept Christ!" means, in effect, "Join a program of reform and behavior modification!" Graham promises that Christ can solve *any* problem—from marital problems to finances. However, this bit of come-on preaching turns out to be no more than the recommendation of a particular human reform program. Christ is found to be, not a supernatural power of transformation, but a word standing for a rather elaborate human program composed of church attendance, praying, witnessing, Bible reading, and taking on new associates. And instead of a supernatural Christ somehow mysteriously working *within* the new convert, the reform program works *on* the convert and puts the convert himself to work on others. Graham's Christ as a supernatural agency is nowhere to be found; in his place are substituted numerous natural influences—from the sounds of hymns and Bible passages to the nods of approval when the convert's behavior measures up to standard, and gestures of disapproval when his behavior deviates too far from the norm.*

---

* There are various kinds of activities that are placed under the heading of "Christ." Moreover, the quest for the historical Jesus is a separate issue of its own.

To be sure, all programs of reshaping, education, and the like are composed of various cues, communications, natural reinforcements, and rituals. There is no other way to change men from one way of living to another way. What Graham claims, however, is that his program has some special ingredient that is beyond the rich realm of nature and human culture. But he no more substantiates this claim than the primitive pagan has substantiated his doctrine of spirits in trees and rocks. The presence of Christ in the lives of men is, in actuality, the effect which the multicolored tradition and reform program has upon them.

Graham is fond of saying that men cannot be changed by the environment. They must, he says, be changed within. But when the air is cleared, what is plain to see is that Graham himself is simply recommending one particular way of using the natural environment of nature and human culture to change human behavior and attitudes. There is nothing inherently mysterious or miraculous about it. When attacking the method of "change the environment in order to change men," Graham in effect is only attacking every other method but his own. His own method is nothing other than the utilization of the natural variables of the environment to reshape human behavior and beliefs. No supernatural phenomena appear on the scene. In a March 1972 sermon the evangelist said that he could not prove scientifically that Christ as a person is alive today. But he said that he believes him to be alive because of the supernatural transformation he brings about in the lives of people. This suggests, however, that the "living Christ" is in actuality Evangelicalism's "living program" operating on the lives of people to change their behavior and outlook. In promising the supernatural, Graham unwittingly is promising simply his own particular procedure and program for manipulating and controlling the natural variables for the purpose of changing the makeup and behavior of human beings.

Sometimes, however, Graham's promises run far ahead of what his program can actually effect. To excuse the program's failure to pay off as promised, Graham is prone to blame the convert himself for not having enough faith or for being sinful in some way. This device is usually very effective, either because it is never clear how much faith is enough or because even the best of converts will, as Graham knows, always be harboring some sort of sin, which may even be secret doubts about Graham's Christ program. In fact, Graham's program, like certain business firms, seems to have a number of devices for explaining away some of the obvious failures to measure up to promises made, which is why Evangelicalism loses a number of "customers," despite its numerous recruitment and advertisement activities and organizations.

The easy promise to solve a problem often becomes obscured by what can best be described as the red-tape runaround. If you have a very specific problem to be solved, the procedures which are classified under the heading "Christ" are in many cases designed to talk you out of an answer to your problem. Because Christ does not have what you want, a substitute is offered. Granted that some specific problems do not deserve to be solved, the fact remains that Graham has promised to solve them. If your problem is financial, Christ will solve it, not necessarily by getting you a loan or a better job, but by encouraging you to be content in whatever state you find yourself.

Imagine a physician who tells you that he can cure your disease. You go to him, and he says, "Well, of course, you must learn to live with this disease and I will teach you how to do it."

"But I thought you could cure it, doctor."

"Well, I can; not in the vulgar, mundane way, however, but in a nobler and higher way. I will teach you how to endure the disease with grace and poise."

"But I want to be cured, doctor."

"I am sorry, but we don't get everything in this world that we want. I ask you, what sort of a world would that be!"

"True, doctor, but you promised."

"You must have faith. Faith can move mountains, you know. And . . ."

Imagine another scene. An evangelical missionary observes a pagan praying to a tree. After a time the missionary, observing no natural phenomena which could be regarded as answers to the pagan's prayer, walks up to him and says, "Your prayer for a new spear seems not to have been answered, my friend."

"You do not understand," the pagan replies. "The tree spirit has answered my prayer."

"How?" the missionary asks.

"By not giving me a spear."

"But I thought I heard you ask your god for a spear."

"Yes, but the answer he gave is that I do not need a new spear. A spear for me was not within his will."

The missionary looks puzzled. "You mean that no answer is the same as an answer?"

"Most definitely. The tree spirit answered. His answer was no!"

"How so?" the missionary asks.

"By not giving me the spear."

"Well," says the missionary, "what is the difference between receiving no answer at all and receiving an actual answer?"

"No difference at all. They are both an answer. The answer is spiritual in nature." Then the pagan asks, "Do you pray to your god?"

"Yes, every day."

"Do you receive answers too?"

"Yes," replies the missionary.

"Then please come with me to my village. My father and sister are very ill."

The two journey to the nearby village, where the missionary, upon meeting the father, proceeds to pray for a cure. After praying, the missionary examines the father and then gives him an injection of penicillin.

"What are you doing?" the son asks.

"I am giving your father medicine that will heal him," the missionary explains.

"Will your prayers not heal my father?"

"Well, the penicillin helps."

"Fine," says the pagan, "I wonder if your medicine will help my god to heal my sister. Come, I will pray to my god while you give her your medicine. Perhaps both of our gods will answer prayer. . . . Say, does your god answer prayer without the medicine?" the pagan asks.

"Well, yes," the missionary replies.

"That is good. But then why do you use the medicine? Does your god answer all your prayers to heal the sick?"

"He sometimes answers by giving the person strength to endure the illness," the missionary explains.

"I see. Your god sometimes answers by not answering. I like your god. He is very much like mine."

The dialogue between the pagan and the Christian suggests how devices used by one religious program to obscure its promises and claims regarding the supernatural may be used by any other program to obscure its promises and claims. Apparently, when Graham studied anthropology at Wheaton College he did so with a view toward showing how evangelical Christianity is the higher fulfillment of all the inferior aims of "lower" religions. But it is possible to view all religions claiming to be supernatural—including Evangelicalism—as unwittingly searching for some more effective and naturalistic way of coming to terms with the natural phenomena encountered on every hand.[24]

Whether or not all religions of the supernatural have in fact been implicitly searching for a personalistic and naturalistic way is an obscure point at best. What is important is that a more effective way of coming to terms with life seems to come, not by relating to some realm beyond nature and human culture, but by coming to terms with the natural phenomena themselves. In short, nature and culture cannot successfully be ignored. Theistic naturalism of the personalistic school will argue that God is known through nature and through man's interaction with the vast interplay of nature. God is in nature in the way that a human is in his walking or his working. God is revealed in the laws and patterns of nature and not through the undisciplined imaginings of supernatural wizardry. Poets, fishermen, farmers, scientists, mystics, engineers, and many others confront nature in a variety of ways at every moment. Each encounter with nature is an encounter with God, not in his totality, but in part. Indeed, men can encounter one another only in part. How could they encounter the everlasting God-in-nature all at once?

Man's understanding of God comes from patient observation of nature, as well as from recording sensitive responses to nature and comparative studies of it. There are also experiments in new kinds of relationships with nature. Novelty and new experiences and new insights must not be reduced to the lust for the supernatural, which is an attempt to jump over the natural process in order to hit God for a very private interview. Longings for supernatural revelations may be compared to the attempts to place a person under an astrological sign as a means of gaining instant knowledge of that human being's whole life-style and character. Most people can hardly see themselves at once. They make all sorts of errors about themselves and their neighbors. What better results could be expected of their knowledge of God?

Even if God should place propositional sentences in the minds of scripture writers, as Graham thinks he did, the real problem would be that of *interpreting* the propositions. But scriptures could not be interpreted until they touched ground somewhere in the natural realm. Even the "call" of God, which some ministers claim to have received as a supernatural communiqué from God, is found to be the result of natural variables that the candidate received in numerous ways. Billy Graham's own call into the ministry was the result of the subtle but effective influence of his mother, as well as the less subtle influence of ministers, the feelings of obligation induced in him by others, and numerous other natural variables, some of which Graham himself openly acknowledges. What the evangelist took to be God's communication of a special and direct message to him personally may be understood as the natural phenomenon of a person "reasoning to himself" about the ideas and messages which came to him in a thousand ways from the realm of nature and human religious associates.

In Billy Graham's film entitled *His Land*, a number of Old Testament prophecies are quoted to the effect that God will cause new springs to flow and flowers to bloom in the arid deserts of Israel. Evangelist Graham, Cliff Barrows, and others of the crusade team believe that God is at this moment in process of fulfilling his prophecies in the land of the Jews. Indeed, the film shows new water spreading along the ground and colorful flowers shocking the Palestinian desert with their novel beauty. But the significant thing to note is that God does not actually fulfill these alleged prophecies directly himself. The new springs in the desert do not appear miraculously, nor do the flowers shoot forth in some supernatural way. In fact, the springs are not exactly springs after all but instead are piped-in irrigation. And the new flowers have been planted and cared for by natural means rather than by God's supernatural intervention. In short, the Jews did the appropriate work, and nature produced appropriately. Today flowers grow and water flows in both Palestine and Nevada because some human beings have learned to some extent how to come to terms with the natural phenomena.

ARE MIRACLES NATURAL?

A careful study of Billy Graham's writings and sermons reveals what he takes to be the distinguishing marks of a miracle. First, a miracle is a direct act or work of God. Second, it is either good in itself or a means of bringing about something good—for example, the blind are made to see, Israel's evil enemies are eliminated (as when God destroyed the Egyptian warriors), the conversion is experienced, or sur-gery is successful when the probabilities of recovery had appeared to be very low. For Graham, a third mark of a miracle is that it is something very important and significant.

Graham regards marriage to be a special miracle because, in the first place, God was the one who initially institutionalized it by a direct act on his part.[25] Marriage therefore, is not simply a biocultural develop-ment.[26] Second, marriage is a good state of being in itself, and it pro-motes additional good as well.[27] Third, it is necessary to the survival and well-being of society.[28] Marriage is that significant.

There can be little doubt that Billy Graham and Oral Roberts have greatly extended the meaning of the word miracle. Some Christians think that they have also diluted it in the process; if the birth of every baby or the cure of diseases is called a miracle, the distinction between the supernatural and the natural is virtually lost. Let us consider this objection by taking the case of a husband and wife who are enjoying sexual intercourse. After the experience, the woman discovers to her dismay that she failed to take the birth-control pill. And at the time of intercourse she was at the most fertile period in her cycle. Already hav-ing all the children they want and can afford, the husband and wife hope and pray that she will not become pregnant despite the fact that she failed to take the pill and he failed to ask her about it. After a month passes, they are assured that she is not pregnant. Is it a miracle that she did not get pregnant?

Let us see whether, by Graham's definition, the avoidance of this pregnancy can be called a miracle. First, is it a direct work of God? In order to be a miracle it must be a direct work. We must postpone an an-swer to this tough question. Second, given the population explosion and other factors in the lives of this particular man and woman, the preven-tion of the birth of another child to them could be regarded as a very good thing. Billy Graham has said on TV that he disagrees with the pope's attitude toward birth control. In his book *World Aflame*, the evangelist, speaking of "the demographic flame," writes: "The popula-tion increase is frightening. . . . Statistics overwhelm us when we take into account the rapidity with which births are exceeding deaths." [29] Presumably Graham does not recommend total abstinence as the best method for birth control among the married, and he says that the sexual experience among the married is good.[30] So the conclusion may be drawn that Graham, on his own principles, would have to say that avoiding pregnancy is a very good thing in many cases.

This then raises the question of whether avoiding pregnancy could be regarded as a significant thing. As noted above, Graham thinks that the population explosion is a very serious problem. Hence, avoiding pregnancy could in some cases be important or significant for the well-being of society, just as it could be a good thing for the individual marriage or family.

So all that remains in determining whether the husband and wife were granted a miracle whenever she did not become pregnant is to show that this prevention of pregnancy was a direct work of God. Unfortunately, neither Graham nor Roberts is very clear on this point of direct intervention. True, they make the distinction, but they do not show how it is made, although they do give one indication. They indicate that God's direct work can be detected whenever something good and significant comes about despite the apparent unlikelihood that it would have come about through regular means. For example, a cancer patient recovers despite the predictions based on available data that nothing further can be done for him. His chances of recovery were slim, yet he is healed. A miracle!

However, Graham and Roberts do not always adhere consistently to this as a way of recognizing the direct work of God; and their view of supernatural intervention, when traced out in detail, seems to become greatly entangled. It may be that the line between the direct and the indirect work of God cannot consistently be drawn. Or if it can, it will have to be done on a basis other than the distinction between the humanly predictable and unpredictable, or the humanly possible and impossible.

Evangelicalism has yet to develop a coherent way of talking about the natural and the supernatural in such a way as to distinguish them clearly, as well as to indicate how they are to be related to one another. Indeed, the way Evangelicals use the word natural is sometimes fraught with difficulties. On one hand, the natural man is considered by Evangelicals to be sinful; on the other, homosexuality and long hair for men are regarded as immoral because they are not natural. Monogamous marriage is regarded by many Evangelicals to be natural—but so is the tendency to sin. The point here is that Evangelicalism has not yet developed a coherent notion of what is natural, much less what is supernatural.

Mormons do not think monogamy is natural. Indeed, the fact that something is either natural or unnatural does not tell us whether it is worthy or unworthy of us as human beings. Some studies suggest that homosexual tendencies are natural to almost everyone, but that is hardly a basis for setting up homosexuality as an ideal. Aristotle thought that women were naturally inferior intellectually, whereas today it is clear that when women have responded poorly to certain tasks, they have done so because they were usually denied proper training, opportunity, and support for fulfilling the tasks.

The practical conclusion to be drawn here is that along with not having been very clear as to what distinguishes the natural from the supernatural, Evangelicals have not clarified the distinction between the natural and the unnatural. Presumably miracles are not quite natural but are supernatural. At the same time, miracles could not give support to what is unnatural or wicked. And if this is not sufficiently confusing, the supernatural is somehow regarded by Evangelicals as an unnatural work of God.

This whole question of "the natural" is utterly fascinating and fruitful to dwell upon, especially in the area of paranormal psychology. It may be that the natural world is the supernatural viewed in a more systematic, comprehensive, and rigorous manner. But that is a whole new area of inquiry. What is important to see here is that our knowledge of the realm of the natural is still growing, so that there is a kind of "progressive revelation" which the inquiring scientific method helps make possible. Perhaps the supernatural is that dimension of the natural world which we do not yet understand in systematic form but which we may hope to understand better as science learns to enrich itself through imaginative and responsive literature and through personal experiences that are sensitively observed and critically evaluated.

SUMMARY

The realm of natural phenomena is rich and variegated, and through the broadly conceived scientific method men are gaining greater understanding of it. But this method depends both on highly sensitive observers willing to let the data "have their say" and on sensitive instruments designed for even finer observation. It also depends on a community of people engaging in perpetual comparative analysis, speculating with one another, checking and double-checking, theorizing, and critically testing hypotheses. The scientific method is simply more refined ways of observing and thinking and problem-solving. The scientific method has its beginnings in human beings' attempts to solve efficiently their ordinary, everyday problems.

One of the long-standing questions regarding the scientific study of any religion or faith is, who can better understand it—the insider or the outsider? The answer would seem to be that a more adequate understanding comes when the insiders and outsiders engage in dialogue in the hope of both informing one another and learning from one another. After all, everyone is an insider to some view of life and an outsider to other views. Everyone is both believer and unbeliever, depending on what view of life or way of life is under consideration. Sympathetic reporting, comparative study, and critical analysis are all essential to a richer and more adequate understanding of any phenomenon, whether it be rock music, communism, or Evangelicalism.[31]

Chapter II
SINNERS ALL

THE MANY FACES OF
ORIGINAL SIN

Billy Graham's doctrine of free will must not be understood to entail that the majority of men have had a choice of whether or not they would become sinners. Presumably Adam and Eve had this choice, but thereafter free will on that issue was extinguished because of Adam's initiating sin. After Adam, every human being born of woman was born to be a sinner without fail. According to this evangelical point of view, God knew that Adam would pollute the whole human race and the environment, but God created Adam and Eve nevertheless. Presumably the Deity either could not or would not arrange simply to eliminate the first couple as a bad experiment and then start with a new couple. Mathematically speaking, the odds were that the second couple would not have sinned. And in any case, God could have created a third couple, a fourth, and on and on, until he hit upon a couple that would choose goodness, not wickedness. And if God could permit the sinful choice of the first Adam to pollute the entire human race, then doubtless he could have permitted a perfect couple's decision for goodness to represent the whole human race. Hence, instead of being born in original sin with an innate predisposition to do evil, men thereafter could have been born with an innate predisposition to do good.

It could be objected that even if the original couple had not sinned, some subsequent couple would have, which would have spoiled everything anyhow. But Billy Graham seems not to go along with that, for he says plainly that had Adam and Eve not sinned, we today would never have experienced hate, greed, prejudice, war, suffering, disease, poverty, or death.[1] The evangelical view holds that all evils—from moral evil to mistakes in logic—are the result of original sin.[2]

This one grand hypothesis of original sin is believed to account for all the evil among men. When the Watts revolt was sparked off in August 1965 many people were asking themselves what the causes of it were. Billy Graham, forcefully denouncing the rioters in language that he has never used to denounce segregationists, announced that he knew the cause of the riot—it was original sin in the hearts of the rioters.

Of course, says Graham, no man is exempt from original sin, which suggests that one reason that Graham himself is often given to excess and exaggeration in his preaching is simply that he is manifesting original sin. A person who criticizes Graham would, of course, presumably be thought of as a brother in original sin, too.

The major trouble with so general a hypothesis as original sin is that it becomes public property, so to speak, for anyone to pick up and use as a weapon against his opponents. But perhaps that practice is also a manifestation of original sin. There seems to be a tendency for those who believe in this hypothesis to begin thinking of some people as either having more original sin than others or at least being more original in their sin. Exactly who those heavily endowed members of the species are depends on who is making the charge. They have been Turks, Communists, white men, black men, New Yorkers, slum-dwellers, Madison Avenue types, "naughty" children, and so on. In the novel *The Way of All Flesh* an irritated father is attempting to persuade his young son Ernest to learn to pronounce a *k* or hard *c*. Despite himself, Ernest keeps saying "tum" rather than "come." The father pronounces the word for the child and tells him to repeat it. But the child is unable to. "Now, Ernest," says the disgusted father, "I will give you one more chance, and if you don't say 'come,' I shall know that you are self-willed and naughty." As expected, the frightened child can only repeat "tum" and cannot say "come."

Of course, whenever failure is observed, especially in others, it is easy to pronounce the phrase original sin or something similar, as if offering an explanation. The failure of a child to say "come" rather than "tum" will most likely lie in the failure of adults to train him properly, and we must not say that this adult failure is simply the result of original sin. Patient parents listen to their children. And when the children happen to speak the correct sounds, then they are rewarded by a smile, nod, or something else. In that way children learn to speak properly. It has nothing to do with original naughtiness or original sin—unless original sin is loosely defined as human finitude.

If the notion of original sin is used to explain every evil and problem in general, it is not a very useful hypothesis. If, however, we use it to explain certain specific evils in contrast to other evils, we must make clear the signs by which we detect it in certain cases and not in other cases. If original sin caused violence in Watts, why was there no violence in the mountains of North Carolina at the same time? Was there a greater concentration of original sin in Watts? Or was the Watts style of sin simply more dramatic, although no more sinful?

Assuming for the moment the reality of original sin in some sense, the practical question, then, would have to do with finding ways to contain or control the impact of this original deposit that is distributed throughout the cosmos, or at least in certain pockets of the cosmos. Some who believe in original sin seem to look upon it as a constant. It will always be around, at least until the Second Coming. Whenever men fail, they are sometimes told that original sin brought about their failure. If men propose to make reforms in society, they are sometimes told that the reforms will invariably fail because of original sin. In Graham's words, "whatever [man] undertakes to do, he succeeds only in corrupting," [3] and some of Graham's evangelical critics point to his own organization as an example of this tendency toward corruption or loss of creativity.

The doctrine of original sin may be compared to the notion of friction. We can predict that, because of friction, the parts of a machine will wear out. But friction also makes it possible for wheels to have traction; ground transportation would be in a predicament without it. Some theologians think that original sin, too, has its useful side and that without it much of human life would remain bland and characterless. The trick then would be to use sin (like friction) in pursuing some ends and to reduce it in pursuing other ends.

Conservatives are more likely to appeal to the notion of original sin to show that attempts at changing the social structures will come to no good. Radicals sometimes think that the settled institutions are riddled through and through with original sin and therefore ought to be changed like an old, worn-out machine. But such general charges are, by and large, useless. They merely postpone questions and proposals of a more specific nature.

Sometimes the doctrine of original sin is a way of expressing the observation that there are unforeseen and inadvertent consequences of human behavior. This is another way of saying that when men act, they do so in an environment of numerous variables, not all of which can in practice be predicted. For example, welfare programs have not always helped the needy; the Vietnam War has probably produced more harmful and unforeseen consequences than what would have resulted had either side been allowed to take over completely from the start; free competitive enterprise has generated an unforeseen air of suspicion and distrust; government intervention has bungled; lack of government intervention has invited lawlessness and considerable waste; the check-and-balance system of government has frustrated legitimate goals as well as despotism; religious conversion has turned a narcotic addict into a narrow-minded fanatic; learning to read has generated greater knowledge of one's plight; and so on ad infinitum. The trouble with the evangelical doctrine of original sin is that it compounds the problem not only by focusing upon great frustration in the world, but also by making men feel *guilty* because of the ontological existence of frustration. In short, the doctrine of original sin says, "Feel guilty! You were born!"

HOW MUCH ORIGINAL SIN?

Evangelicals in the United States are fond of saying that the poor we will have with us always. Their doctrine of original sin says that conflict, ignorance, and frustration will be with us always. Doubtless this is true, whether or not the story of Adam and Eve is taken seriously.

But let us assume for the moment that the poor, frustration, conflict, and suffering will always be present and that this assumption is really a truth revealed from God. That does not tell us *how much* poverty, frustration, ignorance, or conflict will remain or *must* exist among us. In order to meet the letter of the infallibly revealed requirement, only two poor people on earth would be necessary. The rest of humanity could conceivably be at least half as well off materially as Evangelist Graham. Two volunteers could, then, dedicate themselves to being "the poor" on earth. Because of their great sacrifice, they could be rewarded with honor and fame, so that "Blessed are the poor!" would become an international imperative.

The point here is that the evangelical doctrine of original sin does not specify the amount or area of frustration and evil that will plague man so long as he remains on earth or thereabouts. It does not say that men will be defeated in their efforts to gain considerable control over polio, VD, rats, war, the population explosion, crime, poverty, and hatred. It does not say how much progress can be attained short of perfection. In short, the doctrine's practical worth seems doubtful, to say nothing of its dubious metaphysical staging.

It does warn men to be cautious about their utopian ventures into the future. It also warns them not to idolize their present establishment, which is cursed with original friction. But men do not need the doctrine of original sin, with its metaphysics of Adam and Eve, to tell them these things. Scientists do not need to be influenced by Evangelicalism to know that their experiments may go wrong, that glasses will tend to break if dropped, that light bulbs go out, and that the body grows weary. Indeed, by a more scientific study of the natural variables, some of the ill effects of human endeavors can perhaps be controlled for good, although the means of improvement can also be means of producing greater harm and frustration. Granted, the doctrine of original sin says that men will even use scientific means for pursuing evil goals. But that is empirically observable. What is important, however, is that we do not know *how frequently* these evil ends will be pursued. Indeed, with the advance of behavioral science men might gain greater understanding of the variables under which men tend to do more evil and the variables under which they are more humane and rational.

Billy Graham has a sweeping promise regarding original sin. He promises that those who accept the gospel which he and others preach will someday live in an environment free of all frustration, conflict, poverty, and suffering. In short, like the lion and the lamb, the id and the superego will in heaven lie down together in perfect harmony. That is Graham's "answer" to original sin. It is, of course, an answer that cannot at present, if ever, be confirmed.

However, Graham does attempt to offer a bit of verifiable heaven on earth as a kind of token or earnest of what is to come—a "foretaste of glory divine." And that area of heaven on earth is found in the Christian, or at least in the victorious Christian who has a little of heaven in his life.

But does this mean that upon conversion the Christian overcomes original sin? Not exactly. A down payment is made, so to speak, and a promise of more to come is made. In one of his more moderate moments Graham writes of his own conversion: "There was no great change in my life at that moment, but little by little, day by day, I knew that I was a different person. I began to have more concern for the poor and suffering people, and my childhood prejudices disappeared." [4]

These humane attitudes that gradually developed in Graham as he grew into manhood have been observed in other adult Christians. But they have also been observed to be lacking in the lives of people who at least profess belief in the fundamentals of Evangelicalism. Whether or not they are "real Christians" may, as indicated in an earlier chapter, be merely a question of definition. What is more important, however, is the observable fact that these humane qualities exist in many people who either are Christians of another persuasion than Evangelicalism or are not Christians at all. It seems rather clear that being initially converted in Graham's sense is not necessary to the development of humaneness. And there is a serious question as to whether this conversion *guarantees* that this humaneness will come about in a person. A careful scientific approach would seek to learn to what degree this kind of conversion contributes to humaneness and to what extent it is negligible or even retarding under certain conditions. There is also a question regarding the relationship between conversions of other kinds and the development of humaneness in the lives of individuals.

Graham has, of course, seen many lives changed. But so have teachers and probably anyone who has observed people carefully. And the changes come because of a great number of variables. What Graham seems not to grasp so easily is the number of people who, finding Evangelicalism no longer able to inspire them or to provide moral and intellectual direction, gain great relief when they enter into another way. A person may be converted *away from* Evangelicalism as well as converted *to* it. Men have found peace of mind in being converted either to or from Catholicism, Evangelicalism, neoorthodoxy, agnosticism, atheism, humanism, naturalism, Marxism, Jainism, Judaism, and hundreds of other isms. It might be very useful to know what is common to all or many of these conversions. While study has been done in this area, much more remains to be done. William James's remarkable book *The Varieties of Religious Experience*, marks a good beginning, but only a beginning, as James himself was the first to acknowledge.

CAN SIN BE CONTROLLED?

Billy Graham likes to refer to original sin as an inherited disease; except for Jesus, "every other Biblical personality was infected." [5] "Thus we all recognize," he says, "that the human race is sick, that man has a disease that has affected the whole of life. The Bible calls this disease sin." [6] Furthermore, Adam's "sin resulted in a living death. Nature became cursed and the venom of sin infected the entire family." [7] This disease is hereditary. The notion that original sin is a disease is perhaps the most fruitful approach that Graham has taken on the subject. It would appear to be highly suggestive and ought not to be casually dismissed as just another bit of evangelical mythology.

Graham claims that a total cure for this disease of sin has been created. Unfortunately, the claim remains only a claim, for there is no strong evidence to support it. Even the lives of Christians do not appear to be very convincing evidence, and about all that Graham can point to with consistent confidence is that all Christians do have a negative attitude toward what they classify as sin, and feel guilty and repentant when they commit sin. [8]

On a more practical level, some of the more obvious forms of undesirable behavior—for example, violence of various types—can be seen to change whenever certain variables or conditions of the environment change. In approaching violence as a disease in some respects, we may be able to deal with it somewhat more effectively. Some people seem to lie more than others, which suggests that there are environmental conditions that encourage lying, whereas other conditions control it rather well. This again is like looking for the conditions under which a disease flares up in the body. It can be observed that men of certain kinds of background and environment are more prone to violence than men from other backgrounds, [9] just as some diseases seem to thrive better in certain areas of the globe.

Ruth Graham moved her children to a two-hundred acre mountaintop, thick with rich green trees, which she judged would be an ideal physical environment, especially for her boys. With a caretaker to do work outside the house and a live-in housekeeper to do work inside, Ruth Graham has a better environment for increasing her own freedom and contentment. Billy Graham is ambivalent about the question of environment. He sometimes likes to think that the pure free will that everyone is presumed to have is wholly independent of the environment or circumstances. On one hand, he denounces what he calls "the false doctrine that man is a helpless victim of his environment." [10] On the other, he wants laws passed to change some of the environment that is in considerable conflict with Christianity. In fact, he once remarked, "Do not blame the teenagers entirely for any problems they have; their difficulties stem from the environment we have created for them." [11]

It would appear that even if men do have a disease of original sin, the disease may be controlled under a favorable environment, including proper teaching, better living conditions, recognition, and recreation. To be sure, a disease that usually is under control may flare up with a sudden attack. It will do no good to say to the victim, "Ah! Your disease is still there, hidden, but still there. I knew it all along. I told you!" Rather, the practical thing is to find what variables or factors can be changed or introduced in order to bring the disease back under some control. Then a careful inquiry can be made to determine what caused the disease to flare up when and where it did.

It is doubtless wise for a person with such a disease to keep in mind that he is not a god or a superman. He ought to be sensitive to the various conditions that will trigger a new attack against his health. Similarly, men with original sin ought to find out more empirically what specific conditions cause crimes, violence, and deceit to flare up. In this way they may be better able to control their original-sin disease. To be sure, this sort of mundane, patient research and observation is not very exciting and is not as sensational as revival work.

It must be admitted that utopia is most unlikely. Graham worries about "the total answer" to all life's problems, but probably most men can learn to enjoy some improvement in place of absolute perfection. Imperfection will doubtless always be the lot of mankind. But there are degrees of imperfection and degrees of improvement which are worthy of human effort and commitment. Graham sometimes demands from life a "total answer," but every child learns more or less that many of his demands will never be perfectly met. In fact, Graham himself has very recently begun to stress something that he had not greatly emphasized hitherto. Whether it will become a steady theme of his preaching remains to be seen. The new emphasis is on the possibility of a generation of peace. Instead of talking of ultimate and permanent peace only, he now seems more willing to consider the possibility that war can be controlled in finite periods of time and space. Those who worry about Graham's influence on Nixon fail to see here Nixon's influence on the evangelist, for not until Nixon began talking of "a generation of peace" did Graham begin to take up this theme. In the early part of 1972—before election day and just after the president's trip to China—Graham spoke well of the China trip and announced in Melbourne, Florida, that "it is possible we could have a generation of peace." Graham then assured his audience that "there's nothing in the Bible to prevent us from having a generation of peace." [12] What this amounts to is that Graham has made a concession that the doctrine of original sin does not specify how much war is inevitable or how much peace is possible.

It is, of course, unnecessary to burden oneself with the doctrine of original sin with all its evangelical metaphysical overtones. It is necessary only to say that, under certain conditions, natural phenomena—whether organic or inorganic—will behave in certain ways that may be observed. Even human beings, as offspring and members of nature, will respond according to varying conditions and circumstances. This means that it is important to observe and learn as much as possible about those conditions, for therein lies the improved understanding of man's behavior.

This does not reduce men to machines or frogs, for man's responses are uniquely his own because of his special sensitivity, thanks in part to his intricate brain and nervous system. Indeed, creaturely man is perhaps the only religious species on earth, since he is a complex organism which can respond to, and generate, religious questions.

CURES FOR ORIGINAL SIN

Does Billy Graham's "Christ program" work? Does it cope successfully with human evil and failure? More research is necessary to break these questions down and to begin answering them in a more manageable form. We can conclude at present that his program helps in some ways and, like many other programs, has its bad side effects. The program is quite helpful to some and very harmful to others.

Sometimes Graham presents Christ as if presenting a blank check to be filled in by anyone with any problem. Christ can solve any problem. Just name it. If it is a money matter, Christ can solve it. If it is a problem of spirit or body—well, Christ can handle that too. In fact Graham makes the bold claim that Christ can answer all philosophical questions while also resolving marital difficulties. There is absolutely nothing that the Son of God cannot solve or answer.[13] Having set up a background of dismal pessimism with his doctrine of original sin, the evangelist now comes breaking through with songs of euphoria.

Of course, every faith from Marxism to Ayn Rand's religion, capitalism, has an "answer" of some sort. The real question, however, has to do with the extent to which the answer can satisfy the various dimensions of the religious concern—for example, the intellectual, the emotional, and the moral dimensions. Various religions and movements have emphasized one dimension more than another. Ideally, the various ways of life could learn to communicate forthrightly and openly so that each would improve and enrich the others in every dimension of life, whether intellectual, emotional, or moral.

Too frequently, however, each way claims far more for itself than seems justified. When the New Left in America was at its evangelistic peak, a person talking with some of the participants in "the movement" would more than likely be told that moral concern over civil rights, the Asian war, hunger, poverty, and other crucial human matters was initiated by the New Left in the latter part of the 1960's. Before that time no one in "the Establishment" was supposed to have had any social conscience or moral concern at all. In short, morality in our time was presumably invented by the New Left.

Similarly, according to Billy Graham, morality is the specialty of evangelical Christians. On page 161 of his popular book *World Aflame*, which he says is his most important book, Graham claims that "the Christian is the only real light-bearer in the world." Evangelical Christianity is supposed to be the great moral thrust in the world. But it seems more accurate to say that many factors go into making men moral, and none of these factors are supernatural in essence. "Conversion to Christ" sometimes gives men a greater social consciousness. Sometimes it does not. It depends on the ingredients of the program for behavior modification. It also depends on a number of other factors or variables. Graham's own progressive social views—when they are progressive— often seem to be more the reflection of the general progress of the culture than the result of any supernatural "conversion to Christ." Great numbers of Christians are just now beginning to be aroused from social insensitivity, and conversion to Christ hardly seems to be the major factor in this awakening. However, there is evidence that Evangelicals are inserting into their "Christ program" a method for increasing social conscience in areas hitherto neglected by many Evangelicals.

If conversion to Christ is in actuality a reform program rather than a mysterious miracle of supernatural origin, then Billy Graham and other Evangelicals would probably do well to check their program to see if they are getting the results they desire. The same is true of any group with a reform program. Graham likes to quote the late J. Edgar Hoover's famous words about Sunday school as an influence against lawbreaking, but one study in criminology "showed definitely that the tendency to lie and cheat among 3,000 children tested, was in direct proportion . . . to their knowledge of the Bible and scriptural precepts." Indeed, "children who had been exposed to progressive education methods, based on secular premises and modern psychology, appeared to have a far better record as to honesty and dependability." [14]

However, this is only one study and should not be taken without further research, although Graham the supersalesman does not always exercise such caution whenever he can quote a statistic to sell someone on the "Christ program." Studies also have shown that the percentage of believers in God in prisons is much higher than the percentage of believers in God outside prison. Furthermore, the percentage of believers in hell is higher inside prison than outside. However, this too must not be taken without serious qualifications, for it may suggest that a person's religious beliefs are simply not an important factor in helping him to stay out of prison. Rather, it seems more important not to have been born very poor, deprived, and in a setting where education is difficult to obtain. [15]

CHANGE THE HEART

Billy Graham holds that free will is *"a resolve, a sheer act of will within the sphere of an individual's power of choosing and deciding."* [16] As philosophers and psychologists have pointed out, the notion of free will is quite difficult to pin down. To describe free will in terms of "a sheer act of will" is of little help because it is not at all clear what is meant by "a sheer act of will." In fact, in reporting their religious experiences and conversions, many Christians have insisted that they were overwhelmed by divine grace and were transported by some force beyond their human power to resist. Paul claimed to have been overcome by a blinding light despite his own resistance to Christ. J. Harold Smith reported that once when he was about to hurl abusive language at his very godly sister, he suddenly found himself praying to God instead. Smith was "converted" before he knew what hit him. Evangelist Charles Finney insisted that his "baptism of the Holy Ghost" came upon him without any warning whatsoever. He had not been expecting the mighty "waves and waves of liquid love" to flood over him, and he had not even been thinking of such an experience for himself. He did not "resolve" (to use Graham's word) to receive this experience that so changed his life. In ordinary parlance, however, people do use the word resolve. A person will resolve to tell no more lies, or resolve to break the engagement with his fiancée because he thinks that their marrying would be a mistake. We all resolve. But what do we do in exerting free will? Free will has sometimes been defined as "uncaused cause." That is, while free will causes something, it is not itself caused by anything.

This is a dubious notion, however, as Evangelist Jonathan Edwards has shown. The person who resolves to do something seems to realize that a resolve does not appear out of the blue, as if it were uncaused. To get his resolution off the ground, so to speak, he must find some way to influence his own behavior at the appropriate time. To keep from lying, for example, he may ask a friend to be with him when he is most likely to lie. The friend will be an outside restraint on his tendency to lie.

Of course, it could be said that the liar's resolution made him (or caused him to) take his friend with him. But it is difficult to distinguish this resolution from the natural variables which moved him to ask his friend to accompany him. The fear of becoming a pathological liar influenced him to ask his friend to help him. Other causal factors influenced him. So free will becomes just words which stand for the fact that he acted because he wanted to and without doing so under duress or excessively aversive conditions. It seems fruitless to deny that he was moved or stimulated to act. But if he was moved by various causes, then there was no free will in the sense of "uncaused cause."

A psychologist might say that an individual's "resolve is . . . a response to a *stimulus from outside himself* which he did not prompt or cause or perhaps expect." However, some Arminian Evangelicals might reject this stimulus-response language because it suggests that free will is not, after all, an uncaused cause, but instead is a certain kind of response to variables outside the individual. In fact, the above quotation regarding the stimulus originating outside the individual was not taken from a psychology book. It came from one of Billy Graham's own articles.[17]

The problem of the hypothesis of the "inner man" or the "inner free will" or the "inner heart" is that it opens wide the door to a multiplication of "inner selves." The individual person becomes a zoo of inner selves, none of which is clearly named or designated. And the question of stimulating each of them becomes absurd when put into practice.

The notion of the inner free will is at best ambiguous. Because B. F. Skinner makes the mistake of confusing freedom with free will, he understandably wants to move "beyond freedom." Had he not confused these two notions, however, he might have been able to see that human freedom can be discussed rationally. But that is another story.[18]

The major point here regarding Billy Graham's doctrine of free will is that, although he leans heavily on it, the doctrine is found to be a fiction, perhaps a convenient fiction, but one that eventually fades under analysis. This, then, entails that the evil of man is not controlled by free will or willpower. Graham himself rightly criticizes the notion of pulling oneself up by one's bootstraps, which is what willpower seems to imply. Graham knows that outside factors are necessary. The crux of the matter, then, has to do with what those outside factors are. Are they natural? Or are they supernatural? That is, can they be traced and studied, or are they an absolute "mystery"?

Graham says that a "change of heart by Christ" is an absolute mystery. But we have discovered that it is not, because we can track down natural phenomena which Graham places under the heading "Christ." It turned out that the name Christ stands for a collection of many processes, individuals, and programs—like the name American Airlines. If American Airlines will take us where we want to go, we may be tempted to think of American Airlines as something independent of specific things, persons, procedures, and programs—e.g., the plane mechanics, the pilots, airline schedules, the stewardesses, the runways, the terminals, the baggage carts, and all the other natural phenomena lumped under the heading "American Airlines."

Hence, when Graham claims that original sin cannot be solved until individuals first come to Christ, he is in effect saying that they must first go through a good portion of the evangelical reform program of behavior modification before they can be successful in other reform programs. The first few steps in this evangelical program include a confession that one is going to hell unless he "accepts Christ," in the preliminary sense of making proper responses to such questions as "Do you realize that you are a sinner?" "Do you believe Jesus Christ is the Savior?" "Are you willing to commit your life to him?" "Will you simply pray, 'God have mercy on me, a sinner'?" These questions and requests may vary somewhat, but the gist of them is pretty much the same and the responses the same. In order to move people to make the proper responses, it is usually necessary to tell them that they will suffer overwhelming loss and punishment from God if the proper answers are not forthcoming. Great promises are also offered to encourage the proper responses. Both stick and carrot are utilized.

The evangelical reform program urges further activities, such as reading a Christian magazine regularly and attending a church where proper theological words and statements are frequently spoken. By associating with others in the reform program, the new convert may receive encouragement when he attempts to pray, or when he reads the Bible, or announces that he has given up going to all but G- and PG-rated movies. The verbal environment into which the new convert moves may have a steady impact on him over a period of time. In addition, his new friends and associates "in Christ" or "in the program" serve as a powerful social and linguistic environment controlling the individual more than he often realizes at first.

So when Billy Graham says that the inner heart must first be changed before society can be modified for the good, he seems to forget that he and other Evangelicals are very busy endeavoring to change the environment and society in their own particular way in order to change individuals. The only way to change a person is to change the variables affecting him; and, like every other reform program, Evangelicalism seeks to change human beings by changing the appropriate environment, whether inside or outside the skin, whether by medical attention or by appropriate instruction and care.

When Graham says that "society cannot be changed until we ourselves are changed," [19] he forgets that he himself is constantly working to change the variables of society in order to change individuals. The attempt to draw a hard and fast line between society and individuals is often misleading. In some ways it is useful to think of society as individuals responding to one another and with one another in numerous ways. To change certain aspects of society is to change certain variables which affect the way individuals respond to and with one another. And when these new responses come about, then we may say that the individual himself has changed—sometimes slightly, sometimes considerably.

Whether dealing with "original sin" or a number of more definite variables on the scene, the fact seems to be that the evangelical program of reform enjoys only limited success in changing large numbers of individuals beyond a certain point. One reason for this is probably the fact that the evangelical program, like any other, does not have complete control over the variables of society, the economy, the entertainment world, and education. To be sure, the evangelical program does enjoy some success in changing the lives of people for what Evangelicals regard as good. But this success is not enough to satisfy Graham. He longs to change the entire world. One reason for the establishment of "Christian colleges" is to provide an environment for Christians in which their total lives may be shaped even more thoroughly in the evangelical direction. And the desire of many Evangelicals to establish a large "Christian university" in Washington, D.C., sprang from the desire to utilize the university as a source of influence on governmental groups and individuals.

When the evangelical program does not appear to be living up to its advertisements regarding success in changing the behavior of Christians, there sometimes develops a tendency to speak more freely of spiritual renewal and change. This is often so obscure as to thwart rational communication. When the change becomes so inward as to be wholly beyond observation, it tends to be neither confirmed nor disconfirmed. Indeed, the "inward change" becomes so vague as to fade into meaninglessness. In some cases, inward or spiritual change refers primarily to those forms of observable behavior that are peculiar to Evangelicalism—e.g., professing the "fundamentals," talking freely of the Second Coming, singing "Amazing Grace," and offering one's personal testimony to others. Followers of other faiths may attempt to show themselves to be spiritual by manifesting different forms of behavior—e.g., abstaining from meat, avoiding women (or men), sleeping on something hard, humming a tune that is supposed to be the universal note, and all sorts of other special activities, depending on the requirements of the particular reform program.

CONCLUSION

It appears that changes in human attitudes, behavior, and beliefs do not result from an inflow of some ultimately mysterious, miraculous, supernatural force. Rather, they result from the impact of nature and human culture on the individual. Two temptations are strong at this point: (1) the temptation to think that nature is a very simple entity rather than the interplay of sometimes highly complex phenomena; and (2) the temptation to confuse complexity with something supernatural. Indeed, it is a mistake to assume either that simplification automatically means science or that complexity means something irreducibly mysterious and supernatural. To be sure, science seeks to simplify, but this may be done as a means of getting at the greater richness and diversity of nature. If the emphasis upon the mysterious is designed to call attention to the truth that science still has much to explain, well and good. But if the supernatural is supposed to be some realm that cannot be talked about in terms of discoverable natural variables, then hopeless conceptual confusion has set in.

Billy Graham's promises as to what Christ can do for people have been seen to be either a come-on speech or the initiation of a program of reform. The latter is, of course, the more responsible way. Much has been and could still be learned from the evangelical experiment in changing human behavior. We have already seen enough of it to know that it is not like a polio shot with a few infrequent boosters. Rather, it is a lifelong enterprise involving great effort in terms of organization, legislation, finances, a massive amount of literature, schools, armies of volunteer workers, churches, music, and numerous other significant variables. We have also observed counterproductive aspects to the evangelical experiment. The fact that so much time has to be spent in "reviving" and "rededicating" the participants in the evangelical program suggests that, far from being supernatural in origin, it is simply another rather human scheme with some very ingenious and useful methods, as well as some very stupid and fruitless ones.

Billy Graham rightly criticizes what he calls the "Marxist clichés." Like all of us, he is less aware of his own clichés. Graham seems to fail to note that sometimes Marxists keep the old terminology but pump new meanings into it. Of course, this has its limitation and is not meant to imply that the old meanings are wholly eliminated. Similarly, Evangelicalism sometimes pumps new meaning into old words. Another way of saying this, perhaps, is that the old words and meanings are sometimes seen in a broader—or at least a different—context. The point here is that the existing culture affects the way Evangelicalism understands itself and its mission in the world, just as Evangelicalism affects the rest of the culture in various ways. Very gradually the behavioral and social sciences are making their impact on Billy Graham's image of himself and his calling. This is not to criticize him but is simply to say that he who would reform the world must not be surprised to learn that, while he has indeed made an impact on it, the world has in turn exerted its impact on the reformer.

Chapter 12
BILLY GRAHAM AND SOUTHERN BAPTISTS

There are hundreds of Southern Baptist churches in Billy Graham's home state of North Carolina. Yet he placed his membership in a church more than a thousand miles from either his boyhood home town of Charlotte, North Carolina, or his present home near Asheville. Why should he join the large First (Southern) Baptist Church in Dallas, Texas (a church in which Ruth Graham would not be permitted to hold even an associate membership should she want to, for she has not been immersed)? Billy Graham has never lived in Dallas. He has lived near Chicago, in Florida, and in Tennessee. But not in Texas. Why did he choose this particular church in Texas above all others in the United States?

First, this church is "big time," and Billy Graham, as one crusade team member once said, likes to travel in style. The membership of the church is fifteen thousand. Second, and more important, the pastor of the church is W. A. Criswell, who is well known among Texas and Southern Baptists as an outspoken defender of the doctrinal "fundamentals," an enemy of theological liberalism, and a political ultraconservative.

Criswell's ultraconservative theological stance is suggested in the title of one of his books, *Why I Preach That the Bible Is Literally True*, which was published while he was serving a two-year term as president of the Southern Baptist Convention. Until about 1968 he believed in racial segregation, but after becoming convention president, he announced that he had been wrong in his conviction and was changing. For a man like Criswell, such a reversal was not easy to make, for he is not one to question overtly his own convictions. Of course, considerable pressure was exerted on him to exercise moral leadership. To some people this may not seem to be moral leadership, but it must not be forgotten that many staunch segregationists were in Criswell's own church when he was converted from his earlier social views. As president of the Southern Baptist Convention he also had to face some irate segregationists from the deep South.

Another rather drastic change came in Criswell's life at about the same time that his segregationist stance collapsed. Whereas he had previously said rather hard things about some of those living on welfare, in 1969 he publicly supported raising the welfare ceiling in Texas from $60 million to $80 million. Upon hearing the news, one press service reporter exclaimed in surprise, "Criswell for welfare? Man, that is a story!" [1] And indeed it was news. It was no insignificant thing, not in Dallas' First Baptist Church, where H. L. Hunt sits in the audience. A multimillionaire, Hunt stands politically considerably to the right of Barry Goldwater. On his radio program, "Life Line," Hunt employs an emotionless, computer-sounding voice to deliver what he calls "freedom talks," which are pretty much standard-line right-wing politics. For years Hunt has been a well-known member of Criswell's church. One would like to believe that on both the race issue and the welfare issue, it was Billy Graham who exerted constructive influence on his pastor, W. A. Criswell. It definitely was not H. L. Hunt.

Graham and his team are proud to say that Graham was one of the early religious leaders in the United States to oppose segregation. Billy Graham was ordained to preach in 1937, and it was sixteen years later, in 1953, that he resolved never to participate in a segregated crusade or rally if he had anything to say about it. This was his silent witness. After the climate of public opinion began to moderate somewhat, Graham's sermons gradually adopted an unequivocal condemnation of racism. Yet even today adultery seems to be more pointedly and thoroughly condemned than racism. Graham has made it clear that all adulterers will be transported to hell. He has not been so consistently forthright in his views on the destiny of racists. But in all fairness it must be said that Graham can personally understand the racist as an individual better than he can understand the adulterer. He has more compassion for the racist, it seems.

However, in his mind the worst sin seems to be, not adultery, murder, or racism, but not believing in the gospel which he and other Evangelicals preach. That was the fundamental sin of Stalin and Hitler. The second worst sin on Graham's list seems to be adultery. He has never been very clear about when killing in a war is a violation of the commandment against killing. He does not say that war is murder, a term which apparently is reserved for individual killings; collective killings are called battles, wars, and skirmishes.

On the welfare issue, it is very interesting to observe Graham's personal struggle. He does today support the poverty program, although he seems not to be clearly reconciled to it even in principle. What he would like to see is every individual becoming converted to evangelical Christianity, for then the welfare program would be unnecessary. Speaking in the greater Dallas area in September 1971, he was applauded by the audience because of his obvious attempt to belittle those on welfare. He commented that when he himself was a boy on the farm, "we killed our own rats. We did not call on the government to kill them for us." A large portion of his middle-class audience was conspicuously delighted with this comment. But the applauding audience on that day does not necessarily represent the citizens of Dallas and the surrounding areas. The welfare problem is complex, and not all criticisms of it are as unconstructive as was Graham's on that occasion. The rural side of Billy Graham's thinking does at times prevent his grasping some of the more elementary aspects of the practical problems of life in overcrowded slums and inner-city ghettos.

Southern Baptists are currently debating the question of the social side of the gospel they preach. Graham's ambivalence is in many ways a microcosm of the ambivalence of the Southern Baptist Convention as a whole. A Southern Baptist journal reports that in Houston in 1968 Graham said that "the church is going too far in the other direction in its emphasis on social action." Yet the same journal reports Graham as saying that if the Southern Baptist Convention has been lacking in any area, "it has been on social issues, especially the race issue." [2]

Billy Graham, W. A. Criswell, and the Southern Baptists in general want to give the persistent appearance of speaking authoritatively for

God, but behind the scenes many Southern Baptists reveal a certain sensitivity to challenges by "outside" points of view. In order for some Southern Baptist bookstores to obtain and sell copies of Joseph Fletcher's book *Moral Responsibility* it was necessary for the right hand to be ignorant of what the left hand was doing, for some leading Southern Baptists had already denounced Fletcher as a wolf in sheep's clothing—or at least in Episcopalian attire.[3]

W. A. Criswell praised highly the courage of his friend Paul M. Stevens, who sent telegrams to four United States senators—William Fulbright, George McGovern, Fred Harris, and Mike Mansfield. The telegrams read, in part: "If America's problems are too big for you, why don't you go to a country where the problems are your size?" In Fort Worth, which is about forty miles from Criswell's home, Paul Stevens serves as head of the Southern Baptist Convention's Radio and Television Commission. When asked to comment on Stevens' telegram, Criswell is reported as saying: "He's a very courageous and upright man. I admire his courage and his devotion to the efforts on the part of our President [Nixon] and those who support him for the cause of peace."[4]

The Reverend Melvin R. Carter, who is the assistant pastor of the Dallas church to which Graham belongs, protested the use of six high school biology textbooks which presented the theory of evolution as a fact rather than as a theory. This use of the word theory is admittedly slippery, for Carter would not admit that his view of the Bible as the infallible word of God is a theory. For him it is a fact. This whole issue of fact and theory, and related issues, ought to be dealt with carefully in the high schools, perhaps by offering the students an elective course in philosophy. But whether Carter would enthusiastically support such a course is open to question. He did not make it clear if he wanted the evangelical notion of six-day creation (in contrast to the idea of evolution) to be taught as a theory or as a fact.

Melvin Carter, together with six other protesters, presented opposition to four history textbooks alleged to be disrespectful of American heroes. The Texas State Textbook Committee gave Carter and his associates a hearing and also permitted a defense of the books to be made. One defense stated that the issue was not one of disrespect for heroes, but rather a question of what actually happened in the life of, say, George Washington. Did the cherry tree episode really occur, or is it a fictional tale? Although Carter's associates are not prepared to defend the infallibility of stories about American heroes, they nevertheless do not appreciate suggestions that some of the stories might not be true. Again, the issue has to do with the nature of a fact. An elective course in philosophy for high school students might be helpful on this issue too.

As indicated earlier, W. A. Criswell, Graham's pastor, himself a bold opponent of the theory of evolution, is also a tireless opponent of theological liberalism in any shape or form. For him, liberalism is any theological view that does not accept the view of the infallibility of the Bible and all the doctrinal "fundamentals." Dealing with the painful question of considerable change taking place within the Southern Baptist Convention itself, Criswell made a report to the executive committee of the eleven million Southern Baptists. In this report he said, "Somebody is changing; somebody is different. Is it I, or is it they [the liberals]? Are we going to give up the doctrines of faith we hold and be like other denominations?" He then invited those within the Southern Baptist Convention to leave if they did not agree with those doctrines which he considers essential to the SBC. "Leave and join another denomination," he urged.[5]

Billy Graham claims to be as strong a Baptist as he ever was, but he does not appear to want to become involved in this controversy regarding the defining characteristics of a "true Baptist." In Chattanooga, Tennessee, in the late 1950's a Southern Baptist ordination committee rejected a candidate for ordination into the ministry because he said he as a Baptist would take communion with a Presbyterian. Later the candidate was ordained by another Southern Baptist ordination committee and is now a highly respected community leader and pastor in a Baptist church in Georgia. Billy Graham himself could not pass this requirement of strict closed communion, for his wife is Presbyterian and he has taken communion with her.

Graham's pastor, disturbed that "the drift today is to be broad and inclusive and ecumenical," says that Baptists who want the Presbyterian form of church government should join the Presbyterians.[6] He holds to a greater number of inflexible ingredients than Graham does regarding what a "true Baptist" is. Interestingly, a form of Calvinism is very strongly expressed in the Abstract of Principles which must be signed by the faculty of the Southern Baptist Theological Seminary in Louisville. But W. A. Criswell does not insist that the seminary faculty members be Calvinists, for Criswell himself is much more attracted to

Arminianism than were the more Calvinistic founders of the seminary.

In contrast to this exclusivism, the success of Graham's crusades depends upon his team's willingness to work with a great variety of denominations. In fact, an ingenious stroke of public relations by the Billy Graham Evangelistic Association gives the impression that those churches which do not support the crusade in their area are themselves not very ecumenical in outlook. It is sometimes humorous to observe how ecumenical spokesmen who strongly disagree with Graham attempt to excuse themselves from cooperating in the crusade. Indeed, the Billy Graham Evangelistic Association actually uses this embarrassment to its own advantage. What the Graham crusade does, of course, is to place the shoe on the other foot. Those who have declined to join the ecumenical movement for doctrinal reasons have their counterpart in those church leaders who, because of equally legitimate differences in belief, decline to cooperate with Graham's crusades. What is interesting is the failure of each group sometimes to understand the "uncooperativeness" of those who decline to play ball in the other's league, so to speak. Honest disagreement on theological or moral principles is sometimes difficult to acknowledge, and there develops a tendency to think of these disagreements as disguised insincerity or bad faith.

The ultraconservative side of Billy Graham, as well as his remarkable political adaptability, emerged long enough for him to cooperate with Paul Harvey in a "massive Crusade of the Americas," a series of three color telecasts shown in forty cities of the United States. "The three telecasts, representing the largest single evangelistic thrust of the two-continent crusade, were produced by Southern Baptists' Radio and Television Commission, directed by Paul M. Stevens, in cooperation with the evangelism division of the Southern Baptist Home Mission Board." [7] During this same year, 1969, Harvey complained that TV was too liberal and that his own conservative voice was drowned out by liberal voices. Apparently imagining himself to be the sole voice, or bulwark, of TV conservatism, Harvey wrote in one of his newspaper articles: "Even now against the daily avalanche of news seen through the eyes of mostly liberal New Yorkers, my three-minutes-a-day editorial can hardly be considered 'equal time.' " [8] Harvey versus the liberals has a ring of Elijah versus the prophets of Baal. Elijah had to be informed that there were other prophets of Yahweh than himself.

As previously suggested, among Southern Baptists the question is stirring as to whether a conservative theology must necessarily be bound to a conservative political and social outlook. Does the one entail the other? The 1968 Southern Baptist Convention in Houston " 'blended conservative theology with liberal social action in a way that few had believed possible,' observed Editor John Roberts of the South Carolina Baptist Courier in a typical editorial comment." [9]

While the editor of the *Mississippi Baptist Record* steadfastly denied any compromises with liberalism at the Houston convention, the editor of the *Arkansas Baptist Newsmagazine*, Edward L. McDonald, saw things in a different light: "Southern Baptists with liberal, New Testament-oriented views on human relations will now find that they have a new source of moral support." [10] W. A. Criswell, in defending his uncharacteristic support of welfare, stated, "It's not being 'liberal' [theologically] . . . to minister to the needs of the hungry, the disabled, and the sick. It's just simply being Christian." [11]

For the June 1972 annual Southern Baptist Convention both Billy Graham and President Nixon were extended invitations to speak to the convention "messengers." However, according to the April 20, 1972, issue of the *Baptist and Reflector*, Nixon sent word that because of his Russian trip his plans would be too indefinite for him to commit himself to speak to the Convention. The Chairman of the SBC Committee on Order of Business denied that this decision had anything to do with the contention by some Southern Baptist leaders that President Nixon should not be invited during an election year. Billy Graham did accept the invitation and was gladly received by the "messengers." Philadelphia, home of the Liberty Bell, was thought to be the proper location for this particular annual meeting of the Southern Baptist Convention, whose 1972 convention theme was "Proclaim Liberty to All."

Fraught with tragic mistakes and heroic efforts, the body of Southern Baptists has in our time become characterized by both polarization of doctrine and tension regarding its special role in the world. Billy Graham reflects and embodies this tension in his relationship both to Southern Baptists in general and to the current issues which they must confront together. To be true to their heritage, to be a vital force in today's world, and to proclaim faithfully the gospel as they understand it—these are the strings upon which Graham and Southern Baptists seem destined to play in the coming years. And despite the enormous tensions that are emerging within, both Graham and the Southern Baptist Convention continue to increase in numbers and influence. Like Mormons and Seventh Day Adventists, they interpret their growth and influence as a sign of divine favor.

Chapter 13
BILLY GRAHAM'S
CHRISTIAN AMERICANISM

In 1954 Billy Graham was still riding the wave that carried Senator Joseph McCarthy to fame. However, far more discreet than the senator, the evangelist from North Carolina did not allow himself to designate specific clergymen as subversives. Rather, he simply utilized for his own revivalistic purposes the Red scare and general suspicion already generated by such men as Senator McCarthy and J. B. Matthews. The right-wing magazine *American Mercury* was noted for its reckless charges and innuendos directed at many American clergymen, and Matthews was one of its most popular writers, for he seemed never to grow weary of employing such legally loose terms as "pro-Communists," "Reds," and "pinks." In the August 1954 issue of *American Mercury*, Graham called for a revival that would eliminate "the rats and termites that are subversively endeavoring to weaken the defenses of this nation from within." The article was well within the spirit of the times, when many Americans were brewing doubts and suspicions about the patriotism of other Americans.[1]

Only nine months before Graham's 1954 article appeared in *American Mercury*, J. B. Matthews' widely published article "Red Infiltration of Theological Seminaries" had appeared in the same magazine. In that day Americans were only beginning to learn of the ruthlessness utilized by both the left wing and the right wing. Some ministers were naive about the Left, and some were naive about the Right. Graham was in the second category. In 1953, when McCarthyism was a powerful force in the land, Graham came to the defense of McCarthy's so-called investigating committee. Under the naive assumption that the primary effect of the investigating committee was to uncover Communist spies and the like, Graham praised the committee for "exposing the pinks, the lavenders, and the reds who have sought . . . in every subtle, under-cover way to aid and help the greatest enemy we have ever known—communism." [2] Shooting with a political shotgun and utilizing such highly charged and poorly defined words as pinks and Reds was in keeping with the temper of the times. And Billy Graham, far from being above it, was caught up in it and was able to profit from it in his attempts to come across as the prophet of the times.

But as in the days of the French Revolution, the orgy of wild charges became a fire out of control. It was not long before Graham found himself under suspicion and accused of aiding and abetting persons sympathetic to communism. Actually, Graham was much more sensitive to the changing times than were such men as Joseph McCarthy and Carl McIntyre. As the nation began to tire of the ordeal of turning upon itself with excessive suspicion and wholesale distrust, Graham's sermons began to include fewer references to widespread subversion, although he did maintain his close friendship with Richard Nixon, who had made one of his many charges of subversion stick. Both Nixon and Graham were gradually to make fewer references to internal subversion after 1955. Nixon had, of course, charged Adlai Stevenson and other key Democrats with being blind servants of Communist propaganda.

Fundamentalist preacher W. B. Riley was influential in starting the Conservative Baptist Association in opposition to what he took to be the modernism of the Northern Baptist Convention (which later became the American Baptist Convention). Riley served as the president of Northwestern Schools, which served as a center for teaching the "fundamentals." As early as December 1947, Graham had, at the insistence of Riley himself, become Riley's successor as president. But Graham steadfastly refused to yield to pressures to criticize specific liberals and modernists. Graham could see that this would get him in water over his head and that it would be a mistake. Also unwilling to resort to naming specifically the alleged subversives residing and working in the churches, he resigned the presidency in March 1952 in order to devote all his time to evangelism. Mentioning the names of clergymen and then specifying either their precise theological error or their subversive activity was never a part of the Billy Graham style.

During the time that Graham was warning in general of "internal subversion," he also was warning of an external threat—the coming nuclear holocaust. As early as 1951 he came into the political limelight and was quoting newspaper headlines and the book of Revelation as if he were reading off heaven's battle plans. He was preaching the coming of the wrath of God unless America "accepted Christ." Graham's own foreign policy was quite simple. Without God, America and the free world will very probably be destroyed. But if all us Americans would repent and turn to Christ, whom Graham was presenting as America's final hope, then "we would have divine intervention on our side." [3] There is little doubt that in the 1950's, Graham's version of Christianity included the doctrine that America was the land which God had prepared for a chosen people. Rugged individualism was considered to be the mark of both patriotism and spirituality.

However, Graham deserves to be interpreted in historical perspective. Many of the Puritans of the New World were convinced that they had been called of God to find a new land, just as the children of Israel had left Egypt to go to a land of milk and honey. The milk and honey of the New World may be summarized in one word—opportunity. But opportunity had to be rooted in something solid, and so God gave his new people a new land of their own. And many of the early settlers believed that the New World was their land, Indians to the contrary. One of Roger Williams' great "heresies" was not simply belief in religious liberty, but *disbelief* in the right of the "elect of God" to take land from Indians as if Indians were Edomites and Canaanites to be pushed aside by the chosen people.

Most Evangelicals and fundamentalists who make Americanism into a "fundamental" of the faith seem to have a passionate commitment to their version of the Jewish cause in Palestine. They seem to feel a deep kinship with the Palestinian Jews, who are taken to be God's chosen people in the ancient world, while Americans are taken to be God's chosen people in the New World. Arabs and Indians must simply recognize that "the land is ours. God gave us this land."

In his early years as an evangelist, Graham would extol the ideal of "rugged individualism" and "the American pioneer spirit." This was another version of his theme of Christian Stoicism, holding that the new individual can be fully human on the inside, regardless of his external circumstances. Ironically, rugged individualism was unable to grow in Europe. But if such individualism were indeed independent of circumstances, then it should have been able to develop anywhere, no matter what the circumstances. So why did its proponents have to leave their environment in Europe? Why did the pioneers have to move on further west? The answer seems to be that rugged individualism, like any other style of life, depends upon a special and favorable environment. It develops only under supporting circumstances and appropriate conditions. Indeed, much of the uniqueness of the American experiment lies in the fact that in a *new environment*—in a New World, no less—individuals can change their life-styles and can live in ways that the traditional circumstances of the Old World would not permit. Similarly, twentieth-century Jews move to Israel because they seek an environment that will reinforce and sustain the kind of life they want to lead. They understand profoundly how utterly crucial the external circumstances can be to the life of the individual.

The phrase rugged individualism is no longer as popular in the United States as it once was. Billy Graham now rarely uses it, although his quasi Stoicism and folk existentialism may be seen as the old motif in modern dress. Gradually the notion of rugged individualism seems to be giving way to the notion of a silent majority. Some of the sons and daughters of rugged individualists now form a large bloc within America and see themselves as the very backbone of true and genuine Americanism. In them, Christian Americanism is thought to be the heir of this great new land of Zion. They are the Spirit of '76 embodied, the American Way embodied in flesh and blood and automobiles. But recently this sort of Americanism has grown defensive. The old missionary zeal has cooled. The Lord God of hosts has not given swift and sure victory over the powers of evil in Vietnam, and sometimes it becomes difficult to draw the line between the forces of God and the forces of evil. Furthermore, the American nation as a whole seems hesitant to succumb to another seizure of McCarthyism. Indeed, although the silent majority itself is more myth than reality, it does symbolize a new tone of nervous caution. Spiro Agnew, far from silent, has not yet been able to do with the silent majority what Joseph McCarthy did with his followers.

The silent majority symbolizes the lack of confidence of some Americans to speak out as boldly as earlier Americans once did. Woodrow Wilson regarded America as the savior of the world. His was a positive missionary spirit, and World War I was a crusade. In 1957 Graham warned that unless America somehow opposed "the steel of Godless communism" in the captured nations behind the iron curtain, "a day of reckoning is coming" to America. He said, "We cannot ignore the oppressed, suffering and helpless peoples behind the Iron Curtain without paying for it at the judgment of God." [4]

In World War II America's positive missionary spirit was less evident than in the previous war, but because the Nazis were viewed as clearly vile and demonic, Americans could see their own role as the negative but necessary one of destroying this threat to the entire world.[5] When still another evil dragon—communism—appeared on the scene in Russia and China and Korea, Christian Americanism became profoundly confused and frustrated. How could God allow another demonic monster to rise up so quickly after the walls of Berlin had fallen? Soon Christian Americanism, with its simplistic moralism, was having to face the terrible thought that perhaps something was greatly wrong inside America itself! The thunderbolt struck and started a wildfire throughout the land. Just as ancient Israel had imagined itself to be excessively evil when it was not always successful in its conflicts with foreign nations, so Christian Americanism began to search throughout the land for some group of Achans who would confess to their subversive sin and thus restore God's favor to America.

In the book of Joshua the story of the fall of the walls of Jericho is told. The faith of the people of Israel is dramatically vindicated by victory in battle. This is told in chapter 6 of Joshua. But chapter 7 tells us the story of the formerly victorious sons of Israel retreating from the Amorites. The defeat of a small portion of the Israelite army becomes utterly demoralizing. "And the hearts of the people melted, and became as water (Josh. 7:5)." Joshua, the leader, prays immediately to God and complains not only that the band of soldiers of Israel has suffered humiliation at the Battle of Ai, but that the prestige of Israel has been damaged among the "Canaanites and all the inhabitants of the land." Joshua then reminds the Lord that if Israel's name suffers defeat, the Lord's name will suffer too. Joshua boldly puts the question to the Lord: "What wilt thou do for thy great name (Josh. 7:9)?"

In the 1950's Billy Graham seemed to have understood himself to be something of a Joshua of Christian Americanism. He, like Joshua, was worried that the prestige of his nation would sink and that the good name and cause of God would sink with it. According to the ancient story, Joshua, informed that sin moves among the chosen people, begins to search for the source of the sin. Each family is brought before Joshua for examination until finally Achan stands before him. Somehow Joshua discovers that Achan is the guilty person and demands that he confess his sin. Achan is then crushed by stones and subsequently burned with fire. His family suffers the same fate; and "then the Lord turned from his burning anger (Josh. 7:26)." Whereupon Joshua urged his "fighting men" to resume their battle with the soldiers of Ai and God promises them that "you shall do to Ai and its king as you did to Jericho and its king (Josh. 8:2)." In short, now that they have rid the nation of the sinner who was a security risk, God will intervene for the Israelites.

Billy Graham seemed to be working on the same formula. God had given America victory over the British, the French, the Mexicans, and even over the Germans twice in one century. But in Korea, things began to look very bad. Something had gone wrong. Sin must be moving in the camp. Subversion in the land. Sometimes regarding sin and subversion as the same phenomenon, Billy Graham sought to persuade every Achan in America to confess his sin. America's prestige was at stake, and so was God's. Subversion of America was in Graham's mind a sin against God, and sometimes he committed the converse fallacy of thinking of sin (as defined by his evangelical faith) as subversion.

In the past few years Graham has spoken less sweepingly about the Russians, Chinese, and Southeast Asian Communists. And his early leanings toward sending American power into Southeast Asia have given way to a noncommittal stance. Indeed, on *The Dick Cavett Show* on May 7, 1971, he said that if the war in Asia continues, he himself may have to speak out on the matter within six months or a year. Doubtless, it would have been asking too much if someone had requested him to take a firm stand on the matter before election day of 1972.

What is important to see here is that Graham has begun to breathe the air of self-doubt in regard to international matters. Ironically, some of those who favored an immediate pullout from Vietnam borrowed Graham's simplistic moralism and then left the evangelist stranded high and dry. They outmoralized one of America's all-time moralizers.

These new moralizers did not argue that the war was impractical or that it was in fact already lost; rather, they sometimes portrayed America as the Philistine giant. Ho Chi Minh was glamorized as a youthful David clothed, not in Saul's elaborate armor, but in the simple and righteous cause of liberation.

The so-called silent majority grew more and more silent on this particular war as one of its spokesmen, Billy Graham, showed that he could no longer moralize about it. Christian Americanism suddenly discovered itself to be on the other end of the moralistic stick when some of its own rhetoric blew back in its face. The shoe was on the other foot. Christian Americanism's gradual willingness to entertain the thought of pulling American troops out of Asia came, not from a new moral conversion, but from a gradual realization that Asia is not simply a theater of moral display, after all.

The clowns and exhibitionists of the New Left, purporting to make an issue of the war, were mere noise in the background. What eventually exposed the simplistic moralism of Christian Americanism was the cold fact that America's myth of omnipotence had vanished before her eyes. Even William F. Buckley, despite his ability to talk a fog over the obvious, could detect that something had happened. Soon Paul Harvey began to take up the argument that continuing the war was simply impractical and wasteful.

But Billy Graham, always reading the public's mood, has now found a new war and a new enemy, a multiheaded monster—crime in the streets, dope in the schools, sex everywhere, and so on. Adultery is condemned as a national security risk, and only "conversion to Christ" can save America from these new enemies that are not altogether new after all. Once again, he has found a disease for which to sell his "cure."

Only slowly is the United States readjusting to a revised Christian Americanism. According to the older version, on the international scene America was almost omnipotent, omniscient, and omnipresent. But brute empirical facts have cracked the very base of this structure of idolatry. The Korean and Vietnam wars have disposed of the dogma of America's omnipotence. When "America lost China to the Communists," the assumption was that to a great degree America possessed the power to control the Chinese government. When the CIA fell on its face at the Bay of Pigs, the doctrine of American omniscience began to wobble. And now serious talk of reducing America's presence around the globe is heard, for America may not really be as all-pervasive as she once was thought to be. The United States is now seen to be finite; her omnipresence has been cut back. Doubtless the excitement of the moon landing was in part born of the old-time faith in America's omnipresence, a resurgence of Christian Americanism, with the reading of scripture from outer space. For some, however, the lunar trip was partly another expression of the lunacy of a nation that too easily identifies itself with God's universal presence and eternal message. Graham, "God's man with God's message," wanted to make it true that America is God's people with God's message.

But Graham is changing too, slowly but surely. Whereas in 1954 he recommended that Germany be given "the latest and most powerful weapons as [a] deterrent to war," [6] today he is less prone to make specific recommendations regarding international matters. Senator McCarthy's star fell in December 1954, and within a year after that event Graham was questioning the faith that the American version of democracy could be exported around the globe. This does not mean, however, that he thinks that his version of religion should no longer be exported as the exact prescription for every port and village in the world. In fact, he insists that the gospel that he preaches is the *only* hope for the entire globe—now.

It might be suggested that if Graham has cooled in his eagerness to transport the American version of democracy around the globe, then perhaps he could entertain the notion that capitalism is not the ideal economic system for every nation in the world. However, this suggestion goes beyond Dr. Graham's explicit statements. Indeed, it may even be that eventually he would like to see the "pagan nations" adopt capitalism and Western democracy. But apparently they cannot do this until first they "accept Christ." For Graham, it is a mistake to try "to westernize them when they are not prepared for it." [7]

Understanding Billy Graham in greater depth and in historical perspective may help Americans to understand themselves better. Those who like to think of this nation as sick when it does not measure up to its high ideals are sometimes not too far removed from Graham when he hunts for "internal subversion" and "sin within the nation." The popular use of the word sickness to describe an entire nation combines a medical and a theological expression. The danger is that it suggests the need for drastic surgery, with somebody or some group as the lamb on the altar.

Sometimes this surgery is brought off vicariously and mythically. Abraham Lincoln died on Good Friday and, in the minds of many, symbolically atoned for the nation's great sin-sickness. Martin Luther King and the Kennedys are more recent atonements.[8] And Billy Graham is reported by a Southern Baptist to have said in 1968, "If being shot or killed would glorify God, I'll be glad to go." According to the reporter, Graham "added that he almost hoped that he would have an opportunity to suffer for the sake of the Gospel." [9]

Of course this is mythology but sometimes mythology includes very profound ritualization and constructive forms of behavior. However, the lust for saviors and atonement-makers is to a great extent the result of the work of peddlers of guilt and of induced soul-sickness. They peddle it because they want to sell their "miracle drug"—except that there is no conspicuous miracle drug, cure-all, or spiritual snake oil. There seems to be only the possibility of finite improvements and temporary reforms which hold off a measure of hunger, misunderstanding, and tragedy for only a while, until better finite reforms come along or until death levies its heavy tax.

Americans may be going through the process of learning how to lose as a nation in certain areas in order to win more effectively in areas where winning is possible and important. America's "missionary spirit" has both a useful and a harmful side. It has generated hope—and great energy—in the face of overwhelming obstacles. But it has tortured and tormented itself when it has failed to live up to its rather grandiose self-image. The contemporary temptation to wallow in cynicism, defeatism, and resentfulness may perhaps expend itself and begin to develop into a more realistic self-image or set of goals common to great numbers of Americans.

Understandably, it is painfully difficult for a nation, believing in the 1960's that it could exercise precise and far-reaching influence around the globe, to have to face in the 1970's such mundane home problems as smog control and school busing questions. A backlash of defeatism could have been predicted, for a nation who once saw its scope as grandiose in scale needs time and patience to adjust to a more balanced picture of itself. Graham's current Second Coming preaching seems to be a kind of philosophy of resentment which may be stated as follows: If we cannot have great and powerful global influence, then what is the point of going on? Let the Second Coming come. To hell—or to heaven—with it all!

The scientific spirit of limited experimentation, rather than grand cure-alls or sensational cop-outs, needs to be blended with the chastened missionary spirit of the American dream. The call for reforms and improvements would then be, not a call to go forth into the world to make more outlandish promises, but rather a call to make good some of the more realistic and down-to-earth promises. One reason that people find life meaningless is that they have been brought up to think that a meaningful life is impossible unless it is grandiose and cosmic in scope. The simple joys of music, friends, family, silence, and thousands of other finite modes of human experience need to be appreciated more fully, lest they be sacrificed to some cosmic cause that devours all finite forms of life as if they were nothing.

The thought that men die and perhaps may never see life again is no cheerful thought. But the fact of death for everyone does not make the sunset less beautiful, love between man and woman less joyful, or the play of children and the enjoyed work of men and women less real. Graham says that his own life would be meaningless unless he were an evangelical Christian. This is probably true for him. But it need not—and probably cannot—be true for most people. There are other ways, and perhaps a new version of the almost incurable missionary spirit of Americans can be transformed into a disciplined passion for freedom in the sense of permitting greater toleration of certain life-styles, as well as a more thoroughgoing and systematic analysis of their effects. This does not mean absolute toleration, of course, for some things would, if tolerated, destroy great areas of human freedom.

There is, however, probably more room for toleration of the personal convictions and styles of other people than Billy Graham has imagined. This increased toleration need not bring about the end of morality, any more than the emergence of religious toleration in America has destroyed religion. In fact, an increase of tolerance in some directions demands strict regulations. The practical issue is not simply freedom versus controls. Rather, it is a question of the *kind* of freedom and the *kind* of controls we shall have. For example, if some persons for some reason want to receive nude pictures through the mail, while other people do not, then strict regulations would be essential in order to protect the rights of each group. Those who want them should be allowed by law to receive them, while strict laws should prevent firms and individuals from sending this unsolicited mail to those who do not want it. Infringement upon the rights of either group and exploitation of either is unnecessary for a peaceful society. And of course this raises the more far-reaching question of whether there ought to be laws protecting people from unsolicited "junk mail" of all varieties. Graham has had comparatively little to say about the power of advertisements to shape human morality—a complex and mundane problem.

With greater toleration of life-styles, the possibility of a more sensitive and scientific approach to things that greatly matter to men, women, and children will perhaps come into being. And it is possible that some newly clarified common values could emerge through this experiment in new areas of toleration. Americans have a challenge to learn to regard the life-styles of other individuals, communities, and groups as finite experiments in human happiness. When an experiment appears to fail, then the broader society could both learn from the mistakes of the experiment and also accept those persons who have failed. This acceptance would not necessarily be approval but rather a way of helping people to find a new opportunity to start another life-style. This is where religious conversion and koinonia could be of great benefit to people; for when a person has lost his life-style, then *he* is lost until he can find a new way of life. Billy Graham has helped many people to find a new way of life. In a nation that is deeply and incurably religious, he embodies the religious life for many people. At the same time, other men and women have helped former evangelical Christians to find a new way of life. Whether there is one way of life on earth for everyone remains to be seen; it is not an easy matter to settle. It may even be a pseudoproblem. Perhaps it is the ambiguous reality of human life not to be able to settle it. Even if there were only one way, it would tend inevitably to be influenced and modified by its surroundings.

In some respects the Chinese version of communism provides the nearest thing to achieving this goal of one way only. But it has been purchased at an astronomical price, and it does not seem to be greatly attractive to outsiders. Doubtless, the puritanical Chinese Communists think of toleration and pluralism as decadent. But some of us "outsiders" think of greater toleration as simply a way of keeping a few other options alive, just in case the old ones lose their power to satisfy emotionally, morally, or intellectually. In short, men are finite creatures who on various occasions have made serious mistakes even when quoting Science, History, God, or the People. And that is why men do well to keep open a few options just in case they need to appropriate them. If their boat begins to sink, they will be fortunate if they have another boat or two nearby in which to step when the old one has ceased to function. True, there are many supersalesmen offering ships that last for eternity. But that is a very big promise, and the sea of time and experience is unrelenting.

If a ship must keep having old lumber and old parts replaced with new ones, the question eventually arises as to whether it is the same ship afloat or a new one. Christianity is the name sometimes given to a way of life that has kept afloat for many years, perhaps because it has disposed of some of its worn-out pieces and replaced them with newer ones. To what extent it is the same original Christianity is a tricky question.

Perhaps the more important question has to do with knowing how ships keep afloat. Apparently, many ships under many flags seem to manage reasonably well. Whether they like to admit it or not, the crew of each ship seems to be forced to learn from the others some of the techniques and points of keeping afloat. As the earlier chapter on "The Natural and the Supernatural" suggested, Billy Graham has learned that if his way is to avoid sinking, he must borrow from others. And the success that Billy Graham has had in his follow-up programs and in broader institutionalized religion doubtless provides considerable material for instructing others who also wish to keep their ships afloat. If the crews can keep from making literal war on one another, then perhaps the exchange of ideas, insights, criticisms, experiments, programs, and common ideals can be more successfully carried on.

Like the politician, the prophet seems reluctant to admit changing his mind on substantial matters. The politician, on the one hand, is perhaps fearful that his opponent will make him look weak if he admits to having modified his view too greatly. The prophet, on the other hand, stands in the peculiar position of thinking that he is either directly quoting God or accurately paraphrasing divine thoughts. It is quite difficult for the prophet to admit even to himself that his thinking is changing on essential matters, for he does not want to believe that he sometimes misquotes God or does not get the divine message straight.

Those closely associated with Dr. Graham know him to have a very flexible and receptive mind regarding new methods and means of getting his message across more effectively. There is no need to resort to the hypothesis of supernatural variables to explain Graham's success. But neither is it wise to reduce his success to a mere handful of variables. Rather a great number of them, including centuries of cumulative social processes, have contributed to the success of the Billy Graham Evangelistic Crusades. His flexibility of mind regarding changing methods and media is one of those variables accounting for his success.

But does this mean that he is responsive to a substantive change in his theology? Graham does not claim to be flexible at this point. But as indicated in the chapter on "The Faith and the World," changes in the cultural environment do sometimes favor certain variations within the theological structure itself. For example, Billy Graham's Christian Americanism in the 1970's is not altogether what it was in the 1950's. Cultural variations have come about, and Graham's thinking has responded to some of them. In June 1972 his pastor, addressing the Women's Missionary Union Conference of the Southern Baptist Convention, stated, "The whole world is divided into two camps—the East and the West, the slave and the free." He went on to explain that the division is really between Christianity and communism. It is doubtful that today Billy Graham could make such a simplistic statement. He would not want to identify Christianity with the West, or communism with the East. Nor would he want to identify freedom exclusively with the West. Even for Billy Graham the world today is seen to be more complex than Criswell's apocalyptic language indicates.

It would, however, be a mistake to say that Graham and his team periodically sit down and coolly figure out exactly which new movements in the culture will have to be appropriated in order to keep the crusades going full steam ahead. Rather Graham's own consciousness becomes heightened to problems of, say, racism, pollution, poverty, and even the excesses of nationalism by simply living in and reading about his own culture. Graham's passion to put his message across effectively has doubtless contributed greatly to his becoming more sensitive to his social and cultural environment. But this does not entail that Dr. Graham's expanding social consciousness is somehow insincere. Many public figures have been accused of hopping on various bandwagons in order to promote their original cause. Whatever the truth is on this question of motives, it does not nullify the plain fact that once the new cause is confronted, it often evokes new responses and new commitments from individuals.

Sometimes exposed contradictions in our own outlook will bring it to the brink of revision or modification. In his July 4, 1970 sermon entitled "Honor America" Dr. Graham criticized those who "have knocked our courts." When it dawns on the evangelist that he has, for better or worse, contributed to this practice of "knocking" courts—by himself severely denouncing some of their decisions—then he will doubtless have to either reduce his criticism of the courts or accept the conclusion that criticizing the courts may not be always a terrible thing in a vital country such as the United States.

Graham will doubtless continue to increase in certain areas of social awareness. But it is unlikely that he will surrender his image of himself as a special prophet of the Almighty. Graham likes too much the feeling of "speaking with authority." It was once said of Prime Minister Gladstone that he always had a card up his sleeve. And he was sure that God had placed it there for him to use for promoting divine causes. Graham has a similar "God consciousness" which he must somehow adjust to the ebb and flow of his social consciousness.

Notes

Preface

1. Quoted in Alan Levy, *God Bless You Real Good* (New York: Essandess Special Edition, Simon & Schuster, 1967), pp. 54f. Copyright © 1967 Simon & Schuster, Inc. Used by permission.
2. Ibid.
3. Quoted in Glenn Daniels, *Billy Graham: The Man Who Walks with God* (New York: Warner Paperback Library, 1961), p. 27. Used by permission.
4. See Levy, *God Bless You Real Good*, p. 56.
5. Billy Graham, *World Aflame* (New York: Pocket Books, Inc., 1966), pp. 116f.
6. See "Billy Graham: The Man at Home—*Post* Interview," *Saturday Evening Post* (Spring 1972), p. 44.
7. See Sherwood E. Wirt, "The Faith of Dwight D. Eisenhower," *Great Readings from "Decision,"* ed. Sherwood E. Wirt and Marvin R. Sanders (Minneapolis: World Wide Publications, 1970), pp. 347–55. This article appeared earlier in *Decision* (Aug. 1965) and is based on an interview which Wirt had with President Eisenhower.

Chapter 1: Christ, Law, and Order

1. *The Quotable Billy Graham,* ed. Cort R. Flint (Anderson, S. C.: Droke House, 1967), p. 138. Used by permission.
2. Ibid., p. 117.
3. See ibid., p. 170.
4. Billy Graham, "Whither Bound," *America's Hour of Decision* (Wheaton, Ill.: Van Kampen Press, 1951), p. 140.
5. Carl F. H. Henry, "The Marvel of the Rose Bowl," ibid., p. 111.
6. *The Quotable Billy Graham*, p. 169.

7. Ibid., pp. 211f.

8. Graham, "Whither Bound," p. 139.

9. In his book *Without Marx or Jesus* (New York: Doubleday, 1971), the French writer Jean-François Revel argues that the United States is the spearhead of a global revolution in freedom that surpasses both communism and Christianity.

10. See Billy Graham, "Youth, Sex and the Bible," *Great Readings from "Decision,"* ed. Sherwood E. Wirt and Marvin R. Sanders (Minneapolis: World Wide Publications, 1970), p. 32. This sermon appeared earlier in *Decision* (June 1968). See also *The Quotable Billy Graham*, pp. 103–5, 182.

11. Ibid., p. 71; Billy Graham, "The Joys of Family Life," *Good Housekeeping* (Oct. 1969), p. 202; *Decision* (Feb. 1970), p. 12.

12. See *The Quotable Billy Graham*, pp. 101f.

13. Ibid., p. 135.

14. Ibid., p. 62.

15. Ibid.

16. Cf. Bernard Steinzor, *When Parents Divorce: A New Approach to New Relationships* (New York: Pantheon, 1969), p. 239; Morton Hunt, *The World of the Formerly Married* (New York: McGraw-Hill, 1966), p. 293.

17. See Billy Graham, *World Aflame* (New York: Pocket Books, Inc., 1966), pp. 122–23.

18. See William Graham Cole, *Sex in Christianity and Psychoanalysis* (New York: Oxford University Press, 1966), pp. 126–29.

19. See Billy Graham, "The Credibility Gap," *Decision* (Oct. 1971), p. 12.

20. See "Clergy and Congressmen Unite to Fight 'Prayer Amendment,'" *Baptist and Reflector: News-Journal of the Tennessee Baptist Convention* (Oct. 14, 1971), p. 3.

21. *The Quotable Billy Graham*, p. 176.

22. *Baptist and Reflector* (Oct. 14, 1971), p. 3.

23. Quotations and the report are found in *Baptist and Reflector* (Feb. 19, 1970), p. 16.

24. See *The Quotable Billy Graham*, p. 191.

25. See Billy Graham, *The Jesus Generation* (Grand Rapids, Mich.: Zondervan, 1971), p. 170.

26. Richard Owen, "Freedom in Christ," *Baptist and Reflector* (Sept. 26, 1968), p. 4.

27. Ibid.

28. See J. E. Barnhart, "The Question of 'True' Freedom," *Harvard Theological Review* (Spring 1972).

29. See "Billy Graham: The Man at Home—*Post* Interview," *Saturday Evening Post* (Spring 1972), p. 106.

30. Ibid. Reprinted with permission from *The Saturday Evening Post*, © 1972, The Curtis Publishing Company.

31. See "Religious Leaders Ask Congress to Oppose 'Prayer Amendment,'" *Baptist and Reflector* (Sept. 30, 1971), p. 7.

32. See Billy Graham, "Teen-age Vandalism" (Sermon, 1958), p. 12.

33. See John Coyne, "The Voucher System," *Intellectual Digest* (Nov. 1971), pp. 26–27. The original article appeared in *National Review* (March 23, 1971). Evangelical philosopher Nicholas Wolterstorff has carefully outlined some of the options available to those concerned with the question of the neutrality and impartiality of the public schools regarding religion. See his article "Neutrality and Impartiality," *Religion and Public Education*, ed. Theodore Sizer (Boston: Houghton Mifflin Co., 1967), pp. 3–21. Cf. Robert Michaelson, *Piety in Public Schools* (New York: Macmillan, 1970).

34. See Erling Jorstad, *The Politics of Doomsday: Fundamentalists of the Far Right* (Nashville: Abingdon Press, 1970), p. 52.

35. See Ronald E. Osborn, *The Spirit of American Christianity* (New York: Harper & Brothers, 1968), p. 213.

36. "Benjamin Franklin, Articles of Belief and Arts of Religion," *The Development of American Philosophy: A Book of Readings*, 2d ed., ed. Walter G. Muelder, Laurence Sears, and Ann V. Schlabach (Boston: Houghton Mifflin Co., 1960), pp. 67–68.

37. Letter from Franklin to Thomas Paine, ibid., p. 70.

38. See Thomas Paine, "The Age of Reason," ibid., pp. 93–101.

39. See E. S. Gaustad, *A Religious History of America* (New York: Harper & Row, 1966), p. 124.

40. See Jefferson's April 21, 1803, letter to Benjamin Rush, Muelder et al., *The Development of American Philosophy*, pp. 76–77.

41. See Jefferson's April 11, 1823, letter to John Adams, ibid., p. 78.

42. See "Billy Graham: The U.S. Needs 'Spiritual Bath,'" *Baptist and Reflector* (June 5, 1969), p. 15.

43. Ibid.

44. See Sherwood E. Wirt and Marvin R. Sanders, eds. (Minneapolis: World Wide Publications, 1970), pp. 357–60. The preface to this book is written by Billy Graham. Nixon's article appeared in *Decision* (Nov. 1962) during the time he was a candidate for the governorship of California.

45. Quoted in the *Dallas Morning News* (Sept. 30, 1968), p. 5A. Used by permission of United Press International.

46. Ibid.

47. *Baptist and Reflector* (Aug. 27, 1971), p. 3.

48. "Billy Graham: The Man at Home," p. 106.

Chapter 2: The Mountain That Lies to the South

1. Gordon H. Clark, "Apologetics," *Contemporary Evangelical Thought*, ed. Carl F. H. Henry (Great Neck, N. Y.: Channel Press, 1957), p. 137; idem, "Reply to Roger Nicole," *The Philosophy of Gordon H. Clark: A Festschrift*, ed. Ronald Nash (Nutley, N. J.: Presbyterian and Reformed Publishing Co., 1968), p. 484.

2. Stanley High, *Billy Graham: The Personal Story of the Man, His Message,*

and His Mission (New York: McGraw-Hill, 1956), p. 101. Used by permission of Walter F. Bennett & Co.

3. Quoted in Alan Levy, *God Bless You Real Good* (New York: Essandess Special Edition, Simon & Schuster, 1967), p. 58. Copyright © 1967 Simon & Schuster, Inc. Used by permission.

4. Billy Graham, *World Aflame* (New York: Pocket Books, Inc., 1966), p. xv.

5. Karl Popper, *Conjectures and Refutations* (4th rev. ed.; London: Routledge & Kegan Paul Ltd., 1972; New York: Basic Books, 1963), p. 35.

6. See Billy Graham, "How Wise Is Man?," *Decision* (Feb. 1968), p. 1.

7. John J. Hurt, "Southern Baptist Presence Felt," *Baptist Standard* (July 29, 1970), p. 4.

8. Taken from *The Jesus Generation* by Billy Graham (Grand Rapids, Mich.: Zondervan, 1971), p. 177. Copyright © 1971, by Billy Graham. Used by permission.

Chapter 3: The Faith and the World

1. Cf. Howard E. Kershner, *God, Gold and Government* (Englewood Cliffs, N. J.: Prentice-Hall, 1957); R. Carroll, *Jesus: A Capitalist* (sold by the American Council of Christian Churches); Eric Fromm, *Psychoanalysis and Religion* (New Haven, Conn.: Yale University Press, 1950); M. B. Rickitt, *Maurice to Temple: A Century of the Social Movement* (London: Faber and Faber, 1947).

2. See Billy Graham, *World Aflame* (New York: Pocket Books, Inc., 1966), p. 155.

3. *The New York Times*, Mar. 5, 1960, p. 4. © 1960 by The New York Times Company. Reprinted by permission of The New York Times Company and the Associated Press.

4. See Charles S. Braden, *Christian Science Today: Power, Policy, Practice* (Dallas: Southern Methodist University Press, 1958).

5. Billy Graham, *My Answer* (New York: Pocket Books, Inc., 1967), p. 126. © 1960 by Billy Graham; © 1954, 1955, 1956, 1957, 1958, 1959, 1960 by Chicago Tribune-N.Y. News Syndicate, Inc. Reprinted through the courtesy of the Chicago Tribune-New York News Syndicate, Inc.

6. Ibid., p. 211.

7. *The Quotable Billy Graham*, ed. Cort R. Flint (Anderson, S. C.: Droke House, 1967), p. 157. Used by permission.

8. Ibid., pp. 158f.

9. Carl G. Jung, *Man in Search of a Soul* (New York: Harcourt Brace Jovanovich, 1933), p. 284.

10. *The Quotable Billy Graham*, p. 174.

11. Ibid., p. 147.

12. Eleanor Zelliot, "Buddhism and Politics in Maharashtra," *South Asian Politics and Religion*, ed. Donald E. Smith (Princeton: Princeton University Press, 1966), p. 191.

13. Borrowing material from what is known as "the Baptist Press," the *Baptist and Reflector: News-Journal of the Tennessee Baptist Convention* began featur-

ing a series of articles under the general heading "The Jesus Movement." The third in the series (July 29, 1971) deals with the glossalia phenomenon, which has always made Southern Baptists a bit nervous. Like most of his fellow Southern Baptists, Graham has not encouraged spontaneous, unritualized emotional releases in his revivals or crusades. At the Tuett Memorial (Southern) Baptist Church in Long Beach, California, the pastor stopped the first advocates of glossalia among the youths but permitted arm-waving, body-swaying, and clapping.

14. N. H. Ridderbos, *Is There a Conflict Between Genesis I and Natural Science?* (Grand Rapids, Mich.: Eerdmans, 1957), p. 46.

15. Ibid., p. 71.

16. For an important, readable, low-key treatment of the impact of analytic philosophy on biblical exegesis, see John Wilson, *Language and Christian Belief* (London: Macmillan, 1958).

17. See C. E. M. Hansel, *ESP: A Scientific Evaluation* (New York: Charles Scribner's Sons, 1966).

18. "Billy Graham: The Man at Home—*Post* Interview," *The Saturday Evening Post* (Spring 1972), p. 106. Reprinted with permission from *The Saturday Evening Post,* © 1972, The Curtis Publishing Company.

19. See *Decision* (Jan. 1970), p. 13.

20. *The Quotable Billy Graham,* p. 121.

21. Quoted in Vivian Peters, "Mrs. Billy Graham: Crusader's Wife," *Parade, Dallas Times Herald* (Mar. 8, 1970), p. 7; cf. Billy Graham, "The Joys of Family Life," *Good Housekeeping* (Oct. 1969), p. 202.

22. See Dagmar Freuchen, ed., *Peter Freuchen's Book of the Eskimos* (New York: World Publishing Co., 1961), chapter 4.

Chapter 4: The Quick Cure and the Hard Sell

1. For a carefully reasoned thesis that time has become a scarce resource for the affluent and that leisure for them is a fiction, see Staffan B. Linden, *The Harried Leisure Class* (New York: Columbia University Press, 1970).

2. Quoted from "New Crusade in Europe," a copyrighted interview with Billy Graham, *U.S. News & World Report* (Aug. 27, 1954), p. 87.

3. See "Sermons of the Month," published by the Billy Graham Evangelistic Association, Minneapolis, Minnesota, 1951, 1953.

4. *The Quotable Billy Graham,* ed. Cort R. Flint (Anderson, S. C.: Droke House, 1967), p. 62 (italics added). Used by permission.

5. *This Week Magazine* (Apr. 21, 1957), p. 12.

6. Billy Graham, "Will God Spare America?," *America's Hour of Decision* (Wheaton, Ill.: Van Kampen Press, 1951), pp. 125–26.

Chapter 5: The Humble and Moral Man

1. See John Murray, "The Weak and the Strong," *Westminster Theological Journal* 12 (May 1950): pp. 149–50.

2. Sherwood Wirt, *The Social Conscience of the Evangelical* (New York: Harper & Row, 1968), p. 145.

3. One of Graham's teachers when he was at Wheaton College defends this position. See Gordon Clark, *A Christian View of Men and Things* (Grand Rapids, Mich.: Eerdmans, 1952), chapter 4.

4. See Peter Caws, *Science and Theory of Value* (New York: Random House, 1967), p. 13.

5. See Alasdair MacIntyre and Paul Ricoeur, *The Religious Significance of Atheism* (New York: Columbia University Press, 1969), p. 32.

6. In discussing a program for replacing graft with honesty, and prejudice with the Golden Rule, Graham explains: "This can be done *only through an acceptance of Jesus Christ as personal Savior* on the part of the individuals who make up the society of the world" (*The Secret of Happiness* [Garden City, N. Y.: Doubleday, 1955], p. 67 italics added).

7. Quoted in Glenn Daniels, *Billy Graham: The Man Who Walks with God* (New York: Warner Paperback Library, 1961), p. 99. Used by permission.

8. Jean Adams, "A Billionaire's Daughter: I Put God Above My Father's Empire—An Exclusive Interview with June Hunt, Daughter of H. L. Hunt," *Family Week, Denton Record-Chronicle* (Mar. 26, 1972), pp. 6–7.

Chapter 6: Happiness and the Meaningful Life

1. Bertrand Russell, *Why I am Not a Christian*, ed. Paul Edwards (London: George Allen and Unwin, 1957).

2. Cf. Billy Graham, *Peace with God* (New York: Doubleday, 1953), pp. 4–5; idem, *The Quotable Billy Graham*, ed. Cort R. Flint (Anderson, S. C.: Droke House, 1967), p. 89.

3. "The life lived for what this world offers seems futile and empty, tawdry and trivial compared with the utter satisfaction, the glorious joys and lasting pleasures which a person finds in Christ and in the Christian life" (*The Quotable Billy Graham*, p. 41. Used by permission.).

4. Billy Graham, *World Aflame* (New York: Pocket Books, Inc., 1966), p. 220.

5. Ibid., p. 218.

6. From *Moody Still Lives* by A. P. Fitt, p. 20. Copyright 1936. Moody Press, Moody Bible Institute of Chicago. Used by permission.

7. "In Love with the Lover of My Soul," *Youth Sings: A Praise Book of Hymns and Choruses* (Mound, Minn.: Praise Book Publications, 1951).

8. Morton Hunt, *The Affair: A Portrait of Extra-Marital Love in Contemporary America* (New York: World Publishing Co., New American Library, 1969), p. 189.

9. Ibid., p. 118.

10. Ibid., p. 202.

11. Ibid., p. 203.

12. *The Quotable Billy Graham*, p. 96.

13. Bobby Russell, "Honey." Copyright 1968 by Charles Hanson Publisher. Used by permission.

14. Graham, *World Aflame*, p. 220.

15. Ibid., p. 223.

16. Ibid.

17. Cf. E. J. Carnell, *The Kingdom of Love and the Pride of Life* (Grand Rapids, Mich.: Eerdmans, 1960), pp. 18–19, 99.

Chapter 7: Did Hell Surprise God?

1. Cited in F. C. Kuehner, "Heaven or Hell?," *Fundamentals of the Faith* in *Christianity Today*, vol. 12, no. 19, June 21, 1968, p. 28K.

2. See Billy Graham, *World Aflame* (New York: Pocket Books, Inc., 1966), p. 210.

3. *The Quotable Billy Graham*, ed. Cort R. Flint (Anderson, S. C.: Droke House, 1967), p. 96 (italics added). Used by permission.

4. Herschel H. Hobbs, *Fundamentals of Our Faith* (Nashville: Broadman Press, 1960), p. 146. Used by permission.

5. "Billy Graham's Answer," *Chattanooga News Free Press* (Jan. 9, 1962).

6. *The Quotable Billy Graham*, p. 96.

7. E. J. Carnell, *A Philosophy of the Christian Religion* (Grand Rapids, Mich.: Eerdmans, 1960), pp. 380–81. Used by permission.

8. J. A. Motyer, "The Final State: Heaven and Hell," *Basic Christian Doctrines*, ed. Carl F. H. Henry (New York: Holt, Rinehart & Winston, 1962), p. 294, citing Revelation 20:10, NEB.

9. J. A. Motyer, "Hell," *Baker's Dictionary of Theology*, ed. Everett Harrison et al. (Grand Rapids, Mich.: Baker Book House, 1960), p. 267. Used by permission.

10. Ibid.

11. William C. Procter, "What Christ Teaches Concerning Future Retribution," *The Fundamentals for Today*, ed. Charles L. Feinberg (Grand Rapids, Mich.: Kregel Publications, 1961), p. 336. This article was abridged and amended by James H. Christian. Used by permission.

12. See Carnell, *A Philosophy of the Christian Religion*, pp. 357, 377.

13. Ibid., p. 381.

14. Procter, "What Christ Teaches," p. 336, italics added.

15. Graham, *World Aflame*, p. 116.

16. *Decision* (May 1970), p. 13.

17. *The Quotable Billy Graham*, p. 95.

18. Graham, *World Aflame*, p. 101.

19. For a concise debate between evangelical Calvinists and Arminians, see *Christianity Today* (Oct. 12, 1959), pp. 3–6, 14–18. See also W. C. Robinson, "Predestination," *Christianity Today* (Apr. 24, 1961), pp. 638–39; Harvey Buis, *Historic Protestantism and Predestination* (Nutley, N. J.: Presbyterian and Reformed Publishing Co., 1958).

20. Billy Graham, *The Secret of Happiness* (Garden City, N. Y.: Doubleday, 1955), pp. 30–31.

21. Cf. E. J. Carnell, *Christian Commitment* (New York: Macmillan, 1957), p. 271; Gordon Clark, *Religion, Reason and Revelation* (Nutley, N. J.: Presbyte-

rian and Reformed Publishing Co., 1961), pp. 232–41; Carnell, *A Philosophy of the Christian Religion*, p. 339; R. J. Rushdoony, *By What Standard: An Analysis of the Philosophy of Cornelius Van Til* (Nutley, N. J.: Presbyterian and Reformed Publishing Co., 1959), p. 83; Cornelius Van Til, "Christian Theistic Ethics" (Unpublished syllabus, 1947).

22. Graham, *World Aflame*, p. 102.

23. *The Quotable Billy Graham*, p. 95.

24. Billy Graham says that Christ was and is God. If this is true, then it would have been *God* sinning had Christ yielded to temptation in the wilderness. So could Christ have sinned—really? Or were his temptations mere pretense?

25. Graham, *World Aflame*, p. 57.

26. Ibid.

27. Clark, *Religion, Reason and Revelation*, p. 222.

28. B. B. Warfield, *Biblical and Theological Studies*, ed. Samuel S. Craig (Nutley, N. J.: Presbyterian and Reformed Publishing Co., 1952), p. 284. Used by permission.

29. See Clark, *Religion, Reason and Revelation*, p. 227.

30. See Billy Graham, "The Credibility Gap," *Decision* (Oct. 1971), p. 12.

31. John Gill, *The Cause of God and Truth* (Grand Rapids, Mich.: Kregel), chapter 5, p. xiii, italics added.

32. See *The Quotable Billy Graham*, p. 77.

33. See David Augsburger, "Hell," *Decision* (Oct. 1971), p. 4.

34. Warfield, *Biblical and Theological Studies*, p. 323. One contemporary evangelical Christian philosopher, Alvin Plantinga, argues that God simply could not have created free creatures who chose only the good because such is a logical impossibility. Plantinga's case may be found in his book *God and Other Minds* (Ithaca, N. Y.: Cornell University Press, 1967), chapters 6 and 7. Also see his article, "Pike and Possible Persons," *Journal of Philosophy* 63, No. 4 (Feb. 17, 1966), pp. 104–8.

Some Evangelicals claim that God may be said to be omnipotent and omniscient even though there are some things logically impossible for him to do. Unfortunately, this notion of logical impossibility is very loose and obscure and has implications that are concrete rather than purely formal. For example, if it is actually impossible for God to know *personally* what it is like to be unemployed and unable to find a job, then this limitation on God has very real implications for man as well as God. Whether this limitation is to be called logical or something else is of little practical consequence. There are many so-called logical impossibilities for Plantinga's God which have very critical consequences for the doctrine of divine omniscience and omnipotence.

In fact, the route that Plantinga seems to have embarked upon has already been traveled by many previous theologians and philosophers, and one of the judgments that they have been compelled to make is that it is "logically impossible" for God to provide an infallible propositional revelation. Man as God made him could not without reasonable doubt know that the revelation is infallible and of divine origin. Plantinga's appeal to "logical impossibility" saves the Evangelical's God from moral blame by transforming him into a deity that does not harmonize with the traditional evangelical view. Far from being an aid to evangelical theology, Plantinga's case seems to be another ax on this tree that has already fallen.

While Plantinga deals with the question of whether God could have created men both free and beyond doing evil, he does not discuss the question of whether God could have created *only* those whom he foreknew would both fall into sin and subsequently receive redemption. Much of the problem of Plantinga's case is rooted in his confusion of freedom with "uncaused cause," which upon analysis evaporates into a will-o'-the-wisp. In our everyday conversations, when we say that we did something "of our own free will," we mean simply that we did it because we wanted to, rather than because someone else wanted us to or because the circumstances made us go against what we wanted. A person may be caused to do what he does and still be free to the extent that he wants to do it.

Billy Graham seems to think that a person can somehow of free will do something wholly out of the blue, with absolutely no causal explanation as to why he does it. Unfortunately, this leads to the conclusion that not even God can know why he does it, and such a conclusion runs counter to the standard evangelical doctrine of God's omniscience, to say nothing of the doctrine of divine providence. Plantinga's position becomes unnecessarily obscure at this point.

Even if it were possible to say that people who go to hell do so because they want to, Evangelicalism of the Arminian school has yet to face up to the hard question of *what made these miserable souls want to go to hell in the first place.* The Calvinists are at least sufficiently forthright to say that God in his providence arranged their environment in such a way as to produce in them this desire to go to hell. But Billy Graham and Plantinga, while talking of God's providence, steer away from this tough issue and content themselves with affirming a diluted version of providence that allows God to fumble about until perhaps the great majority of humanity is lost to hell. To label as "free will" this fumbling incompetence on the part of a God who is supposed to be the Author of history is a theological misnomer.

Evangelicalism seems to be caught in a dilemma of offering either the Arminian confusion or the Calvinistic notion that God actually wants some people to suffer forever. Fortunately, there are other views of religion and other views of God than what Evangelicalism offers.

Chapter 8: A Question of Holiness

1. *The Quotable Billy Graham*, ed. Cort R. Flint (Anderson, S. C.: Droke House, 1967), p. 85. Used by permission.
2. Ibid.
3. See ibid., p. 81.
4. Ibid., p. 59. The biblical passage referred to is 2 Peter 3:9, KJV.

5. Billy Graham, *World Aflame* (New York: Pocket Books, Inc., 1966), p. 105.

6. E. J. Carnell, *A Philosophy of the Christian Religion* (Grand Rapids, Mich.: Eerdmans, 1960), p. 380. Used by permission.

7. See ibid., pp. 375–77.

8. Ibid., p. 375.

9. See E. J. Carnell, *An Introduction to Christian Apologetics: A Philosophic Defense of the Trinitarian-Theistic Faith* (Grand Rapids, Mich.: Eerdmans, 1948), p. 307, n. 10.

10. B. B. Warfield, *Biblical and Theological Studies*, ed. Samuel S. Craig (Nutley, N. J.: Presbyterian and Reformed Publishing Co., 1952), pp. 8, 11–12. Used by permission.

11. Billy Graham, "Will God Spare America?," *America's Hour of Decision* (Wheaton, Ill.: Van Kampen Press, 1951), p. 125.

12. Carnell, *A Philosophy of the Christian Religion*, pp. 283–84.

13. See F. C. Kuehner, "Heaven or Hell?," *Fundamentals of the Faith* in *Christianity Today*, vol. 12, no. 19, June 21, 1968.

14. Graham, *World Aflame*, p. 221.

15. Ibid., p. 223.

16. Warfield, *Biblical and Theological Studies*, pp. 334–50.

17. Konrad Lorenz, *On Aggression* (New York: Harcourt Brace Jovanovich, 1966), pp. 207–9.

18. Robert Ardrey, *The Territorial Imperative* (2d ed.; New York: Atheneum, 1967), p. 285. Copyright 1966 by Robert Ardrey. Used by permission.

19. See Nels Ferré, *The Living God of Nowhere and Nothing* (London: Epworth Press, 1966), p. 76.

20. Sigmund Freud, *Civilization and Its Discontents*, trans. James Strachey (New York: W. W. Norton & Co., 1961), p. 61. In *The Human Imperative* (New York: Columbia University Press, 1972) Alexander Allander, Jr. denies that human aggression is instinctive. He criticizes especially Lorenz and Ardrey and offers alternative hypotheses of considerable merit.

21. See Arthur Koestler, "The Predicament of Man," *Alternatives to Violence*, ed. Larry Ng (New York: Time-Life Books, 1968), pp. 17–23. This address was delivered as the Sonning Award Address at the University of Copenhagen.

22. Arthur Koestler, "The Initiates," *The God That Failed*, ed. Richard Crossman (New York: Bantam Books, 1949), p. 19.

23. Ibid., p. 39.

Chapter 9: The Inner Self and the Circumstances of Life

1. Taken from *The Jesus Generation* by Billy Graham (Grand Rapids, Mich.: Zondervan, 1971), p. 125. Copyright © 1971, by Billy Graham. Used by permission.

2. Billy Graham, *The Secret of Happiness* (Garden City, N. Y.: Doubleday, 1955), p. 11.

3. See ibid., p. 11.

4. Ibid., p. 32.

5. Ibid., p. 35.

6. Billy Graham, *World Aflame* (New York: Pocket Books, Inc., 1966), p. 153.

7. Ibid., p. 122.

8. Ibid., p. 123.

9. Ibid., p. 143.

10. See ibid., p. 66.

11. See B. F. Skinner, *Science and Human Behavior* (New York: Free Press of Glencoe, 1953), pp. 5, 446.

12. See Graham, *The Jesus Generation*, pp. 61, 152.

13. See ibid., pp. 127, 140.

14. Ibid., p. 167.

15. Ibid.

16. See ibid.

17. See E. Y. Mullins, *The Christian Religion in Its Doctrinal Expression* (Valley Forge, Pa.: Judson Press, 1917), pp. 57–62. Cf. Graham, *The Secret of Happiness*, pp. 10, 29, 84.

18. Graham, *The Jesus Generation*, p. 142.

19. See ibid., p. 108.

20. John Hospers, *Human Conduct* (New York: Harcourt, Brace & World, 1961), p. 61.

21. Graham, *The Secret of Happiness*, p. 84, italics added.

22. Ibid., p. 13, italics added.

23. Ibid., p. 10.

24. E. J. Carnell, *Christian Commitment* (New York: Macmillan, 1957), pp. 11–12. © Edward John Carnell 1957.

25. Graham, *The Secret of Happiness*, p. 13.

26. Ibid., pp. v–vi.

27. Ibid., p. 13.

28. Ibid., p. 2.

29. See "The Case of the Wandering IQs," *Redbook* (Aug. 1967), pp. 31–33, 112–18.

30. Billy Graham, *My Answer* (New York: Pocket Books, Inc., 1967), p. 102. © 1960 by Billy Graham; © 1954, 1955, 1956, 1957, 1958, 1959, 1960 by Chicago Tribune–N. Y. News Syndicate, Inc. Reprinted through the courtesy of the Chicago Tribune–New York News Syndicate, Inc.

31. Ibid., p. 123.

32. See Graham, *The Jesus Generation*, p. 108.

33. See ibid., p. 142.

34. Ibid., p. 126.

35. Ibid., p. 123.

36. Graham, *World Aflame*, p. 122.

37. Carnell, *Christian Commitment*, p. 12.

38. Graham, *The Secret of Happiness*, p. 14, italics added.

39. Graham, *The Jesus Generation*, pp. 126–27. Cf. Billy Graham, "The Mystery of Righteousness," *Decision* (Jan. 1971), p. 12.

40. Graham, *World Aflame*, p. 122.

41. Ibid., p. 146.

42. Ibid., p. 148.

43. See Graham, *The Jesus Generation*, pp. 126–27.

44. Graham, *World Aflame*, p. 148.

45. Ibid., p. 155.

46. Ibid.

47. See Billy Graham, "The Night of Nights," *Decision* (Dec. 1971), p. 12.

48. See Billy Graham, "Stranger in Egypt," *Decision* (Sept. 1971), p. 12.

49. See Sherwood Wirt, *The Social Conscience of the Evangelical* (New York: Harper & Row, 1968), p. 50.

50. Ibid., p. 154.

51. Graham, *World Aflame*, p. 156.

52. Ibid.

Chapter 10: The Natural and the Supernatural

1. Adelle Davis, *Let's Eat Right to Keep Fit* (rev. ed.; New York: New American Library, 1970), pp. 169, 156.

2. *Baptist and Reflector* (Aug. 12, 1971), p. 10.

3. Quoted in *Baptist and Reflector* (Sept. 2, 1971), p. 3.

4. Quoted in Robert Hall Glover, *The Progress of World-Wide Missions* (New York: Harper & Brothers, 1924, 1939), p. 101; cf. S. Pearce Carey, *William Carey* (Philadelphia, 1923).

5. See W. G. McLoughlin, Jr., *Modern Revivalism: Charles Grandison Finney to Billy Graham* (New York: Ronald Press, 1959), p. 11, citing Finney, *Lectures on Revivals* (New York, 1935), p. 12.

6. D. L. Moody, *The Great Redemption* (New York, 1888), p. 439.

7. See John R. Rice, *Prayer—Asking and Receiving* (Wheaton, Ill.: Sword of the Lord Publishers, 1942), pp. 151–52.

8. Carl F. H. Henry, "The Marvel of the Rose Bowl," *America's Hour of Decision* (Wheaton, Ill.: Van Kampen Press, 1951), p. 114, italics added.

9. Ibid., p. 108.

10. Ibid., pp. 107–8.

11. See "Billy's Apostles," *Newsweek* (June 23, 1965), p. 65.

12. Henry, "The Marvel of the Rose Bowl," p. 106, italics added.

13. See J. E. Barnhart, "Natura Naturans," *Philosophy of Religion and Theology: 1971*, ed. David Griffin (Chambersburg, Pa.: American Academy of Religion on the Campus of Wilson College, 1971), pp. 42–47.

14. Wayne Oates, *What Psychology Says About Religion* (New York: Association Press, 1958), p. 67. Used by permission.

15. See Gordon W. Allport, *The Person in Psychology* (Boston: Beacon

Press, 1968), p. 146. This article first appeared in the *Journal of Religion and Health* 2 (1963). See also idem, "A Paradox of Faith: The Religious Context of Prejudice," *The Graduate Journal* (University of Texas) 7 (1966): p. 115–30.

16. Allport, *The Person in Psychology*, p. 144.

17. *Decision* (Apr. 1970), p. 1.

18. Ibid., p. 12.

19. See *Decision* (Apr. 1970), p. 12.

20. See ibid., p. 14.

21. See Don S. Browning, *Atonement and Psychotherapy* (Philadelphia: Westminster Press, 1966).

22. See Anita Stevens and Lucy Freeman, *I Hate My Parents* (New York: Tower Publications, Inc., 1970), p. 194.

23. See Mircea Eliade, *Rites and Symbols of Initiation* (New York: Harper Torchbooks, 1958).

24. It is important to keep in mind that natural phenomena include not only the variables of nature but also of human culture in its various modes.

25. See Billy Graham, "A House in Order," *Great Readings from "Decision,"* ed. Sherwood E. Wirt and Marvin R. Sanders (Minneapolis: World Wide Publications, 1970), p. 23. This sermon appears in *Decision* (May 1967).

26. Ibid.

27. Cf. Billy Graham, "The Home God Honors" (Sermon, 1949); "The Home" (Sermon, 1958).

28. Cf. Billy Graham, "Father" (Sermon, 1956); "The Responsibilities of the Home" (Sermon, 1955).

29. Billy Graham, *World Aflame* (New York: Pocket Books, Inc., 1966), p. 2.

30. See Billy Graham, *Billy Graham Talks to Teen-agers* (Grand Rapids, Mich.: Zondervan, 1958), pp. 24–25. A brief treatment of Graham's view of sex may be found in David Lockard, *The Unheard Billy Graham* (Waco, Texas: Word Books, 1971), pp. 103–6.

31. For Graham's own report and analysis of conversion see "Conversion," *Decision* (Nov. 1969), p. 14; "Only One Thing Wrong," *Decision* (Oct. 1968), p. 14; World Aflame, chapter 15. For a very careful study of some of the difficulties and expectations involved in the scientific study of religion, see J. Milton Yinger, *The Scientific Study of Religion* (New York: Macmillan, 1970). For a readable and informative inquiry into some of the dynamics between science, religious experience, and morality in American history, see Morton White, *Science and Sentiment in America: Philosophical Thought from Jonathan Edwards to John Dewey* (New York: Oxford University Press, 1972). Graham in effect is attempting to live with two world views that have mutually incompatible elements. Some who are sensitive to this strain tend to work toward a kind of new synthesis. Others simply hop back and forth with a kind of skill of their own and do not attempt any kind of creative synthesis. But it is a very risky business (see Peter Berger and Thomas Luckmann, *The Social Construction of Reality* [Garden City, N. Y.: Doubleday, Anchor Books, 1967]).

Chapter 11: Sinners All

1. See Billy Graham, *World Aflame* (New York: Pocket Books, Inc., 1966), p. 59.

2. See E. J. Carnell, *An Introduction to Christian Apologetics: A Philosophic Defense of the Trinitarian-Theistic Faith* (Grand Rapids, Mich.: Eerdmans, 1948), p. 295.

3. Taken from *The Jesus Generation* by Billy Graham (Grand Rapids, Mich.: Zondervan, 1971), p. 30. Copyright © 1971, by Billy Graham. Used by permission.

4. Billy Graham, "The Moment I Felt Closest to God," *Family Weekly, Denton Record-Chronicle* (Aug. 22, 1971), p. 4.

5. Graham, *The Jesus Generation*, p. 64.

6. Graham, *World Aflame*, pp. 56–57.

7. Ibid., pp. 60–61.

8. See ibid., pp. 144–47.

9. See Hans Toch, *Men of Violence: An Inquiry into the Psychology of Violence* (Chicago: Aldine Publishing Co., 1969).

10. Graham, *The Jesus Generation*, p. 121.

11. *The Quotable Billy Graham*, ed. Cort R. Flint (Anderson, S. C.: Droke House, 1967), p. 197. Used by permission. David Lockard, *The Unheard Billy Graham* (Waco, Texas: Word Books, 1971), p. 113.

12. "Graham Says U.S.-China Talks Spur Hopes for a Generation of Peace," *Baptist and Reflector* (Mar. 16, 1972), p. 11.

13. See Billy Graham, "Only One Thing Wrong," *Decision* (Oct. 1968), p. 14; Billy Graham, "Conversion," *Decision* (Nov. 1969), p. 14.

14. Walter Kaufmann, *The Faith of a Heretic* (Garden City, N. Y.: Doubleday, Anchor Books, 1963), p. 269, citing H. H. Barnes and N. Teetars, *New Horizons in Criminology*, 2d ed. (Englewood Cliffs, N. J.: Prentice-Hall, 1951), pp. 184–87. Used by permission of Doubleday & Co., Inc.

15. See Kaufmann, *The Faith of a Heretic*, p. 268.

16. Graham, "Conversion," p. 12, italics added.

17. Ibid., italics added.

18. See B. F. Skinner, *Beyond Freedom and Dignity* (New York: Knopf, 1971).

19. Graham, *The Jesus Generation*, p. 123.

Chapter 12: Billy Graham and Southern Baptists

1. Robert O'Brien, "Criswell and Texas Baptists Help Get Welfare Increase," *Baptist Standard* (Aug. 13, 1969), p. 4. Used by permission.

2. *Baptist and Reflector* (June 20, 1968), p. 12.

3. The Christian Home Life Commission of the SBC created a storm when it invited Joseph Fletcher and a representative from *Playboy* to debate with some Southern Baptists on the topic of the "new morality."

4. Quoted in *Denton Record-Chronicle* (Nov. 10, 1971), p. 2.

5. Quoted under the heading "Leave SBC If Faith Statements Unacceptable, Criswell Urges," in *Baptist and Reflector* (Oct. 2, 1969), p. 7.

6. Ibid.

7. "Harvey, Graham to Share in Crusade Colorcasts," *Baptist and Reflector* (Feb. 20, 1969), p. 12.

8. Paul Harvey, "TV Is a Warped Mirror," *Denton Record-Chronicle* (Sept. 26, 1969), p. 4.

9. "SBC Blends Conservatism, Liberalism, Editorials Say," *Baptist and Reflector* (July 4, 1968), p. 3.

10. Quoted in ibid.

11. *Baptist Standard* (Aug. 13, 1969), p. 5.

Chapter 13: Billy Graham's Christian Americanism

1. Billy Graham, "Satan Religion," *American Mercury*, Aug. 1954, p. 43.

2. Billy Graham, "Labor, Christ, and the Cross," (Sermon, 1953), p. 6.

3. Billy Graham, "Do We Need the Old-Time Religion?," *The Town Hall* (Jan. 2, 1951), p. 9.

4. Billy Graham, "The Signs of the Times," (Sermon, 1961), p. 2.

5. For a study of the missionary spirit during wars fought by the United States, see Sol Tax, "War and the Draft," *War: The Anthropology of Armed Conflict and Aggression*, ed. Morton Fried et al. (Garden City, N. Y.: Natural History Press, 1968), pp. 199–210.

6. "Billy in Germany," *Time* (July 5, 1954), p. 48. Reprinted by permission from TIME, The Weekly Newsmagazine; © Time Inc.

7. Billy Graham, *The Secret of Happiness* (Garden City, N. Y.: Doubleday, 1955), p. 66.

8. See Erling Jorstad, *Love It or Leave It? A Dialogue on Loyalty* (Minneapolis: Augsburg, 1972), pp. 33, 44.

9. Jim Newton, "Graham's Life Threatened? Says He's Ready to Die," *Baptist and Reflector* (June 20, 1968), p. 12.